# THE

# GREAT

# AUDIENCE

"*Master, we have not come*

*through centuries, caste,*

*heroisms, fables, to halt*

*in this land today.*"

WHITMAN to EMERSON

BY GILBERT SELDES

THE

GREAT

AUDIENCE

GREENWOOD PRESS, PUBLISHERS
WESTPORT, CONNECTICUT

*To the people*

*I've worked with*

*in the lively arts.*

*G. S.*

# Contents

viii Contents

# CONFESSION OF ERROR

Twenty-five years ago I made a proposal that seemed modest at the time: that popular entertainment could be accepted and criticized on the same basis as the fine arts. I have now come to believe that this proposal contained a serious error. I didn't perceive then the direction American entertainment was going to take, and while I can make excuses for my failure, I hope this book will correct my earlier mistakes and place the popular arts more nearly where they belong.

In gratitude for the pleasures I had enjoyed, I made large assertions about these arts; what I regret now is my excessive modesty. For I have somewhat reluctantly been forced to the conclusion that our mass entertainments are, practically speaking, the great creative arts of our time. In the traditional sense they are seldom considered as arts and are condemned because they are uncreative. They are machine-made products, they repeat themselves endlessly, using a handful of contrived formulas for plot and stereotyped figures for characters; they are seldom the product of a single powerful imagination but are put together by groups of people who are virtually forbidden to express their own profoundest feelings about the meaning of life. All these things are true, and I can add a more damning indictment still: our mass entertainments are compelled by their own nature to create works that can be promptly forgotten; the work of art as an imperishable object is totally foreign to them.

The creative action of these arts begins after the movie or the radio program has been made: they create their own audience, making people over; they create the climate of feeling in which all of us live. The other arts are private and personal, they influence the lives of those who enjoy them; the effect of the public arts cannot be escaped by turning off the radio or television set, by refusing to go to the movies; neither our indifference nor our contempt gives us immunity against them.

This is what I didn't understand when I attempted to find the right place among the arts for popular entertainment. I think their place among the arts is now well established. The important thing is to "situate" them in their social setting as well, along with education, political debate, propaganda, and all the other means of making us feel and think and act as we do.

The moment we see that our mass media are creative in the sense that they influence our thoughts and feelings, entirely new questions come up. Have these arts any choice as to the kind of audiences they shall create? Is what they are doing now the best they can do? Do they operate in the public interest or are they dangerous to the well-being of the country? Are they in the general framework of democratic capitalism? Are they contributing all they can to prepare us to make those moral and intellectual judgments which will have to be made in the next generation? If they are not, can they change without government interference? Or are they condemned by their economic structure to keep on creating a larger and larger audience whose existence endangers our democratic system?

These are the questions, and I don't pretend to have found all the answers. At the moment it seems to me essential that the questions should be asked as publicly as possible. Occasionally a college president, a political scientist, a parent-teacher group, a psychiatrist, or a preacher suggests that the questions exist; the specific effect of movie Westerns or murder-by-television or the sadism of the comic books is noted and denounced; the *Congressional Record* includes an occasional speech about the misuse of radio for propaganda, and the American Academy of Political Science has studied the media of mass communication. All these single efforts are useful; but they do not bring the whole question of our use of the popular arts to the average intelligent man, so that he can see how his daily life is affected by them even if he is not himself a part of the mass audience. That is what I have tried to do. Bringing the separate problems of various kinds of entertainment into focus is no guarantee that they will be solved, but even if the right answers cannot be found (and in some cases I don't know that there is a single right answer), the right questions at least will be asked. We live more and more in an atmosphere of passive acceptance in which asking questions is becoming a sign of eccentricity; and we are hardly aware of the part played by our mass media in creating this sluggish mood. So long as we think of them purely as suppliers of entertainment, we will not ask the questions that are hard to answer.

In order to ask questions properly I have examined the conditions in which our entertainments are created—the way major studios conduct the business of making and showing movies, the economics of sponsored radio and television—and connected these conditions with the general circumstances of our daily lives; I have then observed the product not so much for the kind of pleasure it can give as for the effect the pleasure has on us; and finally I have tried to find a way to preserve the great virtues of the popular arts without embracing the serious and, as I think, avoidable vices into which they have fallen.

Although I am still prejudiced in favor of these arts, I have temporarily put aside my pleasure in individual programs or pictures, the purely aesthetic interest, in order to concentrate on the effect of the entertainment arts in their mass. For the most part I have applied unfamiliar standards, so that at times I have found myself writing a sort of Elementary Physics of the Popular Arts, considering their quantity, the speed with which they move, their mass and weight and duration, and I wish I had been able to discover the electromagnetic field surrounding each one of them.

A non-prejudice of mine will also become fairly obvious. I do not object to the profits made by the managers of our entertainment industry. In fact, I believe they should make more money by creating genuinely democratic entertainment instead of catering to a sizable minority which they pretend is the mass of the people. I assume that these managers, like most Americans, would like to preserve the capitalist system, and I have obligingly kept all suggestions for change within the basic capitalist framework. I accept neither the radical thesis that the system is too rigid to allow any changes nor the reactionary dodge that the system is perfect and no one but a Communist would want to change it in any detail. I think that the management of our popular arts has been caught in a complicated piece of machinery and hasn't so far seen the faintest necessity for getting out of it. One of the discoveries I made in examining the machinery is that parts of it are not working any too well for the managers; when enough people discover that the machinery may be actively working against the public interest, a double pressure will make itself felt, and the managers will be adroit enough to make a virtue of yielding to it.

I am not only prejudiced in favor of the popular arts, I have also strong prejudices in favor of freedom. I foresee the possibility of serious interference with the free market in entertainment unless the managers of our mass media correct their own errors. We are living in a cross and impatient world, and the temptation is great to use the diversions of the people for political ends. If we decide we cannot afford the luxury of the free market in entertainment, because of domestic troubles or the danger of war, we will lose something of great value in itself and we will be starting on our way to a dictatorial state. I think this can be avoided, but I am also afraid that we will come to it eventually unless the producers of our entertainment reverse their direction. The end product which they are now creating is the mass man. There is still time—but not much time—to make the popular arts serve free men trying to secure a free society.

# The
# Big
# Audience

# Myth: Movies

*THE AUDIENCE VANISHES*

> *"There exists today no means of influencing the masses more potent than the cinema."*
> Pius XI: Encyclical Vigilante Cura *(1936)*
>
> *"For us the film is the most important of the arts."*
> Lenin *(1920)*
>
> *"The businessman desires to think of little or nothing [at the movies]."*
> Congressman Clare E. Hoffman *(1948)*

Except for the makers of baby foods, no industry in the United States has been so indifferent to the steady falling away of its customers as the movies have been. The make-up of the movie audience has been known for a long time; during the past five years statistical research, paid for by the studios, has provided exact figures proving that in one generation the movies have lost two-thirds of their customers and have survived only because a satisfactory birth rate provides new patrons for the seats left empty when people arrive at the years of discretion and stop going to the movies. This information has been received with a nonchalance that ought to make a banker's blood run cold; it has had virtually no effect on the methods of making or distributing pictures, no effect on the quality of the product, which, like baby food, comes in cans. The parallel with strained foods breaks down in one detail: the foods would be worthless if the consumer didn't outgrow them, and the manufacturer virtually guarantees that they will become unnecessary in time and give

9

way to other, more varied nourishment; the makers of movies
pretend that what they offer is a balanced ration for adults also.
But the reason the customers stop buying the product is the
same: in each case the formula no longer satisfies.

At the time Congressman Hoffman spoke, the Supreme Court
of the United States was on his side and against the foreign
ideologists. The Court has never actually reversed its decision
that the movies are entertainment and not a form of persuasion.
The issue was brought before the Court in 1916, in a case involving censorship which the Mutual Film Corporation believed
to be a violation of the First Amendment. The Court held that
as the movies were "spectacles" made for entertainment, they
were not entitled to freedom of expression and could not be considered "as part of the press of the country or as organs of public
opinion." On the other hand, the Pope and Lenin saw in the
movies a form of communication—not an organ of public opinion, perhaps, but a powerful way to *influence* public opinion.
The position of the Court has implied that they were wrong.

The question of free expression has not yet been settled, but it
probably will be by the time this is read, because the authority
of the censors in Atlanta, Georgia, is being challenged by the
producers of *Lost Boundaries*, which treats sympathetically the
plight of a Negro who has passed as white. The Court has indicated its frame of mind in a sort of aside delivered in an anti-
trust suit against the major studios; the essential words are: "We
have no doubt that moving pictures, like newspapers and radio,
are included in the press, whose freedom is guaranteed by the
First Amendment." [1] In the thirty-three years between the two
decisions many things have happened to the movies, but the doctrine of "entertainment" (commonly considered as another word
for "amusement") has not been overthrown.

In business to create illusion, Hollywood has imposed a com-
pound illusion about itself on the American people: that the

[1] A lower court, however, held to the earlier interpretation in 1950.

production of movies is the prime occupation of the movie companies; that movies are America's fourth or fifth largest industry;
and that everybody goes to the movies. None of these things is
true: a mere fraction of the money invested in the movie business goes into the making of pictures; the industry ranks nearer
the forty-sixth place than the sixth; and nearly everybody stops
going to the movies. Nevertheless they are a proper subject for
a statesman to think about. If the Pope and Lenin are right, and
the movies are a supremely powerful instrument for influencing
people, a statesman should decide whether it is good for the
country to have the movies continue in the service of a small
mass minority prodigiously important because it is composed
largely of the adolescent; whether the movies should be encouraged publicly to destroy the audience they create; whether the
country can afford a movie industry which hardly ever functions in the service of the majority of its citizens.

It was not as a statesman that Mr. Hoffman spoke; he was, in
fact, only introducing and spreading on the *Record* an article
on the tribulations of Eric Johnston. But his few remarks are a
good example of common illusions about the movies and will
bear analysis.

In substance Mr. Hoffman appealed to the movies to mend
their ways; as if anticipating the usual reply, he anchored his
remarks firmly in the profit motive, holding out a great hope of
gain if only the movies would cleave to the good and the true.
"The American people like pictures which are clean and whole-
some," he said. "They do not care for barroom scenes. They do
not care for any of those things which a dissolute, decaying
nation sometimes sanctions." He looked for the day when in each
city and town there would be a movie house in which only
"clean pictures, modest actions, were portrayed; . . . where the
rewards went to the decent, the honest. . . ." And he predicted
that the attendance at such houses would soon "educate the
producers as to what the American picture audience really
wanted."

Children and younger people, in Mr. Hoffman's view, might
go to the movies for amusement, but adults go "to forget . . .
some of their pressing problems, to get away from the sordid-
ness of life." That American life is substantially sordid is, in
itself, an un-American idea, and the Congressman softened the
impeachment by making it specific: "The housewife wants a little
distraction from the high cost of living. The businessman desires
to think of little or nothing. He isn't greatly interested in whether
someone's wife or someone's husband was successful in the pursuit of some other individual's husband or wife. He would like
just a little clean fun on the screen."

And for the knockdown cash-at-the-box-office argument, Mr.
Hoffman added: "The real paying audience is made up of older
people."

I must leave it to more worldly minds to correct the picture
of the adult American as sketched by the gentleman from Michi-
gan; even if it were photographically exact, he could not sell it
to Hollywood because the background is out of perspective: the
businessman does not go to the movies—the real paying audience
is made up of younger people. One fact is established: after they
reach the age of twenty or so, people go less and less to the
movies. The movies live on children from the ages of ten to nineteen, who go steadily and frequently and almost automatically
to the pictures; from the ages of twenty to twenty-five people
still go, but less often; after thirty, the audience begins to vanish
from the movie houses. Checks made by different researchers at
different times and places turn up minor variations in percentages; but it works out that between the ages of thirty and fifty,
more than half of the men and women in the United States, steady
patrons of the movies in their earlier years, do not bother to see
more than one picture a month; after fifty, more than half see
virtually no pictures at all.

This is the ultimate, essential, overriding fact about the movies;
around it crystallize all the problems—personal, financial, social,
moral, and aesthetic—of the motion-picture industry, from the

"frustration" of its writers to the "glamour" of its stars. The detailed statistics were presented to the studios by such organizations as the Audience Research Institute, a special branch of the Gallup organization. Their significance has been made clear by outsiders, myself and others, for several years; but it has had no effect on the studios. The dazzling (and inflated) figure of four billion paid admissions a year dwindles into a probable thirty million separate moviegoers, chiefly young people, many of whom go several times a week; and at the end of the statistical hocus-pocus stands the gaunt figure of a mere thirteen to fifteen million individuals who actually see the basic staple commodity of Hollywood, the A feature-picture. (This is three million less than in 1946—a drop of twenty per cent.) The Audience Research Institute estimates that eight of these thirteen million people are under thirty, so that something like two-thirds of the population is contributing only one-third of the A-picture audience.[1]

Face to face with the prime economic fact that the movies kill off their own audiences and live truly on the unearned increment of a steady birth rate, I confess to a sense of shock at the spectacle of an industry, financed by the shrewdest of bankers, contenting itself with a mere third, or at most half, of its potential income. The actual figures have been worked out: if the forty million who have stopped going to the movies would

[1] The statistics about age levels come from the ARI, which made its surveys originally for a movie studio. The thirteen million estimate of the total number of individuals who see an A picture, the most shocking of all the figures, was given in 1949 by the vice-president of one of the most prosperous movie companies and independently noted by the vice-president of another in 1950. On the falling off of audiences, the figures indicate that the rate of decline is leveling, that the thirteen per cent drop in 1948 was the peak, but there was at least a seven per cent drop in 1949 and another of perhaps ten per cent in 1950. Taken in connection with the other figures, this "improvement" offers cold comfort, and it was, in fact, in 1950 that the movie industry began seriously to wonder how to bring in "the hundred million people physically and financially able to attend theaters" and to look for the cause of "the apparent indifference of too many people toward motion pictures." (The quotations are from two vice-presidents, on the business side, of Twentieth Century-Fox.)

be brought back for only one picture a week, the gain at the box-office would be nearly half a billion dollars a year, after taxes; the share of the studios would be a hundred and fifty million dollars. Moreover, with these strays returned to the fold, American movies would, for the first time in years, be making a profit in the domestic market alone and be able to live without the export trade. In recent years about one out of every ten pictures has been able to do this.

It does not follow that we would have better pictures or that richer studios would be more daring in their experiments. All we can be sure of is that to attract a large audience the movies would be compelled to satisfy many more *kinds* of interest; they would have to become a genuinely democratic, instead of a mass-minority, entertainment; and in a democracy like ours, encouragement of individual interests and satisfaction of many various desires are the surest protection against the constant threat of robotization and the ultimate emergence of the mass man.

It will presently appear that so long as the movies neglect the majority of citizens they must actually contribute to the creation of a robotized society; and that is the primary reason for examining the structure that makes this inevitable. But the fact itself is so incredible that we have to inquire why the financiers of movie production have either failed to notice it or considered it insignificant. No other manufacturer of a mass-consumption commodity—cigarettes, soaps, cereals, motorcars—has deliberately cut himself off from the larger part of his market. Why have the movies done so?

The money paid in at the box-office by adolescents is as good as any; during the past decade the gross revenue of the movie industry rose steadily; dividends in 1947, reflecting the peak year of 1946, were over fifty million dollars, an all-time high. It is hard to quarrel with so lordly an annual profit; and any attempt to alter the quality of the movies, in order to bring in more customers, entails a risk which the management may justifiably refuse to take. The investor, cashing his dividend checks, is too grateful to ask whether he might not have gotten a still bigger check; and unless acute inflation renders his dollars worthless, he is unlikely to quarrel with a constantly rising graph.

Yet it is sheer stultification to approach the finances of the movies in this trusting spirit. The critical eye notes that other lines on the chart have been rising also and makes comparisons. The population of the United States went up by over fifteen million between 1941 and 1950; the take-home pay in that period was doubled; the number of families in the five-thousand-dollars-a-year bracket tripled, and the number in the middle group (earning from sixty to a hundred dollars a week) increased almost as much. At the end of that time the inhabitants of the country, taken as a whole, had nearly twice as much money to spend as they had when the war began, *after allowing for inflation;* but they spent a smaller share of their total income on the movies in 1948 than they had spent at any time in the previous twenty years. The amount was high because the average admission price had gone up by forty per cent; but between the great year of 1946 and 1948 actual attendance dropped from eighty to seventy million. (These are Hollywood figures, seriously questioned in the industry; the totals are considered inflated and the drop is estimated as high as twenty-five per cent.)

Financing the movies is done in one of two ways: a bank may put up a large part of the cost of a single picture, on the strength of an independent producer's reputation, the stars he has signed, the story he proposes to make, and particularly the guarantees he can give that his picture will be released by one of the major distributors; or a financial organization—a bank, a holding corporation—may invest in a major studio by making loans or acquiring stock. In the second case, the actual profit of any single picture is unimportant; the studio acts as producer of pictures, but the company of which the studio is one part is also distributor and exhibitor—it owns theaters. At the end of ten years of litigation, two major companies have yielded to the government and agreed to "divorcement"; Paramount, for instance, will be divided into two totally separate companies, one to produce films, the other to own about six hundred and fifty of the fifteen hundred theaters now controlled by the corporation. (The rest must be sold.) In preparation for this fission, Paramount acquainted its stockholders with the facts of life: in recent years two-thirds of its total profit was made by the theaters, one-third by the pictures produced. No other studio has controlled more than five hundred theaters, and a breakdown of balance sheets has not been made public; however, it has been generally assumed that Warners and Twentieth Century-Fox earn between fifty and sixty per cent of their profit as exhibitors, and only MGM definitely made more than half its income in the studios. The importance of the theaters can be measured in another way: in recent years the total investment in the movie business has been around two billion dollars, nearly all of it in theaters; only five per cent of the total was invested in the manufacture of films. An investor in a movie company has been paid dividends out of real estate more often than out of productions in the studio. The bookkeeping is intricate, but the simple fact is that a theater can make money while the picture it shows does not; the exhibitor, who takes as much as sixty-five per cent of the box-office receipts, prefers a smash hit, but he can make a profit by showing less successful pictures for brief runs, while the picture itself may never, out of the thirty-five per cent given to the studio, repay the cost of the negative. The investor in a single picture is vitally concerned with its fate; the backer of a studio, the holder of its stock, doesn't care where his profits come from. He hasn't, in the past, been worried by the fact that out of every hundred average-cost pictures made, only ten have actually made a profit on their domestic rentals alone. He was interested in annual dividends and he got them. He didn't know, or didn't care if he knew, that without its function as a real-estate operator, the company he invested in might be heading for bankruptcy.

The major studios do not completely monopolize either production or distribution, but their influence is predominant. There are many small companies, and from time to time independent producers manage to get backing for a single picture at a time; and there are nearly seven hundred circuits of theaters ranging in size from four houses to several hundred, as well as some seven thousand individuals or small companies managing less than four houses each. But the major studios and the large circuits which depend on them dominate the business of exhibiting pictures, because they control almost all the big city showcases, and, with less than half the theaters in the country, they have about two-thirds of all the seats. The remaining third of the seats, in the hands of small operators, are cheap ones, so that seven thousand small enterprisers, with more than half of the movie houses in the country, contribute only a small fraction of the total revenue and are consequently negligible in influence.

It is not unusual for a picture to gross one-tenth of its total domestic revenue on its Broadway showing and from half to two-thirds in theaters controlled by the studios or by the half-dozen most important circuits. The most famous of the independent houses, the Radio City Music Hall, paid nearly half a million dollars to RKO for *The Bells of St. Mary*, and nearly as much for each of ten other pictures; *Gentlemen's Agreement* and *The Song of Bernadette* did as well, in longer runs, at smaller Broadway houses; and in a special exploitation, running thirty-nine weeks, the Astor Theater paid eight hundred thousand dollars to Samuel Goldwyn for *The Best Years of Our Lives*. These hugely successful pictures went on to magnificent total receipts; in each case not less than one-fifth of the total investment was paid off by showing in a single house.

The large circuits are closely allied to the producing studios and form the channel through which pressure is brought to bear; exhibitors subscribe to annual reports on "marquee value"—estimating the drawing power of a star's name, all by itself—and they also make known their preference as to the kind of pictures they want. As one-third of the box-office receipts goes to the producing studio, these expressions are treated with respect. The

small independent exhibitor has to trail along with the big operators, conscious of his service to the community and perhaps
wondering whether influence must always be in proportion to
income. These small exhibitors have not, in the past, been precisely free in their enterprise; contracts with the studios have
bound them in many ways, and the system of distribution has
by-passed the free competitive market.

The exhibitors make their wants known by criticism of the
current product and at times are shrewd in their comments
(which are liberally quoted in the *Motion Picture Herald*); as
when, during the fatuous cycle of historical movies, one wrote,
"Don't send me any more pictures where the hero signs his name
with a feather." The most conspicuous instance occurred when
a chain of theaters denounced Katharine Hepburn as "box-office
poison"; her spirited reaction to this was to buy *The Philadelphia
Story*, in which she had returned to the stage; she helped finance
the movie version and restored herself as a first-rate "marquee"
property. A great many exhibitors complain that they are without influence, that the studios make pictures without studying
the needs of the exhibitor, and that the system of block-booking
has forced them to play pictures they did not want in order to
get the studios' superior products. The system is now being
abandoned, in the interests of free competition, and it is generally assumed that the studios will have to make better pictures
since each one will be sold on its merits. However, one realistic
observer, after twenty years of experience as an exhibitor, has
expressed grave doubts, saying that by block-booking the studios
often forced the exhibitor to show their finer products and that
now they may not make any exceptional pictures since they cannot be sure that exhibitors will take the risk of showing them.
This gloomy reasoning is supported by the action of small operators throughout the country who declared that the slump in
attendance in 1948-49 was due to the production of too many
pictures "for sophisticated Broadway audiences" and the New
York critics. They called for a return to pictures which would

please the mass audience, darkly warning Hollywood that "some other form of entertainment" (a euphemism for television) might supplant the movies if they became a "class medium." Since the routine studio product, not the exceptional pictures, had in effect destroyed the audience, this comment was notably pointless. Denouncing the exhibitor is a commonplace of all discussion of the movies. In *Life*'s Round Table on the subject in 1949, Joseph Manckiewicz, who has been responsible for many successful pictures as writer, director, or producer, asked, "Who controls the movies? . . . Isn't it true that a real-estate operator whose chief concern should be taking gum off carpets, . . . isn't it true that this man is in control? . . . Here is . . . the real undercover man in the motion-picture industry—the exhibitor." In this indictment no distinction is made between the real-estate department of a major studio, which runs several hundred big-city theaters, and the owner of two or three houses in small towns. If the major companies follow the example of Paramount in "divorcing" production from exhibition, each one will create a powerful chain of theaters—the one developed from Paramount will control six hundred and fifty theaters—and many smaller ones; the owners of medium-size chains will gain in relative importance; but it isn't likely that the individual taste of the exhibitors will influence the production of movies to any revolutionary extent.

From time to time the studios have tried to convince exhibitors that a picture would make money. Pictures have been pretested by telling a selected group of people the story, the title, the names of the stars, and noting the degrees of enthusiasm they express. (As pretesting is more completely developed in the radio business, I will discuss it fully in that connection.)

The Johnston office makes its own sampling of information. It works with committees in the General Federation of Women's Clubs, the DAR, and Protestant, Catholic, and Jewish groups; it learns from them what objectionable features there may be in pictures previewed by its committees, and also gets "suggestions as to pictures not yet in production," which it transmits directly to the producers. By pretesting and getting the criticism before pictures are made, the producers manage to stand the pyramid of creativeness on its head. The imagination functions only after its effects are known.

Pacifying the exhibitor by pretesting is perhaps a symptom of uneasiness in the minds of producers, an awareness that all's not quite right in the movie world. The known facts seem to indicate that the movies subsist on the movie-going habit and that the habit breaks down; neither of these circumstances has ever been fully accepted by producers, who have obstinately held to the principle that people go to the movies to see stars and listen to stories and watch brilliant productions—and that they never stop going.

## "LET'S GO TO THE MOVIES"

Since we now know how few separate individuals make up the movie audience, it is clear that repetitive, unselective, almost automatic attendance at the movies is a prime economic factor. In the formation of any habit, sameness of stimulant and confidence in the effect are required; within the over-all sameness there can be some minor variety—the baseball fan doesn't want to see the Giants play the Dodgers every day; and even some variation of effect is tolerated. A definite additional thrill comes from the appearance of a new sensation, especially when it delivers the faithful and wanted reaction in the end. The reader of mysteries, of Westerns, of comic strips expects the familiar response and is satisfied to delay its coming when material new in its outward appearance takes the place of the old. The simplest stage—of the child insisting that stories be repeated verbatim—gives place to the more sophisticated pleasure of watching the old emerge from a new disguise.

The basic audience, from the start, went to a movie because it was a novelty—and was playing around the corner. They went to all the movies. Later, the sprouting of many movie houses, with small admission charges, ministered to all the inclinations of the addict; he could be sure of getting a seat, he knew more or less what he was likely to get, and he would rather have a bad movie than none. Even the exploitation of the star system did not alter this habit. People went to see Chaplin or Pickford, probably both, when these two were racing through the headlines to see which would sign the first million-a-year contract in the movies; they also went to see the competitors and imitators of these two. There seemed to be an irreducible minimum who went to the movies because they were movies, regardless of stars or story.

Long after the movies had ceased to be a novelty, people continued to go because they were movies; this was true in the movies' first twenty years, when stories might be trifling episodes inflated to five reels or major classics reduced to one; when players were anonymous or stage stars were imported, exploited, and rejected; when famous novelists condescended to write for the screen or actors improvised their plots as they went along. The basic forms of the movies were established in those days: the chase picture (Western or criminal), the historical romance, the biography, the problem play, the slapstick comedy, the spectacle; even polite comedy existed by 1914, with a certain satiric wit; with *The Birth of a Nation* in 1916 the spectacle picture arrived in glory, undiminished to this day.

Personal scandals, protests against the immorality of the "vamp" cycle, and, in the 1920's, a slackening of creative power as well as some overblown investments in real estate, brought the industry to a low point; but stars (including Rin-tin-tin) and the large residual audience that continued to go, no matter what, carried the movies over some rough spots. Sound threatened to destroy the studios but was actually their savior, and a new phase of movie-going began; without sound, the competition of radio, after 1924, would have been fatal. Although the movies went bankrupt in the first years of the depression, movie attendance held at a high level, the public spending a greater share of its

income on pictures in 1933 when it had least to spend than it
ever did before or after.

It isn't necessary to trace the persistence of the movie habit
in further detail. We know now that while it has been, in the
past, strong enough to keep the movies going, it has not persisted
into maturity and middle age; if the movies lose their foreign
markets and stumble over their adjustment to television, the re-
capture of the adult audience will be an absolute necessity for
survival. A few efforts have already been made to discover why
movie attendance has slumped; but they are usually based on
false assumptions about the motive for going or they accept
uncritically whatever catchword is current. During the past three
years the catchword has been more intelligent than most: it is
"maturity." Mr. Johnston has, indeed, warned his clients that
they have not kept pace with the growing intelligence of the
public or with the spread of education as represented by the
number of high school graduates; he has advised Hollywood to
make pictures for adults. The criteria for mature pictures have,
however, not been established.

## COMING OF AGE IN AMERICA

As Americans pass through the stages of courtship and begin
married life, as they go to work, break from the protection and
discipline of their parents, and begin to establish families of their
own, the need for the particular satisfactions given by the movies
becomes less acute. The image of the hero, the throb of passion,
the myth of success, *as conceived by the movies,* are no longer
needed; and as time goes on they become unacceptable.

A good part of the defection from the movie houses is explained by this gradual maturing of the audience. Neither the
friendly encouragement of the dark theater nor the stimulus of
unreal passion on the screen is needed when the ritual of courtship is over; the business of getting on in the world and of setting up a new household absorbs both husband and wife; new

friends and new ways of being with old friends are developed; there is less free time—until the baby-sitter became a recognized social figure, evenings were particularly taken. But the movies cannot put forward these social and economic changes as a complete explanation. The attraction of the movies grows progressively weaker; there is no return to the theaters after business is going well and money for tickets is to be had and the children are growing up and the total habit of life is firmly grounded. Neither the happily married nor those who bump their way over disappointments and divorce seek consolation from the movies; those for whom the success story of the movies was prophetic stay away, and so do those whom it deluded. The habit broken in the first years of adult life is never resumed.

The changes one undergoes in the years when a life pattern is being set make the movie myth irrelevant; when we see that the myth is actually false, it becomes intolerable. In their twenties young Americans not only marry and set up housekeeping and begin to have children; they become aware of new duties and responsibilities: they have to borrow money and meet their debts; they pay taxes and mortgage their homes; they meet the pressure of law and social opinion; they plant themselves, not as irrevocably as Europeans, but firmly enough, and the pattern their lives will follow begins to form. Under compulsion they begin to see what life is like, not the ultimate philosophical essence of life, but the day-to-day actuality. The atmosphere of American life, since the 1920's at least, tends to delay this coming of age; the movies and radio, the entire advertising business, conspire to prolong adolescence until we are in danger of becoming a nation of teen-agers; but biologic and economic pressures still keep to their appointed paths, and at a point where they converge the cross-mark is made, signifying that a young man or a young woman has become an individual, responsible, fairly integrated, and prepared to continue life in a certain direction. This happens to the ignorant and to the well informed; it has little to do with intellectual capacity; it is a consequence not of education but of experience. To see life steadily and see it whole is given to a minute fraction of humanity; but merely suffering and enjoying the small emotions and the domestic trials of an ordinary life have an effect; and those who go through a few years of adult life cannot change themselves back. That is what the movies, which shrink from changing themselves, are asking the audience to do.

The staple commodity of Hollywood is a small group of myths. Unlike the ancient myths, they are not associated with profound religious experience, but, like those myths, they "embody some popular idea concerning natural or historical phenomena." The rest of the definition (in the Shorter Oxford Dictionary) is also applicable: "a purely fictitious narrative usually involving supernatural persons, actions, or events," and one of the meanings of "mythical" is "having no foundation in fact." The mature mind does not reject a myth that corresponds to actuality, because in its origin any myth is an imaginative explanation of a mystery; but the myth must be incarnated into a story to become fiction as we know it, an imaginative re-creation of reality. The myths we reject are not interpretations but falsifications, and the popular ideas they embody may once have been relevant but are so no longer. Grown men and women, and cynics among them, cherish the legend of Galatea, to which Bernard Shaw gave flesh and blood and fundamental brainwork in *Pygmalion*. They insist that the myth must have its own reality; they are as eager as little children to listen to a story, but the story must be true to life either as they know it or as they want it to be; and it must be a story even if it embodies a myth.

Why Hollywood is committed to mythology and can no longer tell a story will presently become clear. For the moment, we can approach the problem of maturity from another direction, observing the movies that are by common consent called mature and inquiring whether they can actually please an adult but not intellectual audience.

## MATURITY, FOREIGN AND DOMESTIC

The accolade of maturity is usually given to European pictures. Some of these are so alien to our modes of thinking that comparisons are useless; but the British product is close to our own in general method and purpose. I take, for my first example, a straight cops-and-robbers picture, *Odd Man Out*, directed in 1947 by Carol Reed for Filippo del Guidice, and *Naked City*, produced by the late Mark Hellinger for Universal (1948).

In each an act of violence is committed at the beginning; in each the police track down the criminal; in *Odd Man Out* a number of people take an interest in the man; some of them hide him, some expose him to his enemies; while in *Naked City* the police are hindered chiefly by accomplices; in each picture the criminal is brought to bay and killed by the police. Having said this much, I have told nothing of the essence of *Odd Man Out* and, at the same time, have said everything worth saying about *Naked City* except that the final chase, along the superstructure of a New York bridge, was excellently photographed and thrilling.

The technical wizards in Hollywood cannot duck the question: By what means did a British variation of our specialty, the escape-and-chase picture, manage to be something like a serious work of art? Why was it profoundly exciting when it stopped being a thriller? Why did its theme seem important, its passions intense, its tragic end so satisfying? The last question is, in a way, the answer to the others. That a cops-and-robbers picture should have a guiding line of thought, that its people should be moved and shaken and reconciled by profound human passions, that the death of the hunted hero-criminal should be tragic—these are the elements our gangster pictures deliberately avoid.

The robbery which launches the story of *Odd Man Out* is undertaken to get funds for a secret political movement vaguely defined as "the Organization." Alien as this is to American experience, it was convincing; the somber fanaticism of the men as

they planned the raid gave the Organization actuality and significance, so that a groundwork of sympathy for the robbers was
laid, and out of this sympathy rose all the later emotions of the
audience. Before we had lived with them five minutes we saw
evil deeds flowing out of a noble motive and were committed
from that moment to pity for good men who could never be
good again because they were involved in murder; we felt hope
and anxiety and fear, the dreadful sense of time running out while
the force of law, admirable in its action and not without pity
itself, closed in; it was not a simple matter of choosing sides, because we had the feeling that both the hunter and the hunted
would give their lives to undo the murder, the feeling that life
sometimes traps the good into evil ways and we are helpless.

In that mood we see Johnny shot by a mill-guard and returning the fire in a desperate attempt to get away; he cannot hold
on to the car and falls; the driver is afraid to go back for him,
and his other companions see him staggering into a side street;
returning later, they fail to find him. From that point the picture
divides into two lines which run parallel, then cross, and finally
converge. One is the story of the wounded man trying to get
away, dragging himself through mean streets, interrupting children at play, fainting in a shelter and waking to overhear the
whispers of lovers, stumbling unseen into a cab in the rainy night
and so passing the cordon of police. The other line brings in all
the people who want Johnny: the police to arrest him; the
jeweled Teresa, smuggler's fence and falsely warm hostess to
the Organization's boys, who wants to square herself with the
police by betraying Johnny; members of his gang who sacrifice
themselves to draw off the pursuers; a nondescript little bird
fancier who finds him and tries to sell him to a priest; the priest
who wants to save his soul; the Samaritans who give him first
aid but no more; the failed medical student who patches him up
so that he can go to his fate; the artist who wants to paint the
look of death in his eyes; the girl who loves him and wants to
save him or die with him.

It has something of the effect of a diagram: faith, science, art, society, love—all competing for the body and soul of man. But with one exception, the artist, all the characters are saved from becoming abstractions, each has a life of his own; they are equipped not with superficial little characteristics but with complete and rounded characters; each has lived before the picture started, and the survivors of the tragedy will live on after it is ended. The streets through which they move are alive with junkyards and bookstalls and charwomen eating fish and chips from greasy papers and trams slewing round corners and factory whistles and men talking politics as they drink beer in saloons and women doing a bit of late marketing; they generate a sense of actuality so that the Belfast I have never seen is more real and palpable to me than the familiar ways of New York in the glossy brightness of *Naked City*.

The instant creation of a powerful emotion and the persisting sense of actuality are two of the three major elements in *Odd Man Out*; the third, the most subtle, is the satisfaction of a profound subconscious need: the picture makes you feel that it exists in time.

This is an extraordinarily difficult thing to do in the movies, which are seen in one unbroken sequence, but it is indispensable. Unless we feel that time is passing, we can have no sense of reality. Whenever we go to the movies we must live in two durations at once; first, our own in the theater, knowing while we sit there that at the end of two hours we must catch a train or stop at the delicatessen; and second, the duration of events on the screen, which may be shorter than our own in a Marx Brothers sequence or many times as long in a biography of Pasteur. (In a remarkable tour de force Alfred Hitchcock identified the two durations; all the events in *Rope* take place in a span of eighty minutes, and eighty minutes is precisely the time it takes the spectator to watch them unroll; the sense that time is passing is not, however, missing.) In *Odd Man Out*, skillful cutting between the two parallel actions, picking up the fugitive not where we last saw him but at a further stage on his doomed way, changes in light and in the pitch of the sound that the streets give off, all contribute; but, most of all, the admirable players themselves make us feel that they are living through events, their voices convey to us the passage of the hours, and we have in the end the final sense of reality, because we have, without knowing it, forgotten our own time, our trains and our errands, and have endured as long as the characters on the screen.

Could Hollywood make such a picture? The answer is that fifteen years ago Hollywood did; in a sense, Hollywood made this same picture, for *Odd Man Out* is a lineal descendant of *The Informer*, and in many ways *The Informer* is the more daring and the more successful. The central character is not a handsome hero played by a popular actor; in place of James Mason's Johnny there is the doltish confused Gyppo played by Victor McLaglen, an actor of known inadequacy upon whom a miracle was worked by the brilliant director, John Ford. Here, too, the minor people are rounded, the streets and barrooms are sound and solid, the alien air (of an Irish city again) is still the air we breathe. Liam Flaherty's book is a finer work than F. L. Green's *Odd Man Out*, and the screen play derived from it by Dudley Nichols is one of the movies' rare instances of creative adaptation. John Ford and Carol Reed have both been influenced by D. W. Griffith, the first man who tried to transmit a dominant emotion through atmosphere on the screen, so the two pictures are technically parallel. *The Informer* also creates the illusion of time passing, and in pace, in pitch of voices, and in lighting, both directors deliberately "underplayed": the murmur of human conversation gives its tone to the pictures, not the projection of dialogue, and dramatic scenes are played for their full value without staccato interruptions of fresh angle-shots. A defect of *The Informer* is that almost all of it is played in semidarkness; the fearful atmosphere of Dublin in the days of The Trouble is impressive, but the picture is hard to see.

The history of *The Informer* is enlightening. Like other distinguished works, it was not a studio enterprise, and an executive of RKO whom I congratulated on the production said, with a rare mixture of grace and candor, "We aren't entitled to credit. John Ford wanted to do it and we let him." As things go, letting a successful director do a picture out of which the studio expects no profit is infrequent, and sometimes the studio is startled by the result. Favorable notices and Academy Awards went to Nichols, Ford, and McLaglen for the best screen play, the best direction, and the best performance by an actor, yet *The Informer* was not, by Academy standards, the best movie of the year, an honor which went to *Mutiny on the Bounty*. (The "Oscars" represent the personal judgment of people in the industry, choosing among pictures proposed by other people in the industry.) *The Informer* continued to be shown profitably for several years and is still revived occasionally.

I have compared one of the best melodramas ever made with a picture considerably above the Hollywood average and have introduced *The Informer*, one of a handful of great pictures, to indicate that the making of movies satisfactory to the adult intelligence is not a national prerogative of the British. For a second set of examples, I choose an English picture which did not give me exceptional pleasure and compare it with an American picture of far more than usual quality: *Brief Encounter* and *Double Indemnity*.

Here, as in the first instance, the two pictures start with the same opening sequence. A man and a woman meet by chance and are instantly swept away by a frightening passion for each other. In *Brief Encounter* the lovers meet once or twice at a railway station restaurant, they go to see an American movie, they are observed by acquaintances who might gossip, and their one assignation is interrupted in a singularly unconvincing and tasteless sequence (the unexpected return of the owner of the flat and an implausible tirade on morality); they part, the man to make the conventional British journey of thwarted love, the woman to return to her husband and family (and the child oblig-

ingly is in bed with a sprained ankle or measles or whatever
occupational disease afflicts children whose parents must be re-
united). Written by Noel Coward, who co-directed with David
Lean, *Brief Encounter* is uninventive and at times inept.

In the picture Raymond Chandler and Billy Wilder made out
of James M. Cain's novelette, *Double Indemnity*, at least three
deaths by violence occur (lover and mistress kill the husband and,
soon after, each other), and there are hints of earlier misdeeds.
The technical virtuosity of the production is a pleasure to be-
hold. The nemesis of the lovers is the claims agent of an insurance
company, and the way his instincts warn him of a fraud is woven
into the story so deftly before he has to act in the central drama
that his intervention is expected, giving the spectator a sense
of threat—and at the same time providing a grotesquely comic
sequence for contrast. The rendezvous in a supermarket is a
masterly handling of all the surfaces of a complicated event. And
the triumph of the picture is that the writer and producer, forbidden by the Production Code from saying anything significant
about the passion between the man and the woman, a passion
almost animal in its instant and exclusive focus on copulation, still
managed to suggest that it did exist. For an American picture,
usually compelled to be false and driven to sly sentimentality
in self-defense, this is exceptional; sensuality is implicit when
Fred MacMurray's eyes follow Barbara Stanwyck's ankle-
bracelet down the stairs as she comes from a sun bath, and it
runs through the early scenes of the picture until the moment
she visits him at his apartment; there, in spite of a slight disorder in the dress, it becomes clear that we no longer are concerned with human beings but with movie characters. From that
point the picture revolves around Edward G. Robinson, who
suspects murder but does not know that the murderer works
in his own office.

Obviously the two pictures, starting from the same event, were
not trying to do the same thing, and it would be as silly to condemn the American for being a melodrama as to belittle the Eng-

lish one for being too taciturn and undramatic. It is not, however, an isolated thing that an American picture turns toward violence and a British toward a more common mood; violence without meaning, according to Max Lerner, is the outstanding characteristic of our film product, and if it is a distortion of the truth of our daily lives, we must face the fact that the Production Code effectively prevents Hollywood from using the truth; in foolish pictures sentimentality takes its place; in serious ones the substitute is a kind of hectic activity which usually turns violent and thus leads to retribution, giving a legalistic and hypocritical "moral" ending. In *Double Indemnity* the mortally wounded hero, after telling his story to a dictaphone, tries to crawl away and save himself, but he fails. Death is his portion. In *Brief Encounter* the hero and heroine have.to live.

And it is possible for them to live because, in spite of the hokum and stale devices of the plot, the principal characters were presented to us with the accent of truth; everything in *Double Indemnity* was made plausible, the surface was brilliant, and you did not have to live in Los Angeles to identify the boxes of soap flakes on the supermarket shelves, the basement garage, the cluttered living room, the daughter going down to a date at the corner. The people were projected larger than life, but they were not filled with the emotions and the significance of life, so that they were really inflated, and when the picture came to an end they collapsed. The highly charged apparition of Miss Stanwyck was correct for the picture; Celia Johnson, who played the woman in *Brief Encounter* (and wore a simple dress throughout) was right as a complete human being. The pitch and the pace of that picture were right for the people in that particular predicament, so that after believing that these events happened to them, we came to believe they might happen to anyone, to ourselves. The scale was life-size.

A third pairing of British and American pictures is *The Fallen Idol* and *The Window*. The first was directed by Carol Reed, using a screenplay written by Graham Greene, who also wrote

the original story. Mr. Greene is a master of the compassionate
escape-and-pursuit story, and Mr. Reed's direction of this picture
is in many ways superior to his *Odd Man Out*. It is a story disclosed to us as it comes before the eyes of a little boy; we see
what he sees; often when adults are speaking and he is not interested in what they are saying, the voices seem to fade and blur.
He worships the butler, Baines, and becomes aware of an attach-
ment between Baines and an attractive girl whom the boy calls
Baines' "niece." Before the boy's eyes, Baines and his wife quarrel and a scuffle follows; running down an outside stairway, the
boy reaches a lower window and sees the woman dead. He thinks
he has witnessed a murder.

The *Window* was produced by the late Frederic Ullman for
RKO. In it, also, a youngster sees what he believes to be a murder; as he is given to telling wild stories, no one believes what he
says. His parents punish him and force him to apologize to the
man and the woman he has accused, delivering him over to them;
since the boy's story is true, the murderers try to do away with
him, and the boy is rescued after a masterly sequence of suspense
which is like a ghastly game of hide-and-seek. In the character of
the parents and in the techniques of telling the story, this picture
is far above the average.

The *Window* shies away from doing what *The Fallen Idol*
does supremely well: it does not tackle the implied moral problem. Both pictures revolve around a child's telling the truth: in
*The Window* the boy that tells the truth is not believed; in *The
Fallen Idol* the boy refuses to talk and then lies to protect the
man he idolizes. The man and his mistress urge the boy to tell
the truth, but the part of the truth the boy knows would condemn his friend. As the inquisition goes remorselessly on and the
boy discovers that Baines' stories of adventure and heroism are
lies, his moral universe is shattered; and in the end an irrelevant
piece of evidence frees Baines from suspicion, leaving the boy
tortured by the refusal of his elders to hear him and lost in a
world of broken faith. It is a complex psychological situation,

reduced to understandable terms by the faultless direction of Mr. Reed; the suspense, as the boy tries to tell his story, is as great as the suspense of watching the boy in *The Window* trying to escape from the murderers; but *The Fallen Idol* touches the heart as well as the nerve-ends and is one of the finest pictures of our time, whereas *The Window* remains only a superior diversion.

I have intentionally passed by the major classics and the grim realistic pictures made in Continental Europe, because I am looking for criteria of maturity in the kind of picture that can be made and successfully presented in America. It is plain that the aversion of Hollywood to mature pictures is based on a fear and a misconception: the fear is that such pictures will not pay and will kill off the present audience; the misconception is that mature pictures must be disagreeable. The melodramas and the love story I have described are not of this order. Before identifying in them the particular qualities that make them mature, it is only fair to look at those pictures which were made in Hollywood and can be called adult.

*The Lost Weekend:* made at the urgent request of Brackett and Wilder, who between them had turned in a dozen or more highly profitable pictures for their studios; at its sneak preview the audience (including many children) expected a Long Island mystery-comedy-melodrama and tried hard to laugh until the nature of the picture became manifest. The studio executives thought it needed a lot of changes but eventually let it stand as made. The motive of homosexuality was perforce eliminated in the treatment of the drunkard, but the story remained grim and frightening; the "happy" ending was not tacked on, it is in the book. The picture had enormous advance publicity and won the Academy Award; it was highly profitable.

*Gentlemen's Agreement:* a superficial, badly acted, woefully directed attempt to bring the theme of anti-Semitism to the screen. The characters were smart stereotypes, the theme was handled gingerly; intellectually the picture was a fraud. A melodrama, *Crossfire*, was more explicit and effective with the same theme. That a subject of concern to the entire world, widely discussed during the war, should come to the screen in spite of the possibility of offending a portion of the audience was the important element.

*Home of the Brave:* a better handling of the theme of prejudice, this time against the Negro. It is interesting to note that while the picture was forthright, the advertising was mincing and timid: "A picture that dares to take a stand—and stands alone." There was no indication anywhere in the ad of what it stood for or against. A simply made war story, using narcosynthesis for shock effect (on the audience too), but not distorted.

*The Best Years of Our Lives:* an overrated, pseudo-realistic story of the reintegration of soldiers into domestic life. Good solid episodes, nearly everything glossy and sliced thin.

*The Treasure of the Sierra Madre:* made at the request of John Huston, with the enthusiastic support of Humphrey Bogart, both of them hugely profitable for Warner Brothers. The story of three men who hunt for and find gold, suspect one another, and come to grief. No women are among the principles, and the oppressive Production Code is evident, if at all, only in the relative purity of the language of the prospectors. Completely honest, directed with a surer sense of the cinematic art than any other American picture in a decade, it was presented in a large Broadway house, received enthusiastic praise, and failed to draw sufficient audiences. When it was nominated for an Academy Award it was again shown, with another nominee, *Johnny Belinda*, without much success. Two awards to Huston (plus one to his father for the best acting in a supporting role) were not enough to give it a new lease of life. The attitude of Warner Brothers was almost hostile; before the Academy nominations were in, Jack Warner compared the gross receipts (about a million and a half dollars) with that of a Betty Grable picture (nearly three times as much) and announced his rule for the future: "Art is out." Mr. Huston in accepting the award thanked

Henry Blanke, his producer; for the studio he had meanwhile done a debased gangster picture based on *Key Largo*.

*Monsieur Verdoux:* nothing of Chaplin's has ever been infantile, and this was a serio-comedy of the first rank. As writer, director, and star in pictures financed by himself, Chaplin is unique; his pictures represent a single, undammed flow of creative effort. His limitations as philosopher, statesman, and analyst of the human heart are serious, but in his great works he transcends them; he simplifies, he transforms his prejudices into tragi-comic motives; he drops his theses by the way, drawn by his genius to create. In *Monsieur Verdoux* this process was not completely successful; some private rancors corrupt the character of Verdoux. Yet as a whole it was an impressive and disturbing work; financially it was a complete failure.

It offended Catholics by the flippant "What can I do for *you?*" with which the man about to be guillotined met the priest; it flouted the current morality of money and murder and sex; it was wildly funny with an overtone of horror. Yet the failure of the picture was not altogether due to its content. Chaplin's political views and private life created a hostile atmosphere; a group of Ohio exhibitors and chain operators refused to show the picture; and Chaplin did not have what the average studio movie does have—a commitment from a sufficient number of exhibitors to show it.

The pictures I have mentioned here are on the serious side, but any picture in which an intelligent adult can take pleasure should be considered mature, and of these Hollywood has made many. *The Great McGinty* and *Hail the Conquering Hero, Hold Back the Dawn,* which had a rare and authentic feeling of romance, *My Man Godfrey, Mr. Deeds Goes to Town, The Farmer's Daughter, The Jolson Story, Hell's Angels*—these are titles picked among the average A pictures. They were made by writers and directors and players steeped in the Hollywood tradition. They are not cited as examples of great art, but they are far from infantile, and they prove that Hollywood not only can make intelligent pictures but can make a huge profit out of them.

The trifles in this random list indicate that maturity is not "box-office poison." They suggest also that both Hollywood producers and intellectual critics should revise their ideas. Maturity does not necessarily imply either the tragic sense of life or an excessive sophistication. The mature picture makes no demand on the audience which the average adult is unable, or unwilling, to meet; and it gives such satisfaction that it can accomplish what the basic childish product has failed to do: it can keep the larger part of the audience coming to the movies instead of driving it away.

The more generalized attitude of the intellectuals, their dislike of domestic movies, their enthusiasm for foreign films, might have some effect on Hollywood if the critics thought out their objections and expressed them clearly. The studios make a distinction between intellectuals and the public: the former want tragedy, the latter want to avoid it. Actually, sound critics know that the true tragic spirit is rare, and what they really want is for Hollywood not to distort character and tragic action in order to send the audience home with a smile as well as a tear. American critics in particular should understand that the sense of tragedy does not rise out of an abstraction but corresponds to the human condition of an era and a country. In the past, poets may have felt the pity of struggling against destiny, the sadness of death taking off the young and the beautiful, the bitterness of injustice; but they were also influenced by the poverty and hopelessness of the common man, by the fatal bars of privilege, by slavery and grinding toil and hunger. If the happy ending was only an aspiration to people in the past, a life free from pressing want is an actuality of the present American economy for such numbers of people that our atmosphere is charged with confidence. The background against which tragedy was written in the past does not exist here, and if we do not create great tragedies it may be because they are not necessary for us. The individual who cannot understand tragedy in the arts may become incapable of facing anything serious in his own life; but this does not mean that the popular arts are under any compulsion to be largely tragic in tone. An aesthete and an intellectual of the first order has even been skeptical of the uses of tragedy: "Because Aeschylus and Sophocles were great poets," Santayana writes, "does it follow that life would be cheap if it did not follow their fables? The life of tragic heroes is not good; it is misguided, unnecessary, and absurd." In this respect, the executives of Hollywood seem to adhere to the life of reason more closely than their critics.

## THE MECHANICS OF MATURITY

The single mark of maturity, stamped like a seal of approval on all the pictures I have mentioned, sunny or somber, is this: the story develops in humanly acceptable terms; even in farcical situations the actions are credible although we could never have predicted them; and the threads of the serious stories are woven logically into their complete pattern. Moreover, the characters are men and women, individuals not types; their motives are understandable, and the fictions in which they appear are stories not myths; whether they are retelling or reversing the legend of Cinderella in *The Farmer's Daughter* or Jack-the-Giant-Killer with Mickey Mouse, they are not escaping from our human predicament, they are only relating the myth to our times.

These pleasant unpretentious pictures are mere flickers of light in the movie houses, passing quickly over the screen, their place taken for months on end by works false in concept and feeble in execution, but so skillful in technique that their emptiness is not sensed until later—at the moment, perhaps, when one decides not to go again without being sure the picture is a good one, the moment when the habit of going to the movies begins to break. These are movies made to be forgotten, and they must be made that way to fit into the system of distribution and exhibition which has for a generation dominated the industry.

The merchandising of movies has passed through many phases

in the past fifty years and is about to enter a new one which will, in the end, take from the studios their control of the theaters. The intricate arrangements by which exhibitors have in the past been compelled to sign up for movies before they were made and, in recent years, to take pictures they did not want in order to get those they did want are relatively unimportant. The significant element is the attitude of the theater owner to the public. The exhibitor, like any other retailer, has a commodity to sell, and the merchandising principle almost universally accepted in the industry is to sell the same product to the same people as often as possible. The product must have no special quality, it must be average, because it is offered to a large, fairly homogeneous group of buyers, who would no more accept an unusual picture under the familiar trademarks than they would accept an occasional bar of green soap in an Ivory wrapper. There is no time to bring in another group of customers; all the regulars must be attracted to the theater within three days or a week, except in the showcases where a picture sometimes may be held for a long time to build up prestige. It is the system of the corner orange-juice stand; it is not the system of the village grocery store or the mail-order house or General Motors.

More than ten years ago Walter Wanger analyzed the ills of the movie industry and called it "co-ordinated to the point of regimentation . . . in its exhibition and distribution setup." In a phase of aggressive independence, he wrote: "The unconscious stifling of experimentation within our industry stems from our mode of distribution. . . . The biggest obstacle to our progress is the super-colossal first-run theater. . . . Each successive feature film must be . . . capable . . . of breaking a dozen records *during the first day* of its run. If it doesn't . . . exhibitors turn the cold shoulder. . . . This is sheer madness. It goes without saying that a film like *Dodsworth* will not gross as much as an Astaire-Rogers musical. Hence a big-theater opening may well ruin its future. But that does not mean that it could not make money if it were properly handled."

Not on the strength of his experience alone, but observing the fate of many other pictures, Mr. Wanger comes to this conclusion: "Our industry should develop an additional first-run circuit of medium-size houses—for which we could produce good medium-budget films which would not have to possess record-breaking mass appeal in order to make money. . . . Movie makers would be in a position to risk the introduction of new ideas. . . . We would also have the opportunity to educate audiences to new types of films—and, indeed, to win entirely new audiences from among those who can't stomach the type of formula film we concentrate on at present. . . . There is a different type of interest growing up—an interest in the realistic treatment of the real issues of the modern world. While . . . continuing to produce the best of the present type of film, the industry can win new audiences by presenting a new type of material more in the modern temper."

Mr. Wanger has produced pictures directly for the studio corporations which own the big theaters; for ten years he was general manager in charge of production at Paramount; he was an executive producer at MGM and later a vice-president of Columbia Pictures. His preferred system of production is to work independently for release by a major studio; he made the remarkable *Private Worlds* and the strange political picture *The President Vanishes* for Paramount to distribute, and the almost outspoken anti-Franco picture *Blockade* and Eugene O'Neill's *Long Voyage Home*, which is still being shown occasionally at large neighborhood houses as well as in art theaters. Perhaps because no secondary system of distribution was ever established, Mr. Wanger has recently been making conventional melodramas for the usual channels and exploiting his *Joan of Arc* through special showings. His talent for the unusual, but not for the radically different, is precisely what Hollywood needed to balance its product; but the edge of his enterprise was blunted by repeated collisions with the stony indifference of the distributors. It is something to make an exceptional picture now and then;

but, like others of the same temper, Wanger has had to waste time on tedious hackwork; his hope for the creation of supplementary audiences, which can be realized only if we have a steady flow of superior pictures, still lies in the future.

The case history of *The Search* is an instance of audience-building. The picture was made by Europeans on a European theme—a mother's search for a lost child. It had exploitable values —Montgomery Clift was on his way to popularity and the story of the child actor, Ivan Jandl, was useful—but theme and direction were alien to our habits and the pace of the story was not exciting. The picture was first placed in a fairly large special house; it was praised, and the appeal to an audience interested in the problems of Europe was prominent. In a year the picture grossed eight hundred and fifty thousand dollars, playing in all sorts of places, and the prospect was for a profit of a million dollars for MGM, which bought all rights to the picture for one-third that amount. At about the same time *Paisan*, spoken in a mixture of languages, was so successful that after a long run in a small theater it became part of a double bill on the Loew circuit. It was also during this period that, as noted before, *The Treasure of the Sierra Madre* failed to meet its obligations in two weeks at a large Broadway house, was pulled, and never had a chance to recover.

Such successes, as well as the failure of mature pictures which did not get "special handling," demonstrate the soundness of Mr. Wanger's approach. His analysis was made before the facts about audiences were known. He spoke, consequently, of educating and winning new audiences, unaware of the failure of the movies even to keep those audiences in whom it had instilled the movie habit. His argument remains valid; the formula movie designed for instant acceptance by the mass audience is not enough: not enough, as he put it, to keep experimentation alive; not enough, as we now know, to keep the movie business solvent as film makers.

The pressure of the big metropolitan house, the urgency to

get the audience, any audience, into the theater *during the first day of a run*, the quick dismissal of a picture if it does not instantly make the grade, are all reflected in subsequent showings. The neighborhood houses work on a known repetitive beat: a new picture or double bill every three days unless a sensational feature is available for a week; smaller places exhaust their current patronage even faster. There is no time to build an audience, and if an exhibitor books an exceptional picture he usually gives it only a few days to prove its drawing capacity. He cannot afford to show it at a loss, and he must offer a new picture to attract his regular customers. Unless a way is discovered to build new audiences, criticism of the exhibitor is futile.

The way suggested by Mr. Wanger ten years ago was more practical then than it is now. When each of the producing studios had a large number of theaters, a certain number of them could have been set aside for the showing of pictures which did not depend on immediate success, and the studios could have made such pictures. A picture could have been held over at a loss for a week or two while its good reputation spread. There would always be the chance that this would not happen, and this would be matched by the chance that some of these specially made and specially handled pictures would become great successes. Now that the studios are losing control of the theaters, the risk can be taken only by the exhibitor, who may have less reserves to invest in promoting a film that builds slowly. It becomes less likely that studios will produce such pictures. Yet the essence of the Wanger proposal is reflected in the conclusions of Adolph Zukor, chairman of the board at Paramount; having weathered wars and the sound track and bankruptcy and inordinate success, Mr. Zukor declared in the middle of 1949 that "pictures with abnormal staying power must be made," and he added, "The public is just not going to a theater for the sake of seeing any picture." "Abnormal staying power" is exhibitor's lingo for attracting fresh audiences. Reflecting on the system of quick turnovers, Mr. Zukor noted: "It is not the number of pictures which will keep the theaters open any longer"—that is to say, feeding a new picture in for a short run is no longer profitable.

The reaction of the chain exhibitors to Hollywood's belated discovery of the vanishing audience was panicky. Giving himself sixty per cent of the receipts at the box-office, the exhibitor can make a profit on routine pictures and does not want to see Hollywood making fewer pictures for longer runs. Afraid that the studios would drop the quantity system of production, a group of important exhibitors announced that if Hollywood interfered with the present rate of supply they themselves would finance independent producers out of a fund of several million dollars. This was a threat; it has not been made good; but it is in keeping with the traditions of the movie industry. A group of exhibitors and distributors, dissatisfied with the conditions imposed upon them, banded together and created First National, which eventually became part of Warner Brothers.

The nucleus of a supplementary system of distribution exists: a few hundred small houses which used to call themselves "art theaters" and were known in the trade as "sure-seaters" because there were always empty seats. Most of them are situated in low-rental areas and compete with the neighborhood houses, not the showcases. Their number is increasing; newsreel theaters have succumbed to the inroads of television and turned themselves into "special" houses, and this may give a clue to the kind of audiences that these houses can attract. It is clear that the mass appeal of television, in its present phase, is virtually the same as the appeal of the routine movie; the movie house that wants to survive during the years of television's growth must attract the audience which has already drifted away from the movies and may not be firmly held by television at its present level of interest. This is the critical point in all plans for the future of the movies: to know what kind of audience can be persuaded to return to the theaters. The success of a small number of houses showing pictures generally called "superior" or "mature" is evidence that an audience exists, but the experience of the past few years is insufficient; we do not know how many such theaters would be supported. At present an unusual picture is placed in a single house and may run as long as six months, drawing customers from all sections of the city; it is possible that more people would go if the picture were shown simultaneously at several widely separated theaters, which would enable the producer to pay off his backers more promptly and free the investment for new productions; but this might exhaust the supply of desirable pictures too rapidly and lead straight back to the quantity system of movie production. Experienced men in the business say that a circuit of first-run houses for exceptional pictures is not required and insist that if the studios turn out the pictures, enough independent houses are waiting to show them. The studios, however, feel that even the steady increase in the number of special theaters gives no assurance that a moderately expensive picture would pay its costs in any reasonable time.

Obviously a double risk must be taken, by the exhibitors and by the studios. If the relative success of a few houses with a few pictures is insufficient data on which to establish a system of production, distribution, and exhibition, the negative evidence is overwhelming. Every inquiry into the reasons why people go less frequently to the movies brings the same answer: there aren't as many good movies as there used to be. According to Elmo Roper, thirty per cent of those who still go to the movies gave this reason. It isn't a scientific statement, but the meaning is clear: people are not sufficiently attracted to the movies that are offered, they do not feel that they have to see them. More than twice as many people say that going to the movies is too expensive, and while this may mean they "can't afford to go to any movies," it also includes the meaning that they "can afford to go only to the movies that seem best" to them. Some of those who stay away because of the cost must be added to those who stay away because the movies no longer satisfy them. When they are asked why they do not go to the movies, people do not say "we have outgrown them," but their specific reasons suggest precisely this.

They told Mr. Roper's researchers that they found movie plots "silly, pointless, and not realistic"; those who did not go disliked some kinds of entertainment that rank high in popularity: horror, murder, and Western films particularly. What they do want is "a humorous, exciting, or true-to-life kind of a story or all three rolled into one." Nothing could be more conclusive on both sides of the usual movie controversy: a large audience exists for the kind of movies made according to formula and a large audience exists for other movies which are not being made in sufficient quantities to keep people going regularly and with confidence to their local theaters. The additional evidence in favor of adding more *kinds* of pictures is that out of every ten individuals four go less often to the movies than they went three years ago and only one goes more often. (The date of the survey was 1949; other inquiries show that the decline in general attendance was probably greater in 1950 than in 1949, ten per cent against seven per cent.)

A sort of mental block has prevented clear thinking on the subject of movie quality. The highbrow critic has given the impression that no good can come out of Hollywood—or, as George Jean Nathan has put it, you can't hope for a Hollywood movie that wouldn't make a coalheaver belch. And the presumably hardheaded businessman has acted as if he had to choose between *The Informer* and Errol Flynn in a hopped-up and hoked-up version of *The Three Musketeers*. The critic has been using the fallacious either-or, answer-yes-or-no technique in the service of an absolute aesthetic ideal, and the businessman has been using it in the service of recurrent profits. The critic, as in the case of Wolcott Gibbs, has washed his hands of the mess, declaring that the rare good picture doesn't justify the waste of an intelligent man's time on the average junk, and the businessman has been afraid to make or exhibit anything out of the ordinary for fear of alienating his regular audience. The critical error is obvious: over the years a number of pictures have been intelligently made, enough of them to give hope, not enough to give satisfaction;

the error of the practical man is, as I have indicated, hidden, because he has made a fair profit. It is a serious error nonetheless; for the break in the movie-going habit has been caused not by the exceptional picture but by the average. The people who have virtually stopped going to the movies still go to see some of the great spectacular successes and some of the pictures honored by the critics. They are disappointed by, and eventually stay away from, the average.

One of the most frequent remarks made by studio executives when they are really exasperated is: "We aren't making pictures for the critics." If the country as a whole is considered, the standards of criticism are not set too high; but if it is true that the critics are more intelligent and more demanding than the average moviegoer, there is a chance that they represent the attitude of the people who have stopped going. A composite report on movie criticism is available in the monthly bulletins of *Consumers' Research*, which tabulates the verdicts of nineteen publications or groups that recommend or fail to recommend current pictures; the publications range from mass-circulation dailies to *The New Yorker* and include the trade press, which is relatively kind to pictures. In a recent issue two hundred and seventy movies were listed; of these nearly half, one hundred and fourteen movies, were definitely not recommended; the nineteen reviewers cast a total of six hundred and forty votes against pictures, and the few that were highly recommended averaged only three votes each. It is, of course, fashionable to write unfavorable notices, but there are only a few intellectual movie critics, and the job of the average reviewer is to let his readers know whether the picture is worth spending money on; his answer is "no" too often for comfort, and the producers cannot impute a supercilious intellectualism to the critic. It is not the critics, but the pictures, that keep people away.

For their own prosperity the movies have to invent a system of making and marketing two kinds of pictures simultaneously: those that will engage the interest of the habitual audience and those that will win back and keep the patrons who require something more than the quantity product can give. The first audience will graduate into the second, and the second will support pictures less expensive to make, pictures that will not exploit stars, but will create them for future use, and profit, in the more popular movies. It may be a hazardous business for several years; the alternative is to go down with no flag flying.

At the moment the chief propagandist for a supplementary system of distribution is Filippo del Guidice, tempestuous Italian-born producer of an impressive number of the most distinguished British films seen in America, ranging from *Tawny Pipit* and *In Which We Serve*, through *Odd Man Out*, to *Henry the Fifth* and *Hamlet*. He begins with the revolutionary principle that management must not interfere with the making of a picture once the talents have been engaged; his second principle is that production must be independent of distribution. Temperamentally incapable of making the established formula picture, which he calls the "habit film," he believes that the British industry should not be too closely tied to American studios and should export to the United States only such works as justify "special handling" and do not compete with the quick-run American product. In his own experience he has seen a picture do well in a medium-sized theater for four weeks, drop below the profit line for two or three weeks thereafter, and pick up from that moment to run for six months; during the critical period the exhibitor was prevented, by his contract, from taking the picture off; del Guidice has also seen one of his pictures fail of the profit margin, in an American house, and vanish after the second week. The two Olivier-Shakespeare productions were made when del Guidice's Two Cities Company had become part of the Rank organization, but their handling in America was altogether special: *Henry the Fifth* was treated as if it were too good for the average man, and the returns were slow and disappointing at the start; but it turned out to be a profitable film; *Hamlet* was placed in a single theater, at very high prices, in New York, and ran for sixty-six weeks.

Similar exploitation in key cities so built up its fame that the picture penetrated even into a drive-in on the Florida coast. In its second year it has already grossed several million dollars in the United States alone, and has gone into the chain theaters; it has a life expectancy probably greater than that of any other film of our time.

It is not by accident that I have cited practical men of the movie industry to describe and condemn the distribution system; I want to dissociate this section, at least, of the total analysis from any imputation of artiness; and I might have gone further and taken the case of the arch-independent, Samuel Goldwyn, who has never to my knowledge made an art picture, or a minority picture, or any picture whatever on which he did not confidently expect to show a thumping profit. Even his commanding position with United Artists, over many years, was insufficient to give Goldwyn the kind of releases he wanted, and he was forced at times into special exploitation, showing his films in convention halls and under canvas, to get them to his audience. For a regular producer who is spending his own money (he is, as far as I know, the only one), Goldwyn is singularly courageous; it is true that he wastes money on some appalling trash, especially in musical adventures and spectacles that may pay off; he is responsible for *The Kid from Spain* and *Kid Millions* and *The Princess and the Pirate* and *The Bishop's Wife*—a list deplorable enough for any one man. But he is also the financer-producer directly responsible for *Dodsworth* and *Dead End* and *Wuthering Heights* and *The Little Foxes* and *The Best Years of Our Lives*. I have no proof that under a plural system of distribution Goldwyn would have limited himself to making pictures as good as his best; I suspect him of having set great store by some of his second-order films while he was making them, but I know he is too shrewd a judge to think afterward that they were worth his time unless they helped finance his better pictures, which were generally quite able to pay handsomely for themselves. His career illuminates the struggle of the independent producer, the difficulties in the way of marketing pictures outside the established order. Because he finances himself, he can make a picture and, if necessary, road-show it or fight the distributors; without such means, an independent hardly dares to buy a story without feeling sure that his release will be forthcoming.

There was a moment at the end of the war when a number of independent producing companies came into existence, some to take advantage of a supposed loophole in the laws governing capital gains and some because men of talent wished to produce movies without interference from the front office. It was a bright prospect, and the brightest spot in it was Liberty Pictures, which combined the talents of Frank Capra, George Stevens, and William Wyler, all of whom had distinguished records before they went into the service; their films for the Army and Navy had been spectacular and had taught them much. With them was a shrewd businessman, and behind them, to release their pictures, stood RKO. Their first picture, *It's a Wonderful Life*, was neither good nor bad; it was too close to the usual thing to be remarkable, and its virtues were completely overshadowed by Goldwyn's *The Best Years of Our Lives*. The company was not encouraged to go on. It was not until almost five years later that anything remarkable came from independent sources. This was *Home of the Brave*, the first feature picture openly discussing race prejudice, independently produced by Stanley Kramer and his associates.

The man who leaves a studio to work independently returns if his venture fails; the independent who succeeds receives, and often accepts, tempting offers from the studios. The exceptional talent is eventually absorbed into the dominant system of production, and that system, as we will now see, has little place, and less enthusiasm, for the exception.

## "HOW TO SPEND A MILLION THREE"

"Do you know what a producer is? A producer is a man who knows how to spend a million three." The definition was given by a studio executive and is notable for its nonchalant attitude toward "three," which means three hundred thousand dollars. But the significant point is the prime function assigned to the man who stands at the top of the pyramid of authority when a picture is being made. He has superiors: the front office, including the executive producer, which is the link between individual producers and invisible financiers. The executive producer may make a picture himself at times, but generally he watches over the shooting of half a dozen movies at once, approving or correcting scripts, watching the daily rushes, ordering retakes. But in the daily work the producer is the responsible authority; he has to know about pictures and has to watch a budget; he has to bring the picture in on or before the appointed day; he has to know how to spend a million three.

In practice, much of his gaudy budget is spent for him the moment he begins work. A fourth or fifth of it is lopped off by the accounting department for overhead; if he has a thirty-day shooting schedule, the wages of all the technicians are calculated to the last dollar. The skillful producer can effect economies by eliminating waste, particularly waste of time; but except in periods of drastic economy, the unwritten rule has been that a picture *must* cost a certain amount; a story bought for a B picture and budgeted at half a million would be automatically rebudgeted at three times that amount if an A star was put into it, since stars will not appear in low-budget pictures. An inventive young man employed by a studio once worked out an ingenious plan for reducing the basic overhead cost by cutting shooting time in half and took it to his superior. The plan was rejected with the remark, "You're trying to make a B producer out of me." From its producers each studio requires results; money has to be spent advantageously. But the formula, a cheap picture is a B picture, held; and, at least subconsciously, the converse was accepted: an A picture must be expensive.

The moviegoer is unaware of the producer's function. By whom is the choice of story made and why? Whose concepts of human relations are embodied in the picture, whose are eliminated? Who creates, and whose creative power is tampered with or destroyed? Only a few of these questions are asked by the paying audience, which, quite legitimately, focuses on the finished product. They are, nonetheless, to be asked by the movie industry itself if it wants to enlarge its appeal. They should also be asked by any statesman who suspects that Pius XI and Lenin are more nearly right about the movies than Congressman Hoffman.

### THE ART OF LICKING

In making the average A picture the producer is in charge of a complex operation; if he is bringing to the screen a popular novel or play, he must preserve what is useful and at the same time make it conform to the mythology of the movies. The original work goes through a series of changes; in addition to those necessary to translate the work into movie terms, there is often a dilution of the strength of the original work, or a change in emphasis, a smoothing away of salient characteristics; it corresponds to the way all character is washed out of women's faces, so that a dull and deathlike beauty becomes the standard of the screen. Story and characters are subtly, or rudely, altered to fit into the established molds, and when a great popular property is bought, if it is at all exceptional, the professional term for reducing it to the screen level is "licking" it. Evelyn Waugh has described the process: "Each book purchased for motion pictures has some individual quality, good or bad, that has made it remarkable. It is the work of a great array of highly paid and incompatible writers to distinguish the quality, separate it, and obliterate it." There have been notable exceptions to this rule, and more in which the special quality has not been obliterated but only smudged over. Hundreds of pictures stick close to their sources because the originals were contrived to be made into movies. Sometimes a book presents few problems, like *Gone with the Wind;* sometimes, as in *Forever Amber*, the licking process destroys the chances of the film.

Licking may involve a major operation, as in the complete removal of the Lesbian theme from *The Children's Hour* to make *These Three*, or the theme of homosexuality from *The Brick Foxhole* to make *Crossfire;* in each case the original situation was unacceptable for the screen, and in each case a good picture was made by using the dramatic elements to carry a new theme. Sometimes the significance of the background is altered, as in *An American Tragedy*, which concentrated on murder and completely obliterated Dreiser's study of the relation between what Clyde Griffith did and the society in which he lived. Or a shift in emphasis may be made to hold the sympathy of the audience: Ring Lardner's *Champion* begins with Midge Kelly knocking down his crippled younger brother; in the movie, Midge is protective and tender. Licking *The Great Gatsby* without giving it a happy ending was a problem; it was solved by draining out the life force of Gatsby himself and providing wedding bells for two minor characters; the Spanish war and its effect on the hero were left out of *Key Largo*, perhaps for political reasons, but no motivation for the hero was substituted. In *Pride and Prejudice* what had to be licked was the sheer creativeness of Jane Austen; her characters had to be refashioned according to movie styles, so Mrs. Bennet turned up as a light-headed mother, and not a fool, and all the irony of Mr. Bennet disappeared, leaving him merely another father who didn't understand his daughters.

I have chosen for detailed analysis a short film, not actually intended for exhibition in movie houses, because it reflects the philosophy of licking to perfection. It is *The Diamond Necklace*, produced by Grant-Realm as the first of a series of television dramas, and it is, incidentally, a grim portent of what Hollywood may do if television production falls into its hands.

What had to be licked in the story was Maupassant's failure to supply a moral; small variations in plot and character were introduced to justify the "moral" ending, an ending, like so many movie formulas, shockingly immoral in its implications. For after the denouement and some added dialogue about the wasted years, the narrator of the story came forward and told the audience that "of course" the necklace was returned and life was easier for Matilda and her husband; emphatically he said that in the years of their struggle they had discovered something more precious than any necklace could be. To justify this, Matilda was shown as covetous from the beginning, even before the invitation to the ball, which, in the original story, motivates her desire for the necklace; she was shown to be heartlessly extravagant *after* they had begun paying for the duplicate; but when her husband was threatened by a moneylender (a new character deftly introduced into the story) she experienced a change of heart and became his willing helpmeet. Since ten years of misery, the consequence of pure accident, could not be shown as a demonstration of divine justice, the event was presented as a sort of retribution for Matilda's vanity and selfishness; and to assure the audience that the improvement in her character and the mutual love of husband and wife were really worth the struggle, Matilda was as radiantly beautiful at the end as she had been at the ball. (Some compunction must have been felt; the ravage of the years was rendered by Maupassant in a single line when Mme. Forestier says, "I hardly recognized you." In the picture the line was broken off after "For a moment I . . .")

This story was made for a commercial sponsor (Lucky Strike), and it is possible that even more than ordinary caution seemed advisable. It is nevertheless an illustration of what happens when a story is forced to conform to artificial standards. An episode that can be read in ten minutes was expanded to some twenty-four minutes of playing time, but the sense of life was not enhanced; the sluggish temperament of the husband was transformed into charm at the beginning and dogged devotion at the end; the social situation of the small functionary in a government office was not worked into the background.

The original story ends with Mme. Forestier's words, "But mine was paste. It was worth at the very most five hundred francs!"—and the imagination of the reader begins to function. In a study course for ex-GIs, over a hundred men and women were asked what they thought happened next; some of them thought Matilda fainted or became hysterical, some that she was too stunned at first to understand what had occurred. That the necklace was returned, they felt, hardly needed explicit statement (after seeing the movie, they heartily applauded one student who said, "They'd have beaten the hell out of her if she didn't return it"). And there was considerable difference of opinion on what had happened to husband and wife, whether they had grown more companionable or had become embittered toward each other, whether they had been so drained of their physical resources that they could not enjoy their sudden wealth, whether the shock of discovery, coming after the strain of the years, might not have made them want to curse God and die. None of this was possible after seeing the TV movie version; the imagination was prevented from going into action, the story was wrapped up in a package.

And finally this case history is typical because no proof was ever offered that the harsh, unmoralized original story would have been unpalatable to the audience. The distorted story itself, agreeably presented, made it less probable that another story, given the same opportunity, would be presented without distortion. In its small way the picture was helping to create the very audience it assumed; it was helping to create the mass.

In the fabrication of stereotypes the major studios have developed an admirable sureness of touch. Occasionally they produce parodies of themselves, as when the Bing Crosby-Barry Fitzgerald pattern of young priest and old was duplicated as young doctor and old; but in the main they set a premium on inventiveness, not original creative power, and the twist is a highly regarded element in any synopsis of a story. The writer whose story is nearly right is asked to keep working at it until he finds the twist; in most cases it involves twisting characters out of their natural shape; sometimes the twist comes first and is the whole picture, as when *Monsieur Beaucaire* was remade with a barber pretending to be a marquis instead of a marquis pretending to be a barber. Manipulation of such mechanical operations is a necessary part of the system of quantity production.

## THE NON-MEN

The high voltage of creative energy is stepped down by a series of interferences, and it hardly comes as a surprise to the salaried writer when he discovers that he has no rights in his own work because "the corporation is the author" of whatever he creates. This phrase (which occurs in the standard contract shortly after a salute to the "unique intellectual abilities" of the writer) may have been introduced originally as a legalistic device to assure the property rights of the contracting studio; it represents, however, an actuality. The picture shown on the screen is the work of a number of people to whom the corporation has given power. The more varied the gifts of any one person, the fewer collaborators he will have; but even if he is a writer-director-producer his work will still represent the corporate demands of his studio.

The creation of a picture usually begins either with the purchase of a property (novel, short story, play), already successful, or with the search for a property suitable to the needs of a star under contract. Occasionally a novel is bought before it is known to the public, and, as a form of insurance, the purchaser will invest in an advertising campaign for the book before the picture is made. A studio may invest in the production of a play and lose the movie rights to a higher bidder; or buy a property and, failing to get the wanted star, trade it to a competitor. During periods of economy the studios hold back and reduce the market price for hits, and at such times we have remakes of old pictures, reissues, and a careful recombing of properties previously acquired. This is usually accompanied by announcements that "original" stories will now be encouraged.

Dore Schary, in charge of production at MGM, the studio with the largest and most expensive roster of stars, has denied that he starts a picture with anything but a story; but, at *Life*'s Round Table, he was challenged by Jerry Wald, producer at Warners, who said, "Rather than wait for the right story to come along, the studio sees the salary mounting up every week and—well, it's not the best story, but let's get him working. You know, Dore, what do you think?" Mr. Schary thought it was a problem. It is a problem constantly solved by looking for the best stories for the most expensive stars, by building up or cutting down stories to fit the star's capacities, turning them into what the public wants to see the star in.

The screenwriter usually begins with the work of an author not on the studio payroll; the probable budget is known and the stars for whom the story is intended. (Sometimes, particularly if there is no pressure of time, a treatment of a novel or play may be made without reference to an individual star; but a common event is for a studio to announce that it has bought a best-seller for a specific star.) Not only the limitations of the star's talents but his or her unique virtues are considered in tailoring the story; it is dangerous to let a star appear in a movie that suppresses his familiar characteristics, the gestures and intonations known to the public; moreover, if the original character is a complex one, those elements must be eliminated which might confuse the image of the star fixed in the public mind; although the movie fan knows that his favorite players eat, marry, have or adopt children, and even possibly vote, the identification of stars with the parts they play is virtually complete. The writer must see to it that the star, whatever character he portrays, will, in the last analysis, be an acceptable version of himself.

When these conditions are imposed, and met, the writer is further obliged to "write out" of the story whatever strong political or social or economic concepts the story reflects, unless they happen to be universally approved. Then he is set to tackle the problem of licking the censorship on whatever sex "angles" the producer plans to keep in the story. Not all of this need be heart-breaking; much of it can be as automatic and subconscious as adhering to policy on a newspaper with strong doctrines; these are the conditions of work. No studio ever pretended that these were the ideal conditions for artistic creation. The studios might, in fact, quote Goethe's saying that the master proves himself when he works within limitations; but Goethe meant something else. He lived before the days of the front office and the Legion of Decency.

The imposed necessity to cut characters down to size, the constant preoccupation with possible objections, the awareness of authority looking over his shoulder as he writes, all combine to harry the writer into using bright tricks; he substitutes violence for passion, activity for strength of character; he invents those twists which surprise an audience at the expense of logical development of plot. Before he is through he knows in his heart that although he has written a script he is not the "author" of the work, and on occasions has been known to ask for the removal of his name from the credit list. At best he has taken part in a large-scale collaboration.

One of the most consistent employers of collaborative writers was Irving Thalberg, a man sensitive to the power of the creative artist, who was compelled by the demands of his studio to hand the work of one man over to another or to add a collaborator who was virtually under obligation to alter the original work. About a year before his death Thalberg acknowledged (in a private conversation) the faults of his system and asked what he could do about it. By the time a production was scheduled the studio already had a large investment in the original play or novel; if the screenplay had been assigned to a dependable writer, the chances were that a considerable number of other experts had also been put to work, making rough plans for scenery and costumes; to remain available the chosen stars may have been withheld from other productions. "A Broadway producer," Thalberg said, "with an investment of five hundred dollars in a dramatic script, puts up another five hundred and tells the author to work on his second act for another couple of months. I can't do that. *I've got a schedule to meet.* If a man brings in a script and it's got good characters and dialogue but no comedy, I get a man that can do comedy—and hope to God he won't spoil the characters. Some people are weak on character building, and I put them to work with a man that's first-rate that way. I know they don't like it, and I don't like it myself. What can I do?" There was an almost morose intensity in Thalberg's approach to all the problems of making pictures; he was, perhaps, too young to conform without a struggle to all the requirements of the vast factory into which MGM was transforming itself. He hoped that every picture turned out under his executive care would be marked by excellence of production, that nothing would seem sloppily done; he took pleasure in an occasional picture to which he gave more than its share of his energies, and he seemed honestly to look toward a time when he could make a few pictures a year, with no other commitments, and with a free hand. He died young, and while Hollywood has possibly turned up equal talents, I doubt whether any of his contemporaries is so likely to worry over the dilemmas of production or is so anxious to find the right solution for its problems.

A solution he would have liked is the steady rise of the versatile creator who is at once writer and director, or writer and producer, and at times all three. The highly technical work of the director lies close to the screenwriter's creative field; the labors of the producer, however, are basically executive and are undertaken by writers as a form of self-protection, to preserve the integrity of their work. The double or triple assignment is not casually made in the studios; for a long time it was hard for a writer to learn anything about directing because he was discouraged from appearing on the set even while his own pictures were being made, being at the time assigned to devote all his time to his next script. As a reward for good work (measured in terms of box-office successes) writers with talent can rise in the hier-

archy of production. The success of George Seaton, of Brackett
and Wilder, and of a few others will encourage studios to give
this reward more often. It couples a large degree of freedom with
responsibility; the further freedom to create pictures entirely
without interference will come only when the need for such pictures is recognized. That is to say, when the system of exhibition
has undergone a revolutionary change.

Parallel to the writer who is not an author stands the star who
is not an actor. The talent is there, and every so often, under able
direction and in an exceptional picture, it comes through as the
real thing, a unified, built-up created character, sustained through
sequence after sequence, combining reality and illusion. For the
most part, the effort is not called for, the rendering of the character may even be dangerous, for the star is expected to present
and project a mask of himself, that part of him known to the
audience: the "charm," the exudation of a mild sexuality, the set
of gestures, the peculiar laugh, the candid look expressive of
nearly nothing, the gravelly voice always saying the same things,
the humorous lift of the eyebrows, the double take that makes
us feel brighter than we are, "the bag of tricks"—these are like
the idiosyncrasies of old friends. And just as our friends, without
changing, seem sometimes to be more themselves, to communicate
more completely, so the movie actor can put together his tricks
with little variations and give a high degree of pleasure. Edward
G. Robinson did this in *Double Idemnity;* the gestures were there,
but they expressed the intentions of an insurance-claims agent,
not of Edward G. Robinson; in *Key Largo* he had no character
to work through, only the old personality. Over a long period
of years James Cagney has used the same nervous flutter of his
hands, the same cocking of his head, the light hoofer's walk, and
once in every four or five pictures they combine to form the man
he is playing, not the image of Cagney itself. The arresting figure
of Humphrey Bogart, always transmitting energy at high voltage,
giving the effect of strong passions under control and even an
illusion of intellectual activity, varies from picture to picture, but

if, as in *The Treasure of the Sierra Madre,* he creates a character
completely, if that character is not one of his limited familiar
types, he must quickly return in a familiar role. In that picture,
said Jerry Wald, "Humphrey Bogart didn't play Humphrey
Bogart" and the public resented it. Bogart was promptly cast as
Bogart in *Key Largo.* In a recent list of the ten stars whose names
had the greatest marquee value, Bogart stands fifth; the men preceding him are Bing Crosby and Gary Cooper; below him are
Bob Hope, Clark Gable, Gregory Peck, and Alan Ladd. It is not
necessary for any of these gentlemen to act, although one of
them, at least, could. The women in the same list are Betty
Grable, Ingrid Bergman, and Claudette Colbert.

The process of preventing women from acting in the movies
begins with the screen test when the face of an actress is west-
mored or maxfactored to a familiar type. Talent is recognized,
but types are important; on occasion a new type enters, a different hair-do suffices, and a new pattern is added to the existing
choices. As an exception, Miss Bergman insisted on playing in
the sweet face that God gave her; most newcomers gratefully
yield their eyebrows and lips and hair to the cosmetician, and
the skill of these men is so great that they can undo the mischief
of nature and reduce to tolerable proportions the broad brows,
the wide nostrils or high cheekbones that give character to the
human face, so that while no actress looks exactly like another,
most of them remind us of someone else—the invisible archetype
of the screen actress, impersonal, inexpressive, but photogenic.
To the newly created face are attached eyebrows and lashes;
with each addition, the purely physical capacity to indicate emotion is lowered; the mask becomes more rigid; the sacrificial rite
is completed by such improvements on the shape and size of the
breasts as fashion, or the censor, dictates.

By calculation or by instinct, the improvers on nature have
fashioned precisely the right mannequin to play the parts assigned
to women in pictures. Since they must not express the reality of
physical passion yet play at love, the stars accentuate the appara-

tus of flirtation, the long eyelashes, and conceal the telltale structure of the mouth; the whole face and the breasts are set off and projected, like weapons in an armory, for provocation and enticement, without promise of response. The accentuation of the full breasts came upon the censors through well-engineered publicity, and it was manifestly impossible to say that the natural endowments of a woman, when sweatered, were not to be shown on the screen; the censor's only victory was in regard to the cleft between the breasts, which has to be seen to be appreciated and is consequently not acceptable. (British costume pictures have to be retaken with a higher line before they can be shown here.) A hoot of derisive laughter follows hard on the appreciative whistle whenever the mounting of the breasts is accentuated, the falsity of the intention being palpable even to the adolescent audience. The breasts, as a sexual symbol or focus of interest, become a gag; and this is natural since sex itself must be played for a laugh, unless it can be involved in violence.

Having reduced writer and actor to manageable proportions, the studios have still to cope with a third talent.

In a recent survey *Fortune* discovered that most college graduates are ready to work at routine professions and trades, and the editors wondered whether the economy of the nation didn't need more adventure, more enterprise, more of the spirit of the old pirates of industry and commerce—"the free-swinging s.o.b.'s" who break molds, strike out new paths, and keep society in ferment. The fate of these exceptional people, as they arrive in the movies, is to be placed beside the fate of the writer who must not write and the actor who must not act.

In the past decade one high-order talent has grappled with Hollywood: Orson Welles. In *Citizen Kane*, the first picture he ever made, he was writer, producer, director, and star. Shrewdly managing his affairs, Welles stayed in radio for some time after he was propelled to fame by his Halloween broadcast of "The War of the Worlds"; he came to Hollywood with experience in the theater, boundless energy, an arrogant self-assurance; he was in a position to dictate his own terms. Into *Citizen Kane* he threw his boyish impudence and his mature iconoclasm; he told his story backward and in parallel segments; he made the camera do all its stunts, never entering a room through the door if he could come through the skylight; he brushed aside the pool of available actors and brought his own company from the East, and introduced them at the end of the picture, not the beginning. He combined elements in the careers of several famous people, blandly presented the result as fiction, and in his late twenties played the part of an old man. His picture even had a new sound, because his training in radio studios suggested the use of dead walls, of echo chambers, of sound effects. Impatient with all the stale tricks, Welles invented new ones, not all of them effective—he seemed so afraid of the movie platitudes that he could not say hello or good-by without trying to be different. He was out to shock all along the line, using scandal, cynicism, technical innovations, and his exuberant energy. He might have been better advised to tell his disturbing story in more conventional forms, or, if he wanted to revolutionize the art of telling a story on the screen, he might have chosen a more conventional plot for the first tryout of his tricks. He may have needed advice, but it is doubtful whether he would have taken any. In the theater and in radio Welles had been a constant experimenter with forms; having found the one that suited him for *Citizen Kane*, he was bound to use it.

Except for Chaplin, no one else in Hollywood made pictures alone; except for his *Great Dictator*, no picture of the time had the stature of *Citizen Kane*. One felt, at its core, a mind, a temperament, a force. Exploiting his highly developed instinct for showmanship, Welles turned out a grim (and premature) obituary laced with the suspense of a mystery, the sudden eruptions of a melodrama; as in a chemical analysis, the picture broke down the massive figure of a tycoon, and in the process half a dozen surrounding figures emerged slowly and fully and came to life. The picture was harsh, it had rough edges, it attacked and absorbed the spectator. It was not a spectacular success, financially. The hostility of the Hearst papers was a minor element in its comparative failure.

In his next picture Welles adapted Tarkington's *Magnificent Ambersons,* which some critics hold in even higher esteem than *Citizen Kane* as a total production. For several years thereafter, his professional career was negligible, the only recurrence of his headstrong and eccentric individuality being in the production of *Macbeth,* on a small budget, in which the speech of Shakespeare was rendered with so strong a Scottish accent that Columbia refused to release it before rerecording the sound track.

It is possible that all the faults but one are on Mr. Welles' side. The one not his is that Hollywood could not put up with his faults in order to use his prodigious talents. It had no rewards to offer him if he disciplined himself, and no tradition of discipline of its own that could be distinguished from mere obedience to the front office.

It is held against Hollywood that by lavish salaries it corrupts men of genius; there is no proof that genius would have flourished in relative poverty, or that characters so easily corruptible had stamina enough to resist even moderate success. A prodigal talent like that of Ben Hecht meets the movie business on its own terms. In addition to preparing for the screen the plays he wrote with Charles MacArthur, he has turned out one of Hollywood's most memorable comedies, *Nothing Sacred;* a distinguished classic, *Wuthering Heights;* a forceful melodrama, *Kiss of Death;* he apparently requires the pressure of studio control because, when he is on his own, his work is insufferably arty, as in *The Scoundrel* and *Specter of the Rose.* His lively intelligence must approach with considerable cynicism the task of adapting *The Miracle of the Bells;* but it is a job that sets him free financially to do other work, not in the films, which interests him more. The failure of Hollywood in dozens of similar cases lies in not absorbing all the energies of talented men, in not making them feel the incalculable possibilities of the film. The never-acknowledged basic concept of the movies as a form of light entertainment for the adolescent minority makes this impossible. There is really little need of exceptional talent. There is no place for the completely independent man.

The men of talent are not without fault. Some of them have had a passion for the movies, others for the prestige and the money they could get from the movies. They have made pictures and felt superior not only to the front office, which interfered with their talent, but to the movies themselves. They have been defeatists about their own opportunities and have caved in under pressure without fighting back. They have developed that "low animal cunning" which characterizes certain other types of businessmen—and they have been rewarded.

These case histories illustrate the means by which the movie departs from its original function, to tell a story, and becomes the great myth medium of our time. To satisfy the only audience on which the exhibitor can count, story must be transformed into myth—the writer's function; from that story the realities of human behavior must be eliminated, the characters must be formalized and idealized even if they become ideal villains—the actor's function. Only the myth, and stories assimilated to myths, can satisfy the demand for the familiar; only myth can by-pass the mind and speak directly to the subconscious; only myth can be endlessly repeated. To make a picture with these qualifications and still make it seem fresh and attractive is the director's function. And if all the talents in Hollywood were free of the compulsions of the front office, they would still be tied in the strait jacket of the Production Code.

## A CODE FOR CONDUCT

> "*Most of our pictures have little, if any real sub-
> stance. Our fear of what the censors will do keeps
> us from portraying life as it really is. We wind
> up with a lot of empty little fairy tales that do
> not have much relation to anything. . . .*"
>
> Samuel Goldwyn

> "*Sharp-eyed Hollywood censor Joseph Breen
> called* [The Bicycle Thief] *indecent and unac-
> ceptable. . . .*"
>
> Time, March 13, 1950

> "*Mr. Johnston said he believed in the judgment
> of the American people to decide on the morals
> of pictures for themselves.*"
>
> AP story, March 15, 1950

From their earliest days the movies have lived under pressure, and
as they grew in power their resistance has steadily decreased.
The pressure has been aesthetic, social, moral, economic, political,
and religious; it has included boycotts, psychological studies, de-
nunciations from bench and pulpit, editorials, legislation and
threats of further legislation, arbitrary use of the police power,
financial chicanery. The surprising thing is that the movies have
survived and from time to time still exercise the right to free expression.

The motives for protesting have varied. Picketers have objected
to political implications or, occasionally, to racial and religious
prejudices. They allow the movies to deal with actuality but do
not appreciate this freedom if their side is not shown in a favorable light. The more persistent censorship is moral; from protesting against the duration of the first movie kiss (30 seconds) to the
imposition of a complete code of conduct, the moral pressure
groups have held to one line: the movies must deny themselves
the pleasure of reflecting the life of our time. The film must not
be vulgar; it must not know that workers strike; it must not

understand the motives of crime; it must not admit that men and women have sexual appetites and enjoy their satisfaction; it must not suggest that corruption in office may go unpunished and that hard work does not always bring great rewards; it must not dwell on any flaw in the accepted social system.

The most effective machine for exerting pressure is the Production Code,[1] which the studios have, in a sense, imposed on themselves. The background of the Code is composed of one part scandal, one part threat of boycott, and one part (I am sure) an honest desire to make the movies respectable. The administration of the Code is in the hands of the Motion Picture Association, now headed by Eric Johnston; the office continues the work of Will Hays, and Will Hays was appointed "czar" of the movies in the wake of gross public scandal in the private lives of a few Hollywood stars; the specifications of the Code, particularly in regard to sex, reflect the principles of the Legion of Decency, and the actual implementation of the Code came after the Apostolic Delegate to the United States challenged Catholics to take action "in the matter of 'immoral films.'" The operation of the Code is, officially, based on voluntary submission by the studios. "No one is compelled to produce motion pictures in accordance with Code regulations. No attempt is made to force producers to accept the service of the Production Code Administration." Pictures which do not get the seal of approval of the Code authorities can be shown in the United States and, in fact, are shown— in about five hundred of the eighteen thousand movie houses in the country. No written contract forbids the other houses to show such pictures, but they would find themselves in difficulties with the studios if they disobeyed the unwritten law of the business. When the Johnston office refused to give its approval to *The Bicycle Thief*, which had already been passed by several

[1] Officially, "A Code to Govern the Making of Motion and Talking Pictures," formulated and adopted by the Motion Picture Producers and Distributors of America (the Motion Picture Association of America, Inc.).

state censorship boards, the picture lost all hope of wide distribution although it was, within the same month, signally honored by an Academy Award.

Writing in *The Motion Picture Almanac*, Terry Ramsaye tells the history of the Code. When sound came to the movies in 1929, he says, Martin Quigley (editor of the influential *Motion Picture Herald*) "observed a growing trend of departure from the level of accepted moral standards." He conferred with the Reverend F. J. Dineen, S.J.; and the Reverend Daniel A. Lord, S.J., "a trained moralist with an interest in the theater," collaborated with them. The draft of a program to guide the industry was prepared by Father Lord, and Mr. Quigley "applied various contributions and qualifications." He also "engaged the interest of Will H. Hays," and in March 1930 the Code was adopted by the Motion Picture Producers and Distributors of America. The Production Code Administration was set up four years later.

Will Hays frequently denied that the Code operated as a means of censorship. Its function was, indeed, to anticipate and avoid the actions of censors. When a script was submitted to his office, competent examiners pointed out precisely how sections of it would run afoul of existing laws or offend moviegoers. Officially the Code Administration reviews a script and points out not only deviations from the printed rules but also "wherein from experience or knowledge it is believed that exception will be taken to the story or treatment." A negative of the completed film must also be submitted, and producers agree not to release a picture until all required changes have been made.

There is provision for an appeal from the Code Administration to the parent body of the Code Administration. (In the case of *The Bicycle Thief* the appeal was ineffective.) In most instances suggested changes are promptly made, but a producer can argue with the Code representative at his studio or go directly to Joseph I. Breen, its director, and occasionally he makes his point. When he was making *To Each His Own* for Paramount in 1946, Charles Brackett persuaded the Johnston office that a young girl caught

in a sudden gust of passion, as if blown by the wash of an air-
plane propeller, need not suffer degradation and death because
she bore a child to a flyer who was killed in action and could
not return to marry her. His argument was that if the wages of
sin for a single impulsive act are death in misery, there would
be nothing left as retribution for a sensual wanton or a deliberate
flouter of sexual morality. Again, Robert E. Sherwood, William
Wyler, and Samuel Goldwyn fought hard—and successfully—to
keep a banker callous to the needs of returned soldiers in *The
Best Years of Our Lives*.[1] (Nothing in the Production Code au-
thorizes the Johnston office even to hint that bankers, or any other
group of professional men, must be treated sympathetically.)
There have been other instances of valor and obstinacy—the
fighter has to be obstinate because merely by delay the censors
can put an intolerable strain on a production.

In general, however, the habit is to try to put something over—
and if that fails, to cave in. And why not? The writer and director and producer know that they can slip in a sly sexual hint,
but it is not worth fighting for, since the whole of their picture
is usually completely divorced from any human reality. There is
only one escape—into the past, into pure myth. If the censor
insists upon twin beds in the time of Queen Elizabeth, a producer
can bring antiquarians to reason with him; but it is more fun to
supply two authentic Elizabethan beds and let the camera linger
a moment on one of them, conspicuously not slept in; but if
(heaven forgive the suggestion) Betty Grable and Alan Ladd are
to play Elizabeth and Essex, it is simpler to yield the point and
trust to Technicolor. If the censor announces that it is permissible
for a man to sit on the side of a bed when a woman is lying in it,
under the coverlet, provided the man keeps *both* feet on the
floor, one raised foot being presumably a symbol of rape, you
can try to get comedy out of a tapping toe (and call it the
Lubitsch touch), but everyone knows there isn't going to be any

[1] "You should have seen the list of suggested changes or cuts that Sam
flatly refused to make." (Letter from Sherwood to the author.)

rape anyhow. So it is better to have the man slap the woman, or the woman shoot the man. Then you can have a brawl for comedy, or the police and a third degree for melodrama, and your picture is sure-fire.

## S–E–X

The Code itself is flanked by "Reasons Supporting the Preamble of the Code," "Reasons Underlying the General Principles," and "Reasons Underlying Particular Applications"; all contain important items, of which the following are the most significant.

From the Code:

"SEX

The sanctity of the institution of marriage and the home shall be upheld. Pictures shall not infer that low forms of sex relationship are the accepted or common thing.

1. *Adultery and Illicit Sex*, sometimes necessary plot material, must not be explicitly treated, or justified, or presented attractively.

2. *Scenes of Passion*

   a. These should not be introduced except where they are definitely essential to the plot.

   b. Excessive and lustful kissing, lustful embraces, suggestive postures and gestures are not to be shown.

   c. In general, passion should be treated in such manner as not to stimulate the lower and baser emotions.

3. *Seduction or Rape*

   a. These should never be more than suggested, and then only when essential for the plot. They must never be shown by explicit method.

   b. They are never the proper subject for comedy."

The fourth item forbids "any inference of sex perversion," the fifth bans the subject of white slavery, and the sixth bars "sex relationship between the white and black races." The seventh declares that sex hygiene and venereal diseases are not subjects for theatrical motion pictures, the eighth opposes showing scenes of *"actual child birth,* in fact or in silhouette," and the ninth says simply that "children's sex organs are never to be exposed."

That is the total of the Code's specifications under the heading of "Sex." Under "Profanity" a few illuminating notes are to be found. Among the words and phrases not to be used are "bat" and "broad" if applied to a woman—also "tart" and "whore"; nor "madam" (relating to prostitution); and "traveling salesman and farmer's daughter jokes" are out. The adjective "hot" is not to be applied to women, and "fairy" (in a vulgar sense) and "pansy" (not so qualified) are forbidden. Under "Repellent Subjects" (after brutality and possible gruesomeness, branding of people or animals) the code notes that "the sale of women or a woman selling her virtue" must be treated "within the careful limits of good taste."

"The Reasons Underlying Particular Applications" begin with the statement that *"sin and evil* enter into the story of human beings and hence in themselves are valid dramatic material." (All italics are in the original.)

Under Sex: "Out of regard for the sanctity of marriage and the home, the *triangle,* that is, the love of a third party for one already married, needs careful handling. The treatment should not throw sympathy against marriage as an institution."

The language of the Code and its appendices is often obscure, and in discussing sex is generally offensive. But the quotation above is a masterpiece of "careful handling" in itself; by this definition the "triangle" is one-sided; it does not involve the love of "one already married" for "a third party," only the reverse. The fixed rule that actuality must be distorted could not be better illustrated. Within this definition of the triangle, romance and sentimentality are possible, as the long devotion of a lover to a married woman who either does not return his love or is merely waiting for her husband to die before yielding. Comedy is possible, since a hopeless love can be made ridiculous. But neither adultery nor divorce is possible. The basic section of the Code, as quoted above, concedes the existence of adultery and allows its use if it is not made attractive: the "Reasons" blandly assume that adultery does not exist. However—

> "*Scenes of passion* must be treated with an honest acknowledgment of human nature and its normal reactions. Many scenes cannot be presented without arousing dangerous emotions on the part of the immature, the young, or the criminal classes.
>
> Even within the limits of *pure love*, certain facts have been universally regarded by lawmakers as outside the limits of safe presentation."

In practice, what the Code calls "pure love" is pure because it is passionless; in day-to-day operations, the Code authority eliminates scenes of passion, and human nature and its normal reactions are not honestly acknowledged. Perhaps the most degrading effect of the Code is the mean and mawkish concept of marriage it has forced upon the movies.

The next explanation concerns the love "which society has always regarded as wrong." This is a wild exaggeration; certain sections of society, at certain times, have held adultery in esteem and considered marital fidelity an evidence of low moral standards, lack of enterprise, or sheer bad luck. The semantics of the Code need study. The additional phrase about love "which has been banned by divine law" refers, presumably, to the Seventh Commandment. This "impure love" must not

> "be presented as *attractive and beautiful;*
>
> be the subject of comedy or farce or treated as material for laughter;
>
> be presented in such a way as to *arouse passion* on the part of the audience;
>
> be made to seem *right and permissible;*
>
> be detailed in method and manner."

The other sections of the Code, the "Reasons Supporting the Preamble" and the "Reasons Underlying the General Principles," supply the moral and philosophical groundwork for the specific commandments on sex. They compose a self-justification of the Code, and in one respect they are cogent and clear. The motion picture "has special MORAL OBLIGATONS" because it affects audiences in special ways. Neither the aesthetes who saluted the movies nor those who despised them were particularly interested in effects and obligations; the churchmen who worked out the Code have the advantage. They saw that

> "this art appeals at once *to every class;*
>
> this art *reaches places* unpenetrated by other forms of art;
>
> the exhibitors' theaters are built for the masses, for the mature and immature. . . . Films . . . can with difficulty be confined to certain groups;
>
> a book describes; a film vividly presents . . . by apparently living people;
>
> a book reaches the mind through the words merely; a film reaches the eyes and ears through the reproduction of actual events."

I refrain from adding italics to those of the Code; if the last words above had been emphasized, they would require much thought; presumably they mean the reproduction of events on the sound stages, as suggested above by "apparently living people." The Code is aware of the remarkable illusion of reality produced by the movies, as witness:

> "the reaction to a film depends on the vividness of presentation;
>
> the film [unlike newspapers which are 'after the fact'] gives the events in the process of enactment and with the apparent reality of life";

and even of the moral effect of the star system:

> ". . . the audience is . . . ready to confuse actor and actress and

characters they portray, and it is most receptive of the emotions and ideals presented by their favorite stars."

Finally, the Code delivers its own fundamental concept of the motion picture. In contrast with entertainment "which tends to degrade human beings or to lower their standards of life and living," the movies are primarily to be regarded as "ENTERTAINMENT which tends to improve the race, or at least to re-create and rebuild human beings exhausted with the realities of life." Reference is made to "the healthy reactions to healthful sports, like baseball, golf," and to the "unhealthy reactions to sports like cock-fighting, bull-fighting, bear-baiting, etc." The gladiatorial combats and "the obscene plays of Roman times" are mentioned to demonstrate the effect they had on ancient nations; wrong entertainment "lowers the whole living conditions and moral ideas of a race."

The vexing question of the relation between Art and Morals is discussed, not lucidly, but with conviction:

"Art can be *morally good*. . . . Art can be *morally evil*. . . . It has often been argued that art in itself is unmoral, neither good nor bad. This is perhaps true of the THING which is music, painting, poetry, etc. But the thing is the PRODUCT of some person's mind and the intention of that mind was either good or bad morally when it produced the thing. Besides the thing it has its EFFECT upon those who come into contact with it; . . . as a product of a mind and the cause of definite effects, it has a deep moral significance and an unmistakable moral quality.

. . . The motion pictures . . . have their moral quality from the intention of the minds which produce them and from their effects on the moral lives and reactions of their audiences. This gives them a most important morality.

1. They reproduce the morality of the men who use the pictures as a medium for the expression of their ideas and ideals.

2. They affect the moral standards of those who, through the screen, take in these ideas and ideals."

The first of these numbered statements is either meaningless or is a gross libel on writers, producers, directors, and actors. The morality of the movies is imposed upon them. If "the men who use the pictures as a medium" refers to the owners of the studios and the distributors of the pictures, it is possible to say that their morality is "reproduced," but not that their ideas and ideals are expressed. The second statement, if it is true, puts upon the entertainment film (which is fundamentally considered to be the same as the amusement film) an intolerable moral burden. Again the Code sidesteps actuality.

Following the Code from its specific thou-shalt-nots to its philosophy produces a strange effect of sympathy; the Code so patently does not say what it wants most to say, that all life must be carefully falsified to conform to an ethical ideal; it acknowledges *"sin and evil . . . [as] . . . valid dramatic material"* and promptly becomes entangled in details of good taste; an amateur semanticist, a logician, an untutored shrewd Yankee of the time of Thoreau, a modern adolescent, could tear the argument to shreds. It is a self-defeating document because if its premises are true, if the movies are responsible for moral standards, if they re-create and rebuild human beings, if like other works of art they are "the presentation of human thought, emotion, and experience, in terms of an appeal to the soul through the senses," then they cannot possibly function under an imposed Code; only movies made purely for distraction, appealing to the mass minority, can be made in this way. The positive demands of distributors dovetail nicely with the negative commandments of the Code; both demand an art from which, as far as possible, all "human thought, emotion, and experience" have been eliminated, and at times the distributors and the backers of the Code have expressed great satisfaction with their success.

I believe that the Production Code, as it operates today, does actual, demonstrable harm to the community; although I do not exaggerate the influence of the movies (or any other art) I think that the Code, its frivolous applications, and the evasions it en-

courages have become a dangerous and destructive element in
American life. I have not cited the passages, more numerous and
explicit, on the handling of crime, since it is well known that
Code approval has been given to pictures of the astounding and
totally meaningless brutality which has become the distinguishing
mark of the American film and has penetrated to comedy and
psychological drama; while the forces of law and order have
become as violent as the criminal whom the Code forbids the
movies to glorify. Here the Code has been either powerless or
indifferent; the rules governing all the aspects of sex are the ones
upon which the Code insists, and on the consequences of these
rules the Code must stand.

The prime effect of the Code is to create a sexual morality
which no moralist, no great religious leader, no church has ever
tolerated. It is as mythical as the social and economic contrivances
of the movies are. "Driven out and compelled to be chaste," the
creative artists in the movies have fabricated a world of fantasy.
Like all imaginary worlds it has its own rules:

> Pure love, as the Code calls it, is not sexual; it may have what
> the physiologists call "secondary sexual characteristics," but it's
> not physical.

> If love is sensual, it is immoral and occurs only between a
> "wicked" character and a weak one.

> Consequently, good women are fundamentally sexless (compare
> any good wife and mother with any old-fashioned "vamp" or
> contemporary "good-bad" woman).

> A further consequence—the sexual relation, the actuality of pas-
> sion between man and woman, exists outside the marriage rela-
> tionship exclusively; within the sacrament of marriage, passion
> is outlawed.

Essential to all of these laws of behavior is the idea that while
men may at times derive pleasure from sexual love, women never
do. This concept was familiar long before the Code was estab-

lished, and from Clara Bow to Greta Garbo the movies presented a series of women who looked with innocence or surprise or distaste, but never with pleasure, upon the advances of the lustful male; at the same time the movies presented endless variations of the vampire, the siren who lured men to their destruction, following some obscure purpose of her own, revenge, perhaps, or ambition, or desire for power, but not for the ecstasy of passion or the simple pleasure of getting into bed with a man.

The word commonly used in describing movies and movie actresses is "sexy"; the word commonly used to describe living people of strong sexual enterprise is "passionate." Since the movies are forbidden to display sensuality, "sexy" is a proper adjective; it implies an as-if state, not an actual one. Just as the word "manly" is never used about a man, as "womanly" is used only for secondary attributes of women, "sexy" refers to the superficial and the immature aspects of the relation between men and women, to the apparatus of seduction and not to the pains or pleasures if seduction succeeds, to provocation not to satisfaction.

Winthrop Sargeant (whom *Life* designated "the most philosophical of our editors") discussed Rita Hayworth and concluded: "It has remained for Americans of the hard-boiled twentieth century to enthrone Aphrodite as the supreme deity of their popular religion, to portray her rather dubious machinations as the most exalting and satisfying of human experiences, and to subscribe with unquestioning faith to her incessant litany that sex is the most important thing in the world." Commenting on these words and the movies' "obsessive cult of love" in general, Lloyd Morris, in *Not So Long Ago*, wrote: "And this . . . seemed to be all that the movies had found to say . . . on the subject of love." Mr. Morris's section on the movies in his book is generally well balanced, bringing in the athleticism of a Douglas Fairbanks against the It Girl and modifying Mr. Sargeant's excesses by noting other, more scholarly investigations which conclude that Hollywood's presentation of love has "very little psychological validity." The point still needs making that the Greeks had no goddess of the non-act of sex. The silver-limbed implacable Aphrodite was caught in bed with Ares, held by the net of chains her husband had forged, and "a roar of unquenchable laughter rose from the blessed gods" at the sight; the girdle she fastened around the thighs of her votaries were unloosed by men as promptly as possible, "and they took their joy of love together." There might be something farcical in love or something tragic; the appetite for love made the gods treacherous and led men and women to heroic sacrifice or to the murder of those who stood in their way. It was not the only desire of humankind, but it was recognized for what it was and faithfully rendered in myth and epic and drama. It was not romanticized and it was not falsified.

It is a possible argument that nothing true or significant about sex can be said in so universal a medium as the movies. It is also possible to take the word of those European novelists who tell us that Americans know nothing of love, because that would at least explain our acceptance of the movie substitute for the real thing. Both of these arguments have the merit of candor; they acknowledge the false image of love presented on the screen. I do not think either has general application, and the simplest explanation of all is, I believe, the soundest: the movies are made primarily for an audience of children and adolescents. The audience begins to go to the movies at the age when myths are sufficient; it continues to go during the romantic phase of adolescence. The presentation of mature passions might bewilder such an audience. Adults who remain fervent patrons have perhaps not reached the phase of reality or have retreated from it. They may find consolation in the bright lies that the movies tell about love, as they may find it in the low-pitched and agonized falsifications of the daytime serial.

The movie substitute for love serves for a time, for some people. The majority of those who know anything about the real thing find that substitute unacceptable. Since the movies have an impressive atmosphere of reality and their version of non-love is presented to adolescents at the formative period of their lives, they may themselves be contributing to the unhappiness in marriage of the American people. Certainly half a century of upholding the sanctity of the marriage bond has not diminished the number of divorces on the grounds of adultery, and if we are approaching a single standard for men and women it is the standard of accepted promiscuity. Perhaps this is the inevitable result of presenting love as trivial, marriage as sexless, and cohabitation as an act to be delayed as long as possible.

There is no question about the sexiness of the movies, their tendency to reduce all other human relations to familiar terms in a sexual equation. In European movies set against the background of postwar rubble and desolation, the actuality of sexual passion plays a part; the most intelligent of the American pictures in that setting, *A Foreign Affair*, is more realistic than most in rendering the atmosphere of a broken civilization, but the picture turns into a charade in which Jean Arthur and Marlene Dietrich represent the familiar figures of the good (cold) woman and the bad one (who is not cold). Cecil de Mille thrives on the sexiness he injects into his Biblical extravaganzas; and other specialists use history or science or the lives of composers to the same ends. To the superficial moralist, this preoccupation with sex is in itself dubious; to our European critics it is ridiculous because the preoccupation is real, the sex is not.

In the depths of the depression Paramount signed Mae West, despite her sensational career as a merchant of provocative sexual tidbits, and, ignoring the threats of censorship, proceeded to make several pictures with her. These constitute the exception; the character portrayed by Miss West always expressed the liveliest anticipations of pleasure from the embraces of men, and romantic love was brushed aside with a knowing wink. The character was promiscuous and friendly, impure love was essentially used for comic effect, and the pictures were as refreshing as if the Wife of Bath had suddenly appeared on the screen. The Code was in existence when Paramount, driven by economic pressure, dared to flout it; a few years later the administration of the Code was fully organized, and Miss West's work, while never reduced to the mincing politeness of the usual screen character, suffered.

The exceptional, almost unique quality of the early Mae West pictures was that by implication she was portraying a "bad woman" who was thoroughly enjoying life. The vamps of the silent pictures were intense and tortured: Miss West's characters were good company. Just as the vamps were followed by Clara Bow, the "It Girl," who suggested that the ideal mate for the American man was the captain of the girls' basketball team in the local high school, the cheerful courtesan of Mae West was followed by the character usually described as the "good-bad" girl. This is not the conventional dramatic figure of the harlot with a heart of gold; appearances are against the girl, but she herself is no wanton, she gets no pleasure out of it; and her goodness lies in the passionless wish to be united in respectable marriage to the hero. In *Movies, a Psychological Study*, Dr. Martha Wolfenstein and Dr. Nathan Leites suggest that the forbidden wishes of the audience are realized in the "false appearances" of the movies, "since we can enjoy the suggested wish-fulfillments without emphatic guilt." I cannot quarrel with this analysis, but I am left wondering what the ultimate effect of all these "false appearances" may be.

A note should be made of one of the rare instances of the appearance of common reality in the movies. At the request of Woody Van Dyke, who directed *The Thin Man*, the writing team of Frances Goodrich and Albert Hackett provided several scenes between William Powell and Myrna Loy which were in the bantering tone that later became standard practice. These scenes managed to suggest, and the director underlined, the important fact that a man and his own wife were in love with each other, took pleasure in each other's company, and (by the single deft motion with which Powell removed the dog Asta from Miss Loy's berth) intended to sleep together.

These exceptions are remembered precisely because they managed to violate the prevailing customs of the films. Or, it might be said, because they correspond to the customs of the country.

One of the customs of the country is divorce, and nothing in the Code specifically instructs the producers on the handling of this subject. In practice the movies have created a mythology of divorce, the essence of which is that divorced couples always remarry. This usually takes place after the husband has escaped from sex, represented by a wicked woman, or the wife has seen through a plausible cad with whom she has been tempted to enjoy impure love.

The minor myths create the proper atmosphere:

Divorce occurs for trivial reasons only; it is the consequence of hasty tempers or misunderstandings or a desire to rise in the world of society or finance.

Divorce does not occur because of sexual incompatibility or incompetence.

Divorce does not occur because of adultery.

The way to prevent divorce is for the wronged partner to pretend to be in love with someone else.

Alternatively, if the wronged partner is the wife, she can take off her horn-rimmed glasses.

Husbands and wives are much together during divorce proceedings; if they are not, and a divorcee marries again, all the forces of nature combine to prevent the consummation of the second marriage, giving time for the first husband to reappear and win the wife back.

The motion-picture equivalent of the old shivaree should provide material for a sociologist. The Production Code says:

"The treatment of bedrooms must be governed by good taste and delicacy";

and the "Reasons Underlying" offer this explanation:

"Certain places are so closely and thoroughly associated with sexual life or with sexual sin that their use must be carefully limited."

In the mythology of marriage this has come to mean that the bridal night is a long series of accidents through which young lovers are kept from entering or staying in the same room after nightfall. It is, in effect, a long strip-tease, a source of merriment innocent only in the technical sense. The ingenuity of picture-makers in creating new obstacles to the consummation of marriage is admirable, unless perhaps it is pathological to set up They Shall Not Cohabit as the great commandment for the legally married.

The devices for keeping lovers apart before they are married fall into a conventional pattern. They are a courteous bow to established morality and can produce delightful moments like the "Walls of Jericho" sequence in *It Happened One Night;* the plotting to prevent man and wife from going to bed has to be more elaborate; the moral system represented is not one accepted by the audience; the play is for laughs that cover a sniggering lewdness. Perhaps as good an example as any is *I Was a Male War Bride,* which had the added attraction of dressing Cary Grant in women's clothes and reduced the whole unhappiness of our postwar armies of occupation to a series of obstacles to co-habitation.

The current interpretation of the Code has drained away from the marriage sacrament all its seriousness; if, in fact, the sacrament hallows and makes acceptable to God and man a passion otherwise brutish, it is only a mockery if the passion does not exist; the small and silly emotions rendered in the movies hardly require sanctification.

That is the suicidal consequence of the Code: it sets out to uphold the sanctity of the institution of marriage and ends by undermining the moral foundation upon which marriage stands. Marriage is—or can be—a profoundly satisfying way to live, full of tensions, hardships, pleasures, excitements; constantly threatened, sometimes triumphant; it persists because it fulfills certain requirements, because in marriage men and women, satisfying their natural impulses, become creators, not only of their children, but of themselves. But this is not marriage *à la* Code. With its fundamentally irreligious concept of marriage, the Code has succeeded in bringing to the screen a relation between men and women which is more ignoble than the meanest marriages of common experience. The economic pressures, the sudden drunken impulses, the vanities and fears and lusts that sometimes drive people to marry are powerful and urgent. Out of them can come hatred or love or degradation; but in any case, life. Out of marriage in the movies nothing can come.

## MODES AND MANNERS

Not even children. The movies do not exist in a social vacuum, and they reflect the temper of our time, when children are considered an economic loss, an obstacle to having a good time, and a threat to marriage itself. Yet the peculiar unreality of the movies gives the relation of parents to children a quality of its own. Children are not conceived in passion and are not born (the Code forbids); they appear miraculously by the side of ravishingly costumed mothers in attractive hospital beds, and disappear again until they are old enough to work in the movies. At that age they are stars of the first magnitude and the earth revolves around them. Their next advent is at the Age of the Constant Bicker, when parents and children outdo one another in discourtesy and wisecracks, the parents regularly receding into the mid-Victorian era for a code of behavior to impose on their children, and the children demanding the freedoms of the early jazz age.

It is impossible to believe that these parents and children are related by blood; they are only connected by plot. The ideals set up sometimes do correspond to the common experience; except for purposes of mockery, no parent is aware of the steady direction of psychology or of education; the ideal school is the one-room building of fifty years ago although the modern high school is represented physically—a big building for dances and romps. Talented children are acceptable, but studious ones are pitied, the butt of ill-natured jokes. Child labor has happily vanished.

And, by a miracle, adult labor has gone also. Without the benefit of an explicit code, the movies have performed a magical transformation of work, corresponding to their miraculous tricks with sex. In a queerly distorted way, the true form of sex can be discerned behind the flowing black draperies that envelop the siren, the bad woman; and the actuality of working for a living can also be made out, dimly, by keeping our eyes on minor characters, milkmen (chiefly used to establish the time of day), taxi drivers, soda clerks, and the like. For heroes more spectacular occupations are found: drilling for oil, building high-tension towers, whatever involves great physical danger or a gamble for sudden wealth. Occasionally, in a thrilling melodrama like *They Drive by Night*, some of the desperation that makes men risk death to earn a living is communicated; otherwise work is not considered "valid dramatic material" and is performed offstage by people of no interest. The stars, in their courses, are professional men; if they are professional women they are smarter than the men around them, but they appeal to our sympathy because, obviously, they want to be but are not loved. Movie women worked in factories during the war—an aberration; they do appear, bright, brash, and attractive, in department stores, and sometimes say their feet are killing them; otherwise they are as happy as larks.

It should be noted that even professional men do not work. When "required by the plot" a doctor goes out on a case, a lawyer appears in court, an art dealer sells a picture, and always a composer writes a great song or symphony in a single blinding flash of inspiration; otherwise work is represented by a brief case carried home at night.

The catalogue of exclusions can be continued indefinitely: people have accidents but they are seldom ill; they do not dose themselves with patent medicines; they are not nearsighted; they do not sweat—they do not secrete at all; below the head, the orifices of their bodies are closed. They are divinities sharing with humanity a few habits: they eat and drink and smoke.

They seem, these attractive creatures, to be characters in romantic fiction, but the surface of their lives is so real that some other sources are indicated. We are haunted by a feeling that we have met this sort of thing before, that somewhere we too have lived as they live—not in the distortion of our dreams or in the soft haze of daydreams either. We look again at all the things they do, the motions so real, the motives so transparently false, and the truth comes to us: *they are "playing house."*

The Code is only one of many pressures brought to bear on the movies, but it is the most important because by imposing its view of the sex relation it creates a general atmosphere of falsehood as opposed to the atmosphere of fiction; it drives the creative imagination from reality to myth. The best the movie can do, in these circumstances, is to repeat those ancient myths which have in them the truth of human aspirations, if not the truth of human existence; it invests the story of Midas or of Venus and Mars with wit and excitement and romance and does it very well, and it would be an evil turn to keep these stories from the screen. But the stock myths of the movies are not so deep-rooted in the memory of the race: their sex myths are those of forgotten Victorian novelists, the social myths come from our own gilded age. They are peopled by characters from stale jokes, the sap of living humor having long ago dried out.

In the prevalent code of behavior in the movies:

A man and a woman, destined to fall in love, always loathe each other when they first meet.

A woman is never absolutely sure a man loves her until he slaps her.

Women are always wiser than men in the conduct of life,

shrewder in business, and craftier in statesmanship; also, often, handier around the house.

The closer a man approaches the status of an "intellectual," the less capable he is of coping with timetables, supermarkets, the weather, laundry, babies, and all the other trifles of daily existence; and the more certain he is to be first baffled and then enchanted by a pushing teen-ager whose glandular attractions he considers signs of abstract intelligence until the end of the sixth reel.

The relation between parents and young children alternates between sentimental indulgence and ill-mannered disputes.

Married couples remain adolescent until their children pass the age of puberty; at that time the parents become miraculously younger than their young and find themselves on the verge, but only on the verge, of sexual adventure from which the children save them.

In marriage the man is constantly servant and suitor; he has gained no privileges, sexual or otherwise, by marriage.

These are some of the myths of domestic life; parallel to them are the social myths:

The principals in any action are always members of the more polite professions—if they work at all; lesser, and comic, characters have jobs.

"The wrong side of the tracks" is still a dominant social force in American life.

All agreeable businessmen made their money "the hard way"; inherited wealth is relatively unimportant; the opportunity to make a million is unlimited; hard work is always rewarded.

There are no economic forces; there are a few unscrupulous manipulators who may bring disaster on many people.

These myths have their own logic and mutually reinforce one another. The hostility of young lovers—whoever loved that loathed not at first sight?—was, at first, refreshing, and Freudians might have rejoiced in this recognition of "ambivalence"; it became a cliché but held on because the love which comes at the end is still only an extended flirtation, carried on with bright remarks, teasing, and a knowing glance. That these lovers are teenagers in their thirties is not surprising, no emotion having stirred them, no experience matured them. The mutual instantaneous and obviously false dislike of the lovers is a substitute for the actual tensions profoundly felt by people when they encounter a powerful attraction, and it has its counterpart in serio-comedy from Congreve to Bernard Shaw. With them it has motive and meaning: in the movies it is purely formula.

"The wrong side of the tracks" formula is, to be sure, a transposition of the Cinderella story, and it is legitimately used to throw up a barrier between lovers. Tabloid headlines and common experience alike indicate that purely social barriers are an obsession with relatively few people, but the formula provides a double satisfaction, assuring us, against all reason, that love conquers all and that all men are born equal. Yet the persistence of the theme in the movies is, again, a substitution for the real thing. The barriers of religion and of race are not touched on in the movies; the social barrier is used instead.

So far as the movies permit the business of making a living to appear at all, they substitute the legends of the past: the genius-inventor, the Horatio Alger hero in opposition to the skinflint banker (complete with mortgage), and the industrial pirate-philanthropist; they appear in contemporary clothes and utter the ideas of the nineteenth century in up-to-date slang. Aversion to the very thought of labor has been carried to such a point that in one vital respect the movies depart from the tradition of the past: success for the hero is not the reward of hard work—it comes by accident, as a natural consequence of his charm. During the early years of the depression Richard Watts, Jr., noted an actual defeatism in the movies: that the hero never tried to find work and was content to marry the rich man's daughter. This was a re-

flection of the great economic crisis of our time in popular pictures; in serious work, King Vidor made *Our Daily Bread*, and
after the New Deal arrived, Nunnally Johnson and John Ford
made the impressive *Grapes of Wrath*; but while the country was
sinking into apathy the movies remained resolutely entertaining,
and in an outburst of courageous realism presented a Robert
Nathan whimsy set in an utterly charming Hooverville in Central
Park. The New Deal, under which several companies reorganized
themselves after bankruptcy, was not much more effective in
turning the movies toward the present; a few isolated pictures
showed an awareness of the changing phases through which the
crisis was passing; but the unity of hope, in the first year of the
Roosevelt administration, inspired the movies as little as the earlier
unity of despair.

The worker—day laborer, machinist, skilled operator, belt-line
automaton, master plumber, whatever he may be—is the most
conspicuous throwback in the movies. Unless inflamed by foreign
demagogues, he is a figure of fun, kindly treated because he has a
beautiful daughter; he is conservative, on friendliest terms with
his boss (an old school friend whom he does not envy), and he is,
if not anti-union, at least not unionized. During the war the
Maritime Union was sympathetically presented in one picture,
but in peacetime the American who earns his living by working
for someone else is, in the movies, not only unaware of the CIO,
he is positively pre-Gompers. Indulgently patting the old contented unorganized worker on the shoulder, the movies have
been safe from the accusation of being anti-labor; they created a
stereotype which represented a number of "virtues," and they
shed over it the sentimentality of the past, giving off, like a fra-
grance, the vague idea that all was well and organization was
superfluous. Apparently everybody was satisfied; the highly organized technicians in the studios did not protest.

This isn't surprising. Undertakers, private detectives, real-
estate dealers, city magistrates, and members of a hundred other
professions may protest if one of their number is shown in a

discreditable way in the movies; but so long as nothing unfavorable is said about them, they and union men and doctors and college professors are as indifferent as all other citizens to the presentation of human beings in an atmosphere totally false to the conditions of their lives.

## CRITERIA OF MATURITY

> "*A wide knowledge of life and of living is made possible through the films. . . . The motion picture . . . builds character, develops right ideals, inculcates correct principles; . . . they can become the most powerful natural force for the improvement of mankind.*"
>
> From the Production Code

> "*The screen will help to keep the mind of the nation young as long as it continues to draw upon the greatest theses of life and of literature, and to use the best which art, music, and drama afford. . . .*"
>
> Will H. Hays

Maturity is not an absolute, and a producer, growing tired of a vague demand, might ask for some specifications. My own list is perhaps more encouraging to Hollywood than some others, and while it is no doubt influenced by my likes and dislikes, I think it is not unreasonable:

1. The tragic ending is required only for tragic themes. Maturity is in itself neither grim nor hilarious; in essence it consists of respect for the integrity of events; it means that if we start to weave a tragic plot we do not at the end catch up the threads and tie them into the bowknot of the happy ending.

2. Comedy can be as mature as tragedy. *Pygmalion* is as satisfying to the adult intelligence as *Hamlet*, though not so moving. From *Nothing Sacred* to *The Paleface*, Hollywood has consistently made first-rate comic pictures; and the creative genius most highly praised by the intellectuals has produced the *series* of pictures most rewarding at the box-office: Charlie Chaplin.

3. There is no need to abandon the tempo of the American

film—only to vary it in harmony with the character of any given picture. There is no need to abandon the star system—only to use stars intelligently, so that they are integrated into stories, not outside them. There is no need to abandon plot—only to develop plot logically out of character instead of distorting character to fit stereotyped plots.

4. A sense of reality is required, and for this the American picture must learn to deal more candidly with the average American in his actual social and economic situation; but the feature film need never be a political pamphlet. There is no restriction on the creative imagination, and characters may be larger than life if only they are not false to life.

5. In any mood—tragic, serio-comic, or melodramatic—the assumptions regarding normal sexual relations must be honest. This means that the current Production Code must be reinterpreted, to say the least; and that the sadistic and senseless violence of the movies will no longer be substituted for the more normal —and more interesting—passions of mankind.

In sum, the motion picture need only go on to its natural fulfillment in the direction it originally took, when it tried to tell stories to people. It has degenerated into telling myths for children. A story is always single, individual, and enhances our understanding of the many-sided mystery of the human spirit; and myth repeated without profound belief tends to become a formula, totally without reference to the actuality of our lives, manufactured without creativeness, and deadening our capacity to see life clearly.

The obstacles in the way of providing a steady flow of mature pictures in addition to the routine Hollywood product have been noted; they are both economic and psychological, and they can be overcome within the industry if sufficient public support is forthcoming. There is, however, another difficulty in the way, which is a form of organized non-support, and it is a serious one.

## PICTURES, POLITICS, AND PREJUDICE

> *"Today there is no event in history and no incident in modern life that cannot be shown on the screen."*
>
> Will H. Hays

The motion-picture industry operates under a constant, often explicit, threat of boycott.

Fifteen years ago the boycott was in a rudimentary state; pickets marched in front of a theater when an offensive picture was shown or a studio was warned that a specific subject would be protested. Today the threat is all-embracing; exhibitors are told that if they show a picture offensive to a political or religious group, the members of that group will not patronize the theater in the future, no matter what pictures are shown, and studios are warned that their total output also runs the risk of boycott if they do not yield.

In 1938, when Will Hays said there was no incident in modern times that could not be shown on the screen, the picture *Blockade* was presented by Walter Wanger. Carefully obscuring the nature of the conflict in Spain, obliterating distinguishing marks as carefully as a murderer in fiction rips out labels from his victim's clothes, the picture still gave the impression that the forces of General Franco were starving innocent women and children; until *Blockade* was attacked by Catholic organizations, liberals were lukewarm toward it; after that, they rallied to its defense. In spite of threats, picketing, and protests, the Radio City Music Hall showed the picture, and the receipts at the box-office were substantial; nevertheless, a large West Coast chain refused to give the picture complete first-run bookings, offering instead the kiss of death, a run as the second feature of a double bill. A further effect was that Wanger shelved production of a serious picture drawn from Vincent Sheean's *Personal History*.

In 1948 Eric Johnston declared that even after the congressional investigation of communism in Hollywood the industry was making controversial pictures. He named *Apartment for Peggy* and *The Boy with the Green Hair*. In the current state of American public opinion, these were as controversial as skimmed milk.

A year later he could have pointed to *Home of the Brave*. The sympathetic treatment of the Negro and the open discussion of trauma caused by race prejudice made this actually a controversial film. One of the less publicized elements of controversy was the distaste of many Negroes for this picture, and for several later ones concerned with Negroes who passed as white; by the earlier standards of Hollywood, however, these pictures were exceptional, the Negro characters were not stereotypes, and the existence of the color problem was recognized.

During the most nervous moments of the cold war in 1948, a Twentieth Century-Fox picture called *The Iron Curtain* was shown and picketed and counterpicketed in New York; it was anti-Communist and it was produced after Congressman Rankin and others had openly warned Eric Johnston that if the movie industry didn't "clean its own house" Congress would do it for them. The picture was important in only one respect: it showed that Hollywood was indeed ready to make controversial pictures —on the popular side;[1] the insistent declaration that films were for entertainment only was smoothly by-passed. MGM's comedy *Ninotchka* with Greta Garbo, which poked fun at the Soviets, was reissued at the same time to prove that Hollywood's heart had been in the right place as far back as 1939.

The congressional investigation of a number of Hollywood writers and directors was specifically intended to unearth Communist affiliations, but Mr. Johnston foresaw the inevitable result. He protested against "labeling everyone who doesn't agree with you a Communist," pointed out the various and very conservative hands through which any screenplay must pass before it is com-

[1] "I am in and out of the State Department every day," Eric Johnston told the writers at every major studio in Hollywood, urging the production of pictures propagandizing for the Truman Doctrine.

mitted to film, and called for the orderly processes of law to deal
with conspiracy and treason, refusing to let contracts be broken
or to get people fired because of political affiliation. Top executives of studios not known for hospitality to liberals also saw
that their freedom might be jeopardized if any outside authority
could interfere in the choice of writers or of subjects. The accused men had, when they started for Washington, serious
assurances of support and, as a mark of confidence, one writer
received from his studio a new contract, although his old one had
still some time to run when the subpoena was served. At the end
of the early sessions Mr. Johnston reiterated his stand against the
Committee on Un-American Activities and insisted that no one
would be fired.

Several days later a meeting of studio executives took place,
and all ten of the accused men were dropped from the payrolls.
When one of them brought suit against MGM, Louis B. Mayer
testified that two investigators for the Committee had conveyed
to him the desirability of "cleaning house" with the threat of
congressional action if he failed to do so, and that this warning
was given several weeks *before* the hearings had begun; Mr.
Mayer quoted his reply: "I wouldn't fire anyone because someone said someone was a Communist, as long as there was no communism in our pictures—and it couldn't get in." What pressures
were exerted later cannot be positively identified. When the
court decided in favor of the writer, the question of conspiracy
became important; if the studios had mutually agreed on a black-
list, punitive damages might rise to the impressive total of sixty
million dollars; the heads of the separate studios stated that they
had each come to a decision individually and that Eric Johnston
had not imposed it upon them. *Variety* then published a circum-
stantial account of the meeting at which the decision was taken,
indicating that James F. Byrnes, former Justice of the Supreme
Court, had advised the discharge of the men and assured the
executives that they could not be sued for more than the salaries
involved. *Variety* added that the executives "agreed they'd be

willing to pay off the coin due, if they lost in court, in order to accomplish the public relations gesture."

Pressure takes many forms, and some are harder to resist than others. A super-patriotic newspaper denounced Hollywood for making a faithful version of *The Ox-Bow Incident*, which outraged the tradition of the Western—the man who was strung up was innocent and the picture was therefore considered radical and un-American; Louella Parsons and Jimmie Fidler often utter warnings to stars and studios about the proper conduct of their affairs; a group called The Motion Picture Alliance for the Preservation of American Ideals made a list of subversive films, which included *The Pride of the Marines, Boomerang, Margie, The Strange Loves of Martha Ivers,* and *The Best Years of Our Lives. Boomerang* was based on the experience of Homer S. Cummings, later Attorney General of the United States, and dealt with doubts that assailed a prosecutor and led to the exoneration of an innocent man; *Margie* was a nostalgic dramatic musical in which a high-school debate on the withdrawal of our Marines from Nicaragua occupied a few minutes. (It should be noted that these charges were too much even for the studio executives; they suffer a certain constraint when newspapers and radio critics attack, but they were exasperated by the Alliance and answered back smartly.)

Clearly we are witnessing the first engagements in a long struggle for control of the ideas in moving pictures. At one extreme are those who insist that the movies are not a proper vehicle for communicating ideas; they trust to indirect pressures to keep liberal ideas out of pictures, and they abandon their principles cheerfully when their own ideas are sympathetically presented. The opposite position is held by those who believe that pictures without ideas are favorable to the present social and political system. Neither side has come into the open; perhaps because neither has thought out the consequences.

The line of battle was drawn in Hollywood itself in the early days of the New Deal. In 1934 employees of studios were told to devote a day's pay to the campaign against Upton Sinclair; they knew that bit players had been rigged out in studio costumes to represent vagrants and criminals in a faked newsreel (to a man, these ruffians were going to vote for Sinclair, whereas sturdy, decent workmen and women who looked like Whistler's mother were on the other side); like the majority of their fellow citizens, many writers and actors were enthusiastic about Roosevelt and were aware of the strong tide carrying America to a new and still unmarked destiny. None of their hopes, nothing of their sense of living in a time of turbulence and change, could get into the pictures they made. It was later said of the Hollywood liberals that their wealth gave them a bad conscience and their devotion to the underprivileged stemmed from a sense of guilt; the screenwriters especially made much of their "frustration." But it must be remembered that the exasperation began when the movies failed to respond to the emotional realities of the time, and that the time was in one way unique: in the bright early years of the New Deal the American intellectual was undergoing the same experience as the American people; with the exception of a few zealots, the writers and artists of America at last reconciled themselves to the wants and the hopes, and, above all, to the energy and the direction of American life. After generations of self-exile, they returned to the mainland; after twenty years of gibes and sneers, they began to love their country. The poets and playwrights and novelists and painters went confidently to their work; some of them were supported by the government, all of them were communicating with their fellow citizens; the wrong-headed and self-defeating drift of the intellectual away from the average man came to an end.

In that renaissance the movie writer did not share; he wanted to, but the movies stood off. The movies had ignored the depression, they would ignore the revival. Under benevolent laws they went through bankruptcy and reorganization, but they did not change their product. The Academy Awards of the early New Deal years went to *It Happened One Night, Mutiny on the*

*Bounty, The Great Ziegfeld;* the only picture with a sense of the destiny of a great nation was *Cavalcade,* and the nation celebrated was not the United States. The early 1930's were a high point in the creation of light comedy and musical shows, ranging from the masterpieces in which Fred Astaire appeared to pictures starring Nelson Eddy and Jeanette MacDonald. It was seven years after the New Deal began before *The Grapes of Wrath* appeared.

The Federal Theater Project put on a dramatization of Sinclair Lewis's novel, *It Can't Happen Here,* in a hundred cities simultaneously; the movies bought the book and shelved it; the Academy Award for the year in which it was to be made went to *You Can't Take It with You.*

The split between the isolationists and interventionists before Pearl Harbor neutralized the films, and the few anti-Nazi pictures produced were denounced as warmongering. When America entered the war the dissension between creative artists and their employers disappeared; the studios rendered a fair account of the American objectives in the war, split fifty-fifty between the Four Freedoms and huckleberry pie. In the cross and contentious postwar world the studios found a fresh and useful theme in psychiatry and reworked the legendary figure of the gangster for new pictures of violence, while the writers fretfully attempted to establish their moral right to have ideas and to see them projected to the screen.

The politics of a large group of writers, artists, and directors were definitely liberal throughout the Roosevelt administrations. Their radicalism stemmed from the Populism of the 1890's, the Progressivism of La Follette, and the New Deal; assaying the precise degrees of Communist sympathy among them has not been tried objectively. The content of films has been analyzed; in addition to the "subversive" films cited by the Alliance, professional anti-Communists point to several pictures made during the war, including *Mission to Moscow,* drawn from a book by a former Ambassador; and principal stress is on the fact that until

*The Iron Curtain* was made "producers consistently ducked anti-Communist themes"—presumably as a concession to their writers. The mother of a star discovered that a line of dialogue her daughter was asked to speak was Red propaganda (the line was, "Share and share alike, that's democracy"); and Congressman Rankin advised Eric Johnston to "read some of these films between the lines" to arrive at their subversive intentions. It is precisely between the lines that radical critics of the movie find the most powerful arguments against any change in our economic or social system; between the lines they hear the silence that signifies consent.

The mildest critic of our social system is aware of this negative force in the movies, and the dictators of Right and Left have kept our pictures out of their countries because inevitably our movies reflect a certain contentment with the capitalist system, they glorify its easygoing ways, and they distract the mind. To the purists a Disney short is an argument for capitalism, a musical show in Technicolor is propaganda against good housing, because billions of man-hours per year are spent observing these pleasant objects, forgetting the wrongs and iniquities we ought to be fighting.

On the fundamental issue the purist is right: there is no entertainment in the void; if it is created by man it reflects, however dimly, the mind of man; there is no entertainment without ideas; and ideas, noble or mean, cannot detach themselves entirely from political and social and religious interests. The gladiators in the arena represented a way of life, and their political significance was recognized; the acrobat in the circus is propaganda for astonishment at the wonders man can perform and an inducement to be satisfied.

The extreme case of religion in the movies illuminates the situation perfectly.

It is, in our common phrase, "unthinkable" that a movie should be made to attack any religion; and theoretically no picture would set one faith above any other. No word or sign in *The Bells of St. Mary* declared that the priest and the nun were more admirable than a Methodist preacher and a Baptist missionary might be; the Catholic Church, represented by a popular American and an attractive foreign star, appeared in an amiable light and cast no shadow on other faiths. Yet non-Catholic dignitaries expressed concern because no comparable pictures showing their religious practices and beliefs appeared. The jaunty priest of Bing Crosby, the athletic nun of Ingrid Bergman, created new images in the American mind, drastically altering old stereotypes; the Protestant minister and the rabbi were denied this freshening contact with the people. The Church in whose history the word "propaganda" first appeared could ask no better example; it would be years before the friendliness generated by these characters would be dissipated; and even if a Cardinal should by a masterpiece of the maladroit bring religious controversy into the political atmosphere, the temper of a vast number of non-Catholics would remain calm because, in the back of their minds, lay the conviction that all priests are Crosbys, genial, full of sentimental charm, and indulgent to other sects.

It is not necessary to assume that any influential Catholic in Hollywood instigated the making of the two pictures in which Crosby plays a priest; the story current at the time is that the first picture was the result of a single sentence uttered, in the blue haze of a story conference, by a non-Catholic producer: "How would it be for Bing to play a young priest?" The second picture was an inevitable response to the box-office success of the first. Certainly no one in Hollywood regretted a friendly tribute to the Church whose Legion of Decency constitutes the most serious threat of boycott; and at the same time some efforts were made to find a satisfactory story "glorifying" a Protestant. The charge that the Crosby pictures were propaganda was eagerly taken up and was disproved by logic: they were popular, so they must be entertainment. The defenders might as well have said that no one was converted to the Catholic Church because of the picture. The essential fact about influence is that it is most effective when indirect, and in the long run the creation of a climate favorable to the growth of an attitude of mind is more important than the planting of any specific ideas.

Minority groups—the Catholics, for instance—are compelled to use pressure, and in a society built on the force of public opinion group pressure is justified if it recognizes the propriety of counterpressures. A reasonable state is one in which all pressures are in proportion to the size of the group, provided no one interest overrides the proper demands of the others. The mathematical problem of the movies in respect to films favoring the Catholic Church is a simple one: the faith of about one-fifth of the population has been attractively presented, the faith of about three-fifths has been neglected but not actively scorned.

This is an example of positive action. For propaganda by inaction we can look to a theme which did not touch the spiritual life of the nation and on which there was virtually no essential dispute.

With the exception of a minority as small as the treasonable pro-Hitler element during the war, the entire population of the United States believed that something on a large scale should be done to provide decent homes for returned soldiers and sailors. No one spoke against housing for veterans. The discomforts and indignities suffered by veterans who could not find homes were universally deplored; the only difference of opinion was on the method of getting houses built.

The housing shortage after the war was treated in the movies precisely as the wartime crowding of Washington had been handled before: in farcical comedy with slight sexual overtones. (The lack of a proper habitation was a "natural" for pictures based on the obstacles to cohabitation.) No important pictures on the subject were made; a matter of immediate daily concern for some thirty million people was not acceptable material. With full respect for the enterprise and acumen of the great managers of public opinion, I still doubt whether the real-estate lobby gave

Hollywood the word; for one thing, the lobby felt reasonably confident about its success in Washington; for another, the word would have been almost insultingly superfluous. Because the thought of treating the housing shortage in terms of the hopes and resentments of actual GIs and their wives, and in terms of the breach of faith with their children, would not normally occur to the producers of pictures. The only myth to which they could attach the subject was that of the pioneer, gladly suffering hardships; in that myth man fights nature or Redskins, not his fellow man. Neither government nor lobbies could figure as the deliberate creator of obstacles to happiness. The theme most talked of in the studios at the time was the situation of husband and wife, agreeing to divorce, compelled to live under the same roof (and perhaps under the same ceiling). It was a good comedy situation —it always had been.

The argument in Hollywood ran that light entertainment, grossly exaggerating the discomforts of the housing situation, would cheer the actual sufferers by contrast; it was also supposed that "no one would go to see a serious picture about the housing shortage." The possibility of a genuine emotion within a comic situation was not canvassed. One thought of the British picture, *Love on the Dole*, and of the remark of an acute critic in London, Miss C. A. Lejeune, who wrote: "British picture-goers want adult films about people in whom they can believe, people who behave credibly and humanly in possible circumstances. They have come to the conclusion . . . that Hollywood is functionally incapable of giving them that sort of picture." And Hollywood is convinced that Americans are fundamentally unwilling to see that kind of picture. If that is true, how much of the blame can be traced to the pictures Hollywood did create in fifty years?

Assuming that the argument mentioned above is well founded and that the lives of many GI families were made tolerable by being distracted from their own troubles, didn't this distraction actually slacken the demand for political action on housing? Wasn't the four-year delay in getting a housing program through

Congress partly due to the artificially induced sense that the matter wasn't important after all? Did Hollywood, by refusing to
take the side of those who demanded action, actually take the
side of those who conspired to prevent action? Weren't the farces
a help to the real-estate lobby, and wasn't the absence of a strong
dramatic treatment equally an action *against* the American Veterans Committee and the other groups who needed the kind of
help that radio occasionally gave them? And isn't it understandable that these ex-GIs, who trudged miles in the jungle to see an
American movie during the war, are precisely the adults who are
drifting away from the convenient hometown and neighborhood
movies today? Are they perhaps thrown off by a suspicion,
hardly formulated, that the movies have let them down?

The questions crowd one upon the next. Is it Hollywood's
function to create public apathy? We know the answer: "Our
mission is to entertain." The next question brings us up against
a solid wall: Must entertainment create apathy?

The Committee on Recent Social Trends appointed by President Hoover declared that "the motion picture is primarily an
agency of amusement," and in Hollywood amusement and entertainment are interchangeable terms. In spite of its deviations into
horror and psychiatry, the picture industry thinks of itself as a
creator of laughter and can see no alternative except to make
glumly depressing pictures on topics of the day. This feeble concept of entertainment sounds plausible; it omits only the laughter
that has rung down the ages, from Aristophanes through Rabelais
and Molière to Mark Twain. It omits the laughter of Charles
Chaplin.

I asked Chaplin one day, while he was shooting *Modern Times*,
to tell me how he had come upon the idea of making the picture.
He told me that a friend had described to him vividly and with
deep indignation the functioning of the belt system in Detroit.
"I knew there was a great comedy in it," Chaplin said, "if I
could only find it." What he had to say about a system he feared
and hated had to be expressed in his own comic terms; he is pre-

eminent as a comic spirit because his terms have grown more complex and subtle but remain always his own, always essentially in the tradition of comedy. His occasional lapses can be traced to the injection of ideas not completely integrated into his basic comic pattern. That kind of translation into comedy is not the habit of the feature-film makers; for Chaplin, with all his grotesquely conventional and sentimental characters, holds to the truth of his themes, whereas the usual film brings into action people who are true to life on the surface and betray all that is human inside them—for a laugh.

The abstract subject of religion and the immediate material concern of good housing illustrate the kind of problems that propaganda in the movies can present. Another instance must be mentioned.

In 1949 the British-made picture *Oliver Twist* was announced for exhibition in America. It was not shown. The incident was a remarkable example of the interaction of pressure-politics and finance and was so important that a large part of a session of the Civil Liberties Union annual meeting was devoted to it. In its complexities, *Oliver Twist* exhibits the grave difficulties under which the movies labor, the desperate passions they can arouse, and the conflict of irreconcilable ideals.

It was reported from England that the physical characteristics of Fagin, the Jew, were modeled closely on the original illustrations—the ancient kaftan, the sickle nose, the small, mean eyes, the unkempt beard—and it was recalled that these stigmata of hatred had more recently been used in the caricatures published by Himmler. Protests against showing the picture were overruled by the J. Arthur Rank organization, but before the picture arrived in New York, the Sons of Liberty, which had previously been active against the British policy in Palestine, began a boycott of other Rank pictures and presently extended it to pictures made by other British firms. (An announced counterboycott of American films in England was completely abortive.) The close connection of the British film industry with the British government gave a strong political tinge to the boycott here, and it was actually part of a campaign to stop buying British goods, the American boycotters arguing that they were unable to vote the responsible British officials out of office and were therefore compelled to take economic action. It was later explained to them that the earnings of British films in this country went to American firms releasing the pictures; and on this ground the Sons of Liberty called off their pickets; the Rank organization, without making a specific commitment, set aside its plans to show *Oliver Twist*.

Obviously the basic argument never came into the open in these negotiations. The situation was awkward for both sides; the Civil Liberties Union felt bound to ask for the free exhibition of a picture which might stir the basest passions; and the boycotters found themselves obligated by their argument to set harsh limits to freedom of expression on the screen. The position of the Union was that picketing, boycotts, and all other forms of pressure would be legitimate after the picture was made public; the opposition held that by that time serious damage might have been done, and, in any event, if the boycott was justifiable, it should be used at its most effective point, before the showing, and it should have been used before the picture was ever made. To this the Union's reply was that in the present situation the public could not see the picture and judge for itself or weigh the merits of the boycott; and the response to this was that the picture constituted a clear and present danger, that it could be used by interested organizations to create strong anti-Semitic feeling and must not be shown.

Not one of those who wanted the picture to be shown had the slightest respect for a producer who would, in the years after Hitler, put upon the screen a figure that might rouse latent feelings of religious hatred; not one denied the possible danger, although all questioned how clear and present it was. And on the other side, many of the protesters were uncomfortable because they were themselves adherents of the Civil Liberties Union and felt the danger of compromising its basic position. Uneasiness was, in fact, the dominant mood, perceptible below the vehement assertions of broad principle, a fear that the movies had brought a new element into the field of communications and a suspicion that perhaps the modes of safeguarding freedom of expression might have to be changed if the fundamental principles were to be saved.

The problem of freedom and fairness comes up with more challenge and complexity in radio than it does in the movies, and I will not anticipate the argument here. The special circumstances of the movies are these:

> what is communicated is emotion, more than reason;

> the audience is peculiarly receptive because the emotion is conveyed through a special kind of fiction, the myth, and usually in an atmosphere of relaxed enjoyment;

> the interaction of the Production Code and the system of distribution have eliminated from this audience the mature and the thoughtful;

> the movies have in part accepted and in part created in this audience a dulled perception of the meaning of present events;

> the movies make their impressions slowly, they work on the subconscious, through images, and their effects are long-lasting.

There is a further point which applies to all the entertainment arts which are also forms of communication: the postwar world has not yet built its foundations, and for the first time in its history the United States is anxious, without confidence in the future, aware of commitments but ignorant of their consequences; in that atmosphere a determined struggle for control of popular emotion is going on, and "the free market of ideas" is being rigged as deliberately as any other market. The manipulators who are successful are those who understand the new machinery of communication and who know that the velocity of ideas is at least as important as their specific gravity. At sixty miles an hour, a car weighing two thousand pounds needs a road graded and banked, and if it hits another car going at the same speed the result is more serious than the coupling of two freight cars, weighing ten times as much, but going at the rate of half a mile an hour. Those who are creating the emotional tone of our time know that today words and images travel with the speed of light. It is probably the prime fact of our social life, and until the dynamics of radio and the movies are understood by citizens and statesmen as fully as they are by engineers of propaganda, we risk being controlled by people who have no responsibility to us, to whom we answer yes obediently, not knowing we have consented to place our lives, our liberty, and perhaps our sacred honor in their hands.

Doctrinaire orations on the abstract principles of freedom of expression are worthless in the situation; we need eternal vigilance to make sure that the working principle is not compromised. Actually, the defenders of free expression have proved themselves flexible enough to cope with some of the new conditions. In the past decade the right to hear has been fought for as often as the right to speak, particularly when commentators of liberal temper have been edged away from the microphone; and without infringing on free speech, defenders of free speech have asked whether speakers are really free or are paid to express the opinions of others. In general, the principle of the free market is still accepted, the idea that competition is the life of trade, and that the truth will ultimately prevail. It is interesting to find this confident trust in the "somehow good" among those who are most aware of the dangers. For instance, Morris Ernst, an able propagandist for the principle of freedom, is also the author of many books and magazine articles proving that the free market does not exist, the control of movies being a small, tight concentration of power, and the actual (if not the legal) control of newspapers and broadcasting moving to fewer and fewer individuals.

As I have suggested, not ideas but emotions are created by the movies as a by-product of entertainment. The effect of the movies is not diminished by this, nor is it even diminished by the absence of the mature from the audience; seen in the formative years of adolescence, they create a permanent background, the romantic scenery against which we set the real places and people of our lives. Because of the way they are made and sold and seen, the movies contribute more of certain elements to our lives than radio does, and less of others; but both of them are parts of the entertainment-communications system, and it will be better to observe their effects after we have looked into the business of broadcasting.

*"Nothing will kill the movies except education."*
*Will Rogers*

# Oracle: Radio

## IN THE PUBLIC INTEREST

> *"To criticize radio, why, that's un-American!"*
> Victor Ratner (then vice-president of CBS)

Everything in the movies exists in the past tense: in radio and in television everything is in the present. The screen is primarily significant as a medium of fiction: broadcasting as a medium of fact. Our myths are fabricated in Hollywood; radio is the modern oracle.

The voice comes through the air, the speaker unseen, answering questions of statecraft, propounding riddles, explaining and foretelling events, denouncing the enemies of the state. There is a hierarchy of oracular voices; at the top are those announcing war and chaos, and at the bottom the veiled sibyls, Big Sister and Aunt Jennie, comforting, advising, a guide to life. Like the ancient oracles, the modern can be bribed.

Radio has a split personality: the broadcasting business is licensed by the federal government to operate in the public interest and is, itself, a huge private enterprise; it is devoted to the prodigious sale of commodities but manufactures none. It brings entertainment, most of which it does not itself create. The day-to-day reconciliation of its various activities has compelled the business to analyze itself, and broadcasting is probably more aware of its nature, its obligations, and its possible doom than any other American business. It came into being after Theodore Roosevelt and Woodrow Wilson had reworked the Populist platform into a system of checking private enterprise against public rights;

but it was unhampered by bureaucracy in its formative years, getting its growth in the happy-go-lucky days of Harding and Coolidge. It was, consequently, in its lusty manhood when Hoover, who had tried to lop off its commercial aspects in 1924, became President, and the depression left hardly a scar. The machinery of regulation was working long before the New Deal arrived; it had a moderate conservative rather than a radical complexion; and the faint threat that the FCC would actively interfere with broadcasting, to place the public need above all considerations of private profit, was dissipated when some of Roosevelt's appointees to the Commission departed after his death. The broadcasters fretted under the ill-defined powers of the FCC; occasionally they dodged a sniper's bullet from an educator or an anti-monopolist, but they never had to go through the galling experience of public discontent or the heavy fire of such commissions as set standards of service and rates of payment for railways and telephone companies. It is, in fact, a prime article of the broadcasters' creed that they operate in the public interest but are not a public utility.

There was a moment when radio almost became a ward of the government, and even this turned to its advantage. As Assistant Secretary of the Navy, Franklin D. Roosevelt helped to form a kind of patents pool, so that radio escaped the kind of internal bickering that entangled the movie industry for years. The threat of serious rivalry between industrial giants ended in an agreement between the Radio Corporation of America (RCA) and the Bell Telephone Systems, by which the latter withdrew from broadcasting and the former agreed to use Bell's long lines for transmission.

Good fortune continued. For a long time David Sarnoff, the dominant power in RCA, felt that the costs of broadcasting should be a charge levied upon the manufacturers of receivers and that no advertising should be permitted; and Mr. Hoover, as Secretary of Commerce, deplored the possibility of commercializing this great medium (and incidentally said that the American people would not stand for advertising on the air). The industry was rescued from such capitalistic idealism when advertisers forced their way in. It was good fortune too that Sarnoff was a practical visionary who, as early as 1916, foresaw that in every home there would be a box out of which music and drama and news and information would come; and that the first great rival to Sarnoff's NBC was created by William S. Paley, an enthusiast who at a certain time developed a large sense of social responsibility. But the best good fortune of radio lay in its critics.

For a decade the sharpest attack on broadcasting was directed at the commercial message which used to be called by the ugly name of "plug"; and the irrelevance and inevitable failure of the attack can be measured by the disappearance of the pejorative word, its place taken with honor by "the commercial." The public response was negligible; even so powerful an organ as *The Reader's Digest* received written support from only three-tenths of one per cent of its readers, and in Cleveland a thoughtful and energetic campaign by Robert Stephens, radio editor of the *Cleveland Plain Dealer*, turned up an equally low manifestation of dislike. The circulation of the paper was then four hundred thousand; only five hundred and fifty-one persons, in one hundred and two different communities, showed any strong feeling about commercials. Without explicitly making the point, broadcasters could shrug off criticism as purely highbrow, and later, when the critics learned their lesson and began to worry about what radio really did to people, the broadcasters associated criticism with bureaucracy and government control of the pleasures of the citizen—in effect, socialism en route to the communist state.

The fault of the critics was that they had not analyzed the nature of radio and took it for a form of entertainment, like the movies. It does entertain, but its essence lies elsewhere. The broadcasters themselves rationalized their equivocal public-private character and came closer to the mark. Secure in the affections of the people and under pressure from a federal authority (which can deny, or refuse to renew, licenses), the broadcasters escaped the confused thinking of the movies. As necessity requires, the movies call themselves either an art or a business, capable of inspiring the loftiest actions or merely entertaining the masses. Radio has taken its stand: *everything* it does, from analytical newscasts to giveaways and symphony concerts, is in the public interest; when the daytime serial—one of its most vulnerable services—is under fire, it is defended not primarily as a diversion but as a lesson in living, an alleviation of the anxieties of the audience; and proof is forthcoming in the worthy testimony of the listeners: by the example of "John's Other Wife" they forgive errant husbands, and from "Our Gal Sunday," perhaps, they receive guidance in their own lives.

With the skill of a Chicago semanticist, the broadcasters have argued that the public interest is whatever interests the public; unlike the movies, radio is legally recognized as a medium of communication and can therefore appeal to the Bill of Rights for protection against interference with free expression, and broadcasters have always reacted vigorously against any effort of the FCC to look into the programs they transmit. They alone can decide what to send out and what to reject. While, in practice, sponsors create programs, the networks and the stations consider themselves responsible to the people. In practice, also, broadcasters do not attempt anything as complicated as an appeal to all the interests of all the people; they transmit, primarily, programs which sponsors believe will interest sufficiently large sections of the public. It is a comedown from the broad general statement of public interest, but it holds to a principle, and by the virtue of that principle radio stands or falls.

Sober criticism of radio can usually be reduced to variations of a simple statement: the broadcasters do not satisfy enough minority interests and in admittedly few types of program may harm the vast majority who do listen. The defense can also be encapsuled: radio is a mass medium and, in the name of democracy, it must serve the vast majority. Taken together, these offer a good working basis, even though the hypothesis is wrong. Radio seldom reaches the vast majority; it is a mass-minority medium. The attack and the defense start from the wrong premises, and it isn't surprising that they wander off in the wrong direction.

I propose to examine the programs, the conditions of production, and then the public, remembering always that the entire program structure, not merely the newscasts and the documentaries, are theoretically of service to the public.

## SATURATION

In a totally unexpected development, the number of broadcasting stations on the standard band almost doubled between 1946 and 1948, and the number of Frequency Modulation stations rose from six hundred and eighty-eight to one thousand and five (including authorizations). By now there are, in spite of the inroads and threats of television, some two thousand AM stations, few of which are on the air less than twelve hours. Many of these stations must broadcast the same programs, and all but a few resort at one time or another to playing recorded music, many of them doing hardly anything else. Only a few isolated sections of the country receive the signals of fewer than three stations, and in large communities or well-situated small ones citizens have their choice of half a dozen or more programs for the greater part of the day and night. Technically these programs are divided between sponsored and sustaining, but the differences in content do not correspond precisely to this division; generally the sponsored programs approach an ideal of "pure entertainment" but include news, news analysis, and some educational and cultural programs (such as symphonic orchestras); sustaining programs on networks tend to be strictly educational and documentary, and on smaller stations consist of quarter-hours of recordings for which a sponsor has not yet been found.

Another consequence of the amount of broadcasting is that

the programs must be repetitive. That the same newscaster appears every night at the same hour is merely a convenience, but the sameness of Jack Benny's program week after week or of the action in "Young Widder Brown" day after day is a necessity imposed on them by the impossibility of creating something new every day or every week. It has been proposed that the popular comedians appear once every two weeks, alternating with other equally popular comedians; but the repetitive program has its parallel in repetitive listening, and sponsors are afraid to break the rhythmic spell of "same time, same station." No similar proposal has yet been made for the daytime serial in which, because listening is sporadic and often interrupted, repetition is of the essence.

To present the same thing day after day or week after week and still to hold an audience is no small accomplishment. It is done by ingenuity, by making the old seem new, by adding small portions of actually new elements from time to time; above all, it is done by making each individual program as easy to forget as possible. Men have written before this without the expectation that what they wrote would outlive monuments and brass; but to write *in order to be forgotten* is something new in the world, and, in the long run, this pumping out of never-ending waters of oblivion may be the most serious count against radio as a public service. It reduces the created entertainment to the level of a commodity, and the process is parallel to that of the mass distribution of commodities: the paper plate, the razor blade, are sold to be quickly used and thrown away. There is an almost hypnotized repeated action in the manufacture, an uncritical contentment, an almost apathetic acceptance on the part of the consumer. The justification of the quantity system is in the hidden concept that nothing is too good for the average man, and in spite of the aesthetes who long for the handmade and the de luxe edition, the system proves itself; but we are not dealing now with plates on which our food is to be served, we are concerned with the nourishment, the entertainment and diversion of the human spirit. Is it in the public interest to be smothered in stale pillow-feathers?

The large-scale production of entertainment which is meant to be forgotten does not correspond to the inherent nature of radio, only to the way it is now used. Economy of commercial effort dictates the sale of time Sunday night at seven to the same sponsor for thirty-nine weeks a year, and economy of creative effort makes the occupant of that hour use the same material week after week; five different sponsors at ten forty-five each weekday morning might result in five different programs each competitively trying to be more memorable than the other.

To make individual programs forgettable, yet hold the audience, means that the format must be the link between one program and another. Sometimes this format is a simple device to connect elements which are superficially different each week—as different, let us say, as the radio version of one Hollywood picture is from the next. A master of ceremonies, like the *compère* of Molière's time, sets the scene, introduces the players, makes way pleasantly for the commercial, and at the end thanks the players and announces joyous tidings for the following week. Sometimes an atmospheric connection is established; the first series of "The Theatre Guild on the Air" had something of the Guild's quality, and Orson Welles did a series in which the recurrent element was himself as principal actor and "narrator-in-character" of each play. The format of a comedy show is more elaborate: for Fred Allen it became so fixed that each element seemed precisely timed, and only his irrepressible ad libs could be counted on to make the program come off the air late. There was the introductory remark, the meeting with Portland (and by some miracle the never varied "Mr. Al-len" and "Why, Portland" had always a sense of fresh delight), then Portland's report on items in the news or notes from Momma's latest letter, the visit to Allen's Alley with the characters acting according to formula; then the break and, after the commercial, Fred and his guest.

The manipulation of the elements on a Benny show has been far more astute; Benny has something different occasionally. Once he ran a contest for the best ending to a sentence which began, "I hate Jack Benny because . . ." For half a year each program asked the listener to go back to last Thursday to witness the preparation of the program they were listening to; it was an awkward device since the sense of the past is lacking in radio, but it served to introduce the real framework, the sequence of loosely connected episodes in which Benny as a miser, as a dupe, as a dope, performed his various roles. He rotates a number of subsidiary characters, giving them most of the laugh lines, and works up situations which are funny because they are invisible (it turns out that Mary is helping Jack across the street, not, as you suppose, the reverse); he is a masterly technician in the medium; age has only given him another permanent joke, about his baldness, and apparently custom cannot wither him, the old jokes being, as always, the best.

Drama and the big popular comedy programs are in the upper reaches of radio; lower down, format is purely a matter of packaging, wrapping other people's goods in new paper. When the quiz shows suddenly spurted, energized by "Information Please" (which was essentially more a conversation than a quiz), dozens of variations were tried out. The success of Ralph Edwards' "Truth or Consequences," on which he gave a prize to a listener to whom he telephoned, revived a type of program tried, and abandoned, several years earlier—the "Pot o' Gold." Immediately the format of the quiz was adapted to the giveaway; on hundreds of local stations rewards of ten dollars were given for answering questions little harder than those on "It Pays to Be Ignorant," while on the networks the format which required a contestant to identify a song was changed so that he had to identify a song played backward. An entertainment in the ordinary sense was not offered, the programs were precisely on the level of the pinball machine; the mechanism of each program, its dynamics, speed, energy, became supremely significant—how often clues were given, how much time was spent rehearsing the list of prizes, how valuable they were. It was a triumph of format.

## "AND TELL SAD STORIES"

But not the greatest. It is hard to say this without the appearance of mockery, but, in sober truth, the great invention of radio, its single notable contribution to the art of fiction, is the daytime serial; and the phenomenal thing in this case is that the format has been essentially the same for virtually all of the fifty most successful serials which have appeared. About thirty network serials were offered daily, almost equally divided between NBC and CBS, in 1950. "Vic and Sade," a remarkably shrewd and lively series of dialogues, with minor characters, all of them speaking in a highly personal version of the American idiom, stood outside the canon; "The Rise of the Goldbergs," in which the characters were vastly superior, was well within the structural formula; the serious work of Sandra Michael in "Against the Storm" deliberately used the form, omitting some of its debased elements, for good social purposes. But the scripts turned out by the Hummert factory and the skillful individual work of Elaine Carrington, the stories by Irna Phillips with their undercurrent of hysteria, and dozens of others, were cut from the pattern originally set by "The Jordans" and "Myrt and Marge."

The master stroke is the way the daytime serial fitted itself to the actual habits of listening and evolved a technique of narration as skillful as that of Joseph Conrad and, in its way, as complex. There is nothing in the daytime serial for the occasional listener, except mystification; and a careful observer, listening every day for weeks, is astounded at the slow pace of events, wondering how anyone can listen so long to so little. Actually serials are heard over a long period of time but not always consecutively; even devoted listeners hear their favorites perhaps not more than three days out of five; routine as their days are, breaks and interruptions occur, and listening goes on while housework is being done, so that sometimes a phone call or a pot boiling over may blot out a significant moment. The serial takes these accidents of listening into account; the immediate past is reconstructed before each installment, and an event is divided and subdivided, so that the thread can always be picked up. In one serial it took a man a full installment to decide that as the last house on the block was numbered 1676 and the first house, two blocks farther, was 1800, the place he was looking for, number 1700, must be the big house occupying the intervening block; and this was the fourth of five installments in which the man set out to call at the house in order to see his estranged wife; having discovered the house on Thursday, he spent all but the last minute of Friday in conversation with a friend, giving a résumé of the events that had caused the separation; in the final minute he saw her step into a car and drive away—providing the necessary week-end "suspense." In one of Elaine Carrington's rather charming domestic serials of a few years ago, the better part of a week was spent in deciding the proper height of a young girl's hemline. The historical weekly serial, "Roses and Drums," lasted longer than the Civil War it described.

The techniques of the serial are founded on the assumption of immortality. The characters in them were born and grew to their present estate, but as the serials exist outside of time, their people do not grow older and the listener is expected to know them forever; hence the slow pace of development, the absence of dramatic solutions; we are supposed to get to know these people as we get to know new neighbors, becoming more familiar, each time we see them, with the intonations of their voices, the way they laugh, what they are interested in; and we are supposed to care for them in the same way. We do not expect old friends to be dramatic or amusing every time we see them; the longer we know them the more content we are merely to be in their company; they populate our world, they are landmarks on our journey through life; and if we don't see them for several days, we want to know what happened to them and quite expect them to be a little repetitious when they tell us.

The serial began with characters, with real people telling what had actually happened to them that day; the formula was adequate for the creation of interest. Upon it was presently grafted the principle of suspense. This was probably an importation from the action serials of the movies, but it soon became clear that the format of the daytime serial was not right for suspense. The "Perils" formula on the screen was excellent to carry over a week; it presented the heroine in deadly danger at the beginning of an episode, got her out of it, and started her well on the way to the next item of jeopardy—but each week it got her out. The radio version could not get its heroine out each day; moreover, with the emphasis on her as a character, it was necessary to continue each situation for a long time because any triumphant resolution of her difficulties would make her temporarily less interesting. Suspense had to be continuous; it went through a process of fractionization. The purpose was to create not excitement but anxiety.

To create anxiety, or fractional and unresolved suspense, the daytime serial capitalizes on its technique of delay; it gives a minimum of action in each installment, actually cutting itself down at times to two desultory conversations of about four minutes each, the rest of the quarter-hour being taken by résumés, musical bridges of the most revolting quality, and commercials; and like some of its own characters (and many people known to its listeners), the serial has the faculty of total recall: it is the only dramatic art form in which nothing ever happens between the acts, nothing is compressed and composed and foreshortened. It has a kind of realism, it uses long pauses, hesitations in speech, it goes back on itself and repeats and remembers, it welcomes irrelevances and interruptions, all for the purpose of going ahead as slowly as possible, of postponing the inevitable hour when it must get somewhere. A French dramatist once demonstrated the principle of realism by writing a play for two characters, both old men, in which nothing happened for three acts; it is the only instance of a slower movement than that of the daytime serial.

The admirable technique of the form has not received its due because critics have been appalled by the characters and plots and by the substandard production from which the serial suffers; brilliance of presentation, good music, background effects, and good radio acting are the exceptions. The serial is, nonetheless, a first-class creation, supplying a form flexible enough to take any character and any plot that is worth developing over a long period of time. The Scheherazades who tell these stories scorn the idea of coming to an end after a thousand and one installments, but they are in the great tradition. Their form is excellent; what they pour into it is another matter.

In addition to the Fabian technique, the writers have been forced to use materials which lend themselves to the long pull: happiness they know is brief in this mortal world, and their stock in trade is linked sadness, long drawn out. A lingering illness, a long and interrupted journey, the law's delay, accidents that prevent action, letters that fail to arrive and when they do arrive remain unopened (excellent for the additional twist of suspense needed to carry over the week end)—all these become the natural properties of the serial and have, in turn, an effect on the characters. The woman at the center of the serial is a strong character, but if she were permitted to function in strength, the plot would blow up in a few days; she has to be harried and chivvied and above all prevented from taking action. This means that she cannot confront a strong character as her adversary. Not clash, but slow tension, is required; so Medea must deal always with the irresolute and reluctant Jason, never with Creon, who can banish her from the scene; and it would be superfluous for Hedda Gabler to commit suicide, since neither the Judge nor the poet will be central to her life, only her irresolute husband.

So the technique of production, parceling out small bits of action from day to day, has given to the daytime serial one of its most remarkable qualities: it abounds in weak characters, usually men, who cannot make up their minds and stand undecided at every fork in the road. The will has atrophied, they are at the mercy of events, torn by indecision, pushed into action without the sinew and fiber to carry action through. These are the people closest to the heroine, and they may be characters of considerable violence, but even if they are criminals they act out of weakness, not strength; minor characters, often without motive, provide the bad, to contrast with the good, but the main action is not in the black-and-white area of good and evil, it is in the cloudier realm where strength is held back by weakness. In serial life, God wot, no villain need be; and though it isn't exactly passion that spins the plot, we are delayed by what is weak within.

The weak man required by the structure of the daytime serial is peculiarly useful because he is, obviously, impotent, and although a woman may weep at suspected infidelities, she is never deceived; her long self-examinations to decide whether she loves him conceal what she knows, that he cannot make love to her. The obstacles to cohabitation between man and wife are not the same in the serial as they are in the movies—the general moral tone is different. In the movies illicit love is represented by a fadeout, if it is permitted to exist at all; in the serial, amnesia is the substitute for adultery, a bigamous marriage being the natural consequence of losing one's memory. But the confessed unworthiness of the male reduces these and all serial marriages to social arrangements; the happy consummation of marriage for the heroine is unthinkable. Vast impedimenta of jobs and errands and phone calls and ailing relatives stand between her and a man, or she is swept by her employer into an exploration of Africa or must rescue a failing bank or newspaper; underneath all this activity the truth remains: the man is no good, she will not marry him. Perhaps it is as well. The evidence is not so overwhelming, but one suspects she is frigid.

This is the end to which the boldest invention of radio has come. I shall return more than once to other aspects of the serial. For the moment I note that from time to time the serial form has been used in sustaining programs by networks chafing under criticism or by bolder sponsors; the stories were a little more reasonable, the characters had some natural intelligence, and occasionally a few inventive techniques were used. The sustainers usually fell by the wayside, and sponsors almost invariably began to insist on a "stronger story line," which meant that they wanted their prestige serial to sound like all others. The only hope for the daytime serial was that a writer of some creative power would recognize the possibilities inherent in the form and its vast influence. Several works of fiction have become the basis for serials, but, so far as I know, no established writer has attempted to work in the medium. The unimaginative snobbery of American novelists has blinded them to the remarkable virtues of the serial; even during the war, when a chance was offered to write a patriotic serial with overtones of racial and religious brotherhood, one of the best known of American novelists, and not a highbrow, refused even to consider the proposal, although perfectly willing to write hour-long dramas for the night-time audience. Today the incalculable influence of the serial is being transferred to television, and there is a chance that a new set of technical requirements will create a new atmosphere; the dreary ruminations of the characters may become boring, action will be required, and to satisfy this need the weak, impotent hero may have to acquire some hormonic virtue. The most hopeful developments have been the quick failure of several attempts to carry over the typical daytime serial and the triumph of such programs as "The Goldbergs" and "Mama." These half-hour weekly programs use the form for an easy exfoliation of character and are seldom driven to the intricate plots and the artificial creation of anxiety; they are of exceptional merit; and as television will, like radio, follow the leader, there is a chance that a new style has been established.

## "THE CONTEMPLATION OF THINGS
## AS THEY ARE"

The other field in which radio has been powerfully inventive is the documentary, the presentation of fact. Except for direct news and commentary, all fact programs need showmanship if they want to stay on the same air as the smartly presented programs of pure entertainment. Sponsors are reluctant to buy a period directly following a dull program; networks and stations are reluctant to spend money on programs without prospect of sale, but they cannot fill all the open spots with costly packages intended for sponsors. The fact program fills the vacancies.

The original style of the radio documentary was set by "The March of Time." This program was so successful that when *Time* magazine no longer needed it to build circulation, public demand brought it back to the air. At first CBS gave the time; later it attracted commercial sponsors. In its earliest appearance it was a re-enactment and dramatization of the news, a formula so simple that documentaries have followed it ever since. It provided what radio at that moment needed: a new sound on the air, a new tempo, and an alert feeling for the radio medium itself. Particularly the sense of the present, that whatever you heard was happening at that moment, was energetically exploited by "The March of Time," and the mixed sense of adventure and doom, the crackling of cellophane mingled with the sound of the last trump in the portentous voice of the announcer, made this program exciting. It was one of the small number of inventions that gave listeners the experience of radio as a thing in itself, not merely a new way of transmitting the old.

The further career of the documentary is odd: it divided into informational presentations of important subjects, usually disagreeable ones like syphilis, housing, and communism; and, parallel to this, a kind of poetic exhortation to stand fast for democratic principles and a saner international order. The second was largely the work of Norman Corwin, who began his career in radio with a rare perception of its nature: sounds, human or mechanical, and silence are its only elements, and Corwin made notable use of them. His grouped and divided voices, the neatness of attack he got from his actors, the timing of his pauses, the integrating of music, and the elaborate nicety of his sound effects made his rendering of poetry remarkably exciting. He carried his talents and enthusiasm over when he began to direct more commonplace programs, including a series of documentaries on "Americans at Work," and gave them, as far as the writers permitted, something of the dazzle and glamour with which he later surrounded his own politico-poetic programs. Others did realistic documents of men at war, true to the sound of guns and motors, reproducing human speech with more accuracy than is usual on the air, and peopled by stock GIs—the Texan, the boy from Brooklyn, the small-towner, the Negro or the Jew (not both on the same program), the hard-bitten sergeant, the malcontent whose buddy is killed and who becomes a hero (Achilles as rendered in the movies by John Garfield). Corwin took for his own the field of ideas. He was, in fact, an admirable carrier for the liberal-patriotic ideals of the time, an admirer of the New Deal, a mature anti-fascist, with a poetic sense of the dignity and worth of the individual life, who did not want himself or his countrymen pushed around by anyone, even the National Association of Broadcasters. (When the president of that organization said, in 1944, that radio is a product of American business, comparing it to vacuum cleaners and washing machines, Corwin said, "This stuffy kind of Babbitt stands responsible for the dreadful mediocrity of so much of American radio.")

For a time Corwin held the fate of the documentary in his hands. Although he worked exclusively for CBS, he was the political conscience of the broadcasting industry; the emotionalism of his work responded to the deep personal emotions of the war years, and few were aware that he used a fact, a position in latitude and longitude or the gross annual tonnage of flatboats on the river Rhine, as a poet might, to startle, to set the imagination working, to make the heart beat faster—never as a fact in relation to other facts. Passages in these declamatory works rang and reverberated, so that the listener was carried on a sea of sound; it was good to feel that he was in the main current of contemporary thought, but the listener could not think himself. When Corwin tackled controversial subjects he presented them through symbols and a group of characters who became as stereotyped in their way as the familiar characters of other radio programs; he documented their birth and education and first job and first appearance on the breadline, but he lacked the dramatic instinct to make them single individuals; they were more voices than people.

Corwin took the documentary into a moonlit garden; it was a romantic interlude, honorable to both, but the girl's good name was never the same thereafter and no sponsor would make an honest woman of her. In his campaigning for Roosevelt and later when he made his One World tour, as a winner of the award established in honor of Wendell Willkie, Corwin brought the microphone and the recorder to men and women, sympathetically drawing from them some affirmation of belief, some murmur of hope or of bewilderment. He was well publicized and brought prestige to CBS; but no one thought that the documentary as he practiced it could ever be anything but special; with good publicity he attracted substantial audiences, and there was once a wild rumor that he was actually cutting into the Hooper rating of Bob Hope, against whom he was spotted; but as Corwin himself remarked, it was always Hope 40, Corwin 8. A few years later, when he left to do some programs for the United Nations at NBC, a CBS program executive declared that the era of the poetic documentary was over.

Its place was taken by massive social studies, running as long as an hour, usually on subjects "about which the listener can do something, either by taking some action or by changing his attitude." [1] An hour on marriage (NBC), on communism (ABC), on mental hygiene (CBS), on splitting the atom (Mutual), indicate the range. "Split the Atom" was an attempt, not the first, to use the current techniques of radio in order to impart scientific information; it was a quiz show, "sponsored by Nature, spelled N-A-

[1] Davidson Taylor, then in charge of such programs at CBS.

T-U-R-E, world's greatest manufacturer of energy." Contestants who failed to answer correctly were punished by a mild electric shock; a radioactive hundred dollar bill was hunted by a man with a Geiger counter. *Time* quoted Sir Arthur Salter: "In England we had a series of talks on atomic energy . . . but without any . . . music, applause, and the impersonation of isotopes to hold the flagging attention." But Mutual received over a thousand letters after the broadcast.

Several years before the Mutual experiment a sponsor took over the series called "The Human Adventure," and the first program enlisted the oddly assorted talents of Clifton Fadiman, Colonel Stoopnagle, and an actor impersonating Albert Einstein; production was in the hands of Sherman H. Dryer, formerly director of the radio office of the University of Chicago and until then archenemy of commercial broadcasting. ("The walls of Yale and Chicago," he once prophesied to an audience of educators and radio executives, "will still stand long after Radio City has crumbled into dust." The audience laughed—I don't know why; perhaps hopefully.)

With the perspective of five years Mr. Fadiman might have been describing this program when he wrote in "The Decline of Attention": "A successful, technically admirable attempt is made to *attract* the attention without actually *engaging* it; to entertain rather than challenge . . ."

Worse than that. An exchange of puns between a radio comedian and a literate intellectual goes beyond attracting attention; it actively distracts the listener from the subject, and this is a constant danger in all attempts at popularization. Norman Cousins has written: "We now have the Triumph of Distraction. Thought replacement is already a giant industry. . . . An open hour in a day's schedule without access to radio, movies, television, or absorption devices produces a feeling of helplessness and boredom . . . bordering on personal panic." [1] Using the in-

---

[1] T. S. Eliot describes a further stage: "Distracted from distraction by distraction."

strument of distraction to focus the attention is like using a mirror as a burning glass.

Among the early attempts at the documentary, before it found its name and form, were the educational programs. The history of this type is illuminating and, to the cynic, very satisfactory. It is not true that educators failed to see the possibilities of radio; they saw clearly, and their only reservation was that radio must not impose any conditions upon them; they were perfectly willing to deliver hour-long lectures to an unseen audience. College professors did not survive the competition of gross-minded comedians who were not so obstinate about techniques. When the college radio stations failed, the broadcasters began to prepare straight educational programs to be received in schools or at home. They were not intended to train the mind; dramatizing the functions of the genes and chromosomes was not offered as a substitute for work with the microscope; the purpose was only to attract attention and arouse interest and curiosity, to create the atmosphere in which education could occur.

These experiments lived in perpetual jeopardy. "The School of the Air" (CBS) was for years a morning program, available in classrooms, highly praised by educators and offered as an example of public service by the company. The fatality was that a half-hour of education broke the mood of the morning program schedule, which was primarily the mood of the daytime serial; sponsors who wanted to buy a block of quarter-hours, letting the audience flow from one to the other, could not tolerate this dam in the stream; and no one wanted to start from scratch after the educational program was over, knowing that the home audience was committed elsewhere. "The School of the Air" shifted to late afternoon, and a philosophical explanation was issued to prove that this was more advantageous. Presently the programs were shifted off the air entirely; it had been discovered that a lot of education was tucked away in many commercial programs so no special ones were necessary, and besides radio was not the proper medium for education in the strict sense.

This is quite possibly true. It still leaves the feeling that the broadcasters as a whole have not been enthusiastic about creating a well-informed citizenry, perhaps because they suspect that an educated public might be less "radio-minded" than the one they now serve. Certainly the industry, which is so extremely proficient in other fields, has failed to find techniques to make the documentary or the cultural program widely acceptable. Perhaps it can't be done. Perhaps it can be done only by broadcasters who are not instinctively afraid of the critical intelligent mind.

Nothing illustrates the split personality of the broadcasters more strikingly than the clash between their prestige programs and their popular ones. Their documentaries are tributes to the scientific method, they use and applaud the work of sociologists, they hold up for admiration the researcher, the teacher, the idealist, the trained mind, the thoughtful citizen. And in commercial programs these people are constantly presented as figures of fun, the butts of practical jokes, victims of the verbal hotfoot inflicted on them by the real heroes, the willful and invincibly ignorant. The way radio reaches us, the bits and pieces thrown together in a comedy program, the abrupt change of subject, the disconnection between one program and another are in themselves conditioning us away from seeing anything steadily or whole; in addition, the irresponsibles who create the actual programs defend themselves against the latent intelligence of the audience by glorifying the happy ignoramus who can always be counted on to give the intelligent man his comeuppance. The sympathies of the audience must be manipulated for this purpose; the man of wit must be cut down to the size of a smart-aleck, and the trained mind must be assimilated to ancient stereotypes—the absent-minded professor, the sexually unattractive schoolteacher, the philosopher who cannot understand a comic strip, the mathematician lost in the intricacies of a timetable. This is so pervasive that it even gets into the Henry Morgan and Fred Allen programs, which are fundamentally based on the principle that an intelligent man is more intelligent than a stupid one; the

average program works on the opposite assumption, and the
hearty hillbilly (female), the illiterate Brooklynite, the rustic, and
the man who spent four years at Yale as janitor, are the sympathetic and triumphant characters. They are holdovers from the
1850's, when universal education was beginning, when the shrewd
untutored individual had to defend himself against invasion by
the educated; they perpetuate a prejudice as harmful in the
present state of the world as the prejudice against medical science
was in the days of cholera and plague. I shall return to this phenomenon, in another connection, later.

The dilemma of the broadcaster is that he must defend the
sponsors' standards and at the same time adhere to loftier ones
himself. The excellent radio critic John Crosby noted a prime
instance of the double standard in the NBC documentary "Marriage in Distress": ". . . Narrator Ben Grauer spoke out against
the American habit of acquisitiveness. 'We drive ourselves harder
and harder . . . in order to be able to afford cars, refrigerators,
deep freezers. . . . This acquisitive passion . . . is one of the many
reasons why so many modern marriages founder. . . .' " Mr. Crosby
felt that "the most treasonable expression of all" was a glancing
blow at soap opera. As he mildly remarked, NBC devotes virtually all of its time to stimulating a thirst for the mass-produced
luxuries upon which this program frowned and derives a sizable
share of its total income from soap opera.

It is not hypocrisy for NBC to turn a shining, earnest face to
the public once every three months and proclaim its independence of the sponsors; the bedrock principle of American broadcasting is that the prosperity and freedom and happiness of the
people all demand sponsored programs free to communicate any
attitude of mind, within the limits of propriety, and that no one
but the broadcaster can determine what shall go out on the air.
Even if stations and networks were certain they could escape
punishment, they would have to approve the scripts of commercial programs because listeners would blame them for any offense
—the uproar over Mae West's broad Garden of Eden scene with

Charlie McCarthy and the sensational response to Orson Welles' "Invasion from Mars" proved that the public took its protests directly to the broadcasters, regardless of sponsorship. It may be illogical for the broadcaster to demand absolute freedom of expression and to give only limited freedom to those whose money he takes—but in practice it works out well. The "Commercial Editing" or "Continuity Acceptance" department of any network is on the alert for suggestiveness, for advertising which may offend another sponsor; it may question the appearance of political ideas in a script; but it is not authorized to impose standards of social desirability upon sponsors.

With this freedom, sponsored radio has created or taken over the programs familiar to all of us. It is not important that few of them are aesthetically interesting; a good vaudeville show and a well-balanced popular magazine have no special aesthetic value rising out of their internal structure, but they are perfectly satisfactory. It may, however, be important that the entertainment upon which Americans spend more of their time than any other should be so little creative, should live so much on borrowings and reworkings and imitations. Apart from the daytime serial and the documentary, the inventiveness of radio has gone into creating new atmospheres, the noise and the worked-up excitement of the giveaways, the pretended spontaneity of the comedy shows; the material comes from the old parlor game or from vaudeville. There are mere traces of novelty: in the comedy shows, the vaudeville happens around an invented character or the projection of the star's personality; in the quizzes and giveaways some play is made for the human interest supplied by the contestants.

## CHATTER—MUSIC—MURDER

There is no predecessor directly responsible for the chatter programs of Mary Margaret McBride, several married couples, Arthur Godfrey, and many disk jockeys. They are the Midwestern visit and the gossip of the supermarket brought together informally, and they serve as an antidote to the keyed-up excitement of the prize contests and the nervous instability of the serials. Some of these programs last an hour or more and are evidently intended for background noise while the housework is being done; a serviceable noise on local stations is often a shopping tour, with no entertainment or only an occasional playing of a record, the rest of the time being given over to description and praise of various articles to be found in department stores or chain groceries.

Such programs also are on the quiet side, as is most of radio music; a considerable amount of hot music, on records, is played, and in large cities there is often a "music station" devoted almost entirely to classical and semi-classical recordings. Symphony orchestras were heard and had sponsors a long time ago; then they remained as sustainers, and during the war achieved sponsorship again (the Philharmonic) and an unwonted prestige (the Toscanini concerts on NBC).

In connection with music, it should be noted that when listeners are asked what kind of programs they would want more of, the leader is almost always "good music." It may also be noted that good music attracts substantial, but not overwhelming, audiences.[1] It may be merely a coincidence that during the same period the quality of popular music has perceptibly gone off. Two of the great popular composers, Gershwin and Kern, died within a decade, leaving the work of composing good popular songs to Berlin, Porter, and Rodgers, all of whom are of the previous radio generation; a few other composers for the musical theater, Weill and Duke and Arlen, have done admirable work; but the casual singing style of Bing Crosby, further weakened by the almost inanimate utterances of Sinatra, has taken the life out of popular

---

[1] As it is universally assumed that listening to good music is a superior way of passing the time and probably proof of a cultivated mind, it may be futile to do more than record a dissenting vote: "We have had a radio installed, I never listened to one before, there is a deplorable amount of music going on in the world, if they would suppress most of it perhaps the world would be more peaceful." The writer is Gertrude Stein.

songs, and the best thing to be said of radio in this connection is that it kills off the bad ones pretty rapidly. Radio's mortality rate is almost as high for popular songs as it is for human beings.

It is estimated that some fifteen hundred murders take place each week on the air. This does not include murders meditated or suspected in daytime serials, but does take in manslaughter specially arranged for children's programs. (In Los Angeles ninety-seven deaths by violence were reported on one week's television programs.) Regularly the National Association of Broadcasters announces a code of ethics in which violence is deplored as bedtime fare for the young, but the God-given right to broadcast horror and mayhem is little disturbed. Some of the programs of violence make the police or the G-men their heroes and all of them, without exception, accept as gospel the dictum that crime doesn't pay, carefully noting it for the benefit of the young at the end of each program.

Neither the crime programs nor the adaptations of plays, books, and movies have shown much ingenuity in recent years. A number of conventional techniques have come into existence, such as the handling of audio-perspective (to help the listener "see" where people are placed) and the use of musical bridges and sound effects. There is a high level of competence and a dead level of sameness. In each type of program the same intonations are used to identify the characters; each type has its prescribed tempo. A considerable amount of experimental work was done ten years ago, and the results have been absorbed, but radio now needs the invigorating effect of a new production style, which would do for it what George Abbott did for the musical show or Jed Harris for melodrama some years ago; it needs also to break from its stereotyped characters and to discover a new and psychologically more realistic approach.

## STARS AND SPONSORS

The economics of experiment in radio was dramatized for the outsider by the famous CBS raid in which the major comedians of NBC were captured. For many years NBC had been the commanding power in broadcasting and CBS the aggressive second; even during the war, when virtually all salable time was sold, NBC held its position because it had almost a monopoly of popular comedy, and as a result it attracted the most powerful affiliated stations. The situation was favorable to experiment because CBS needed to draw attention to itself and, at the same time, was making enough money to invest in programs that might not pay off. Its economic position allowed fairly young people in both the executive and program branches of CBS to work out their ideas; Corwin, William N. Robson, Irving Ries, and other directors had a workshop at their disposal; at the same time the network worked on programs for sale. Unfortunately, the hardest thing in radio is to develop a comedy program; Benny, Allen, Cantor, Burns and Allen, Hope, Durante, had all come to radio with long experience in other fields; by a strange fatality, if they ever were placed on the CBS network, they did not stay there, and no new talent quite measured up to them in appeal. Although CBS sold as many as twenty program packages to sponsors (six of them news, four quiz and giveaways) the network had to establish itself more firmly; it had to meet the expenses of television and the reduction in radio income which success in television would bring. By seducing the great comedians away from NBC in 1949, the network fortified its entire schedule; the periods before and after the famous programs became more desirable, and a sponsor taking one of these might also buy a period on another night, at a sizable discount. The CBS atmosphere of enterprise, success, and optimism came to station-owners at a low point, when they were beginning to lose faith in radio and were still afraid of television; a paralysis of the will was spreading to them when they were galvanized into action by the spectacular business deals and the exceptional publicity that centered around Jack Benny's capital-gains problems; a new excitement was generated, and broadcasting was the better for it.

The situation of the two chief rivals had been reversed. It was not observed that when CBS bought out the stable of NBC stars it virtually confessed its failure to raise winners itself. Psychologically this was a fatal blow to creative enterprise, although CBS announced that it would continue to build its own shows and NBC assured its affiliated owners (many of whom might switch to CBS as soon as their contracts permitted) that it had saved millions by not competing for the comedians and could spend freely for new programs. Actually CBS had been tailoring programs to the needs of sponsors for several years, with only occasional pioneer work; and NBC did not have the tradition of experiment. Although it produced an imposing educational series, in the year after the comedians went to CBS most of its new programs were in the old ruts of commercial radio, and its major effort "opposite Jack Benny" was a "giveaway," an attempt "to buy the audience."

Both networks, as well as ABC and eventually the key Mutual stations, were sinking large sums of money and much of their creative energies into television, which, in a sense, was all experimental; naturally the barometer of radio hovered around dead calm. It was perhaps superfluous for CBS to announce, on a note of triumph, that there would be *no change* in the Benny program itself when it moved to the new network. Until a new concept of the audience, and the broadcasters' relation to the audience, was developed, there could be no change in any essential of radio.

If change must come, the broadcasting business is more happily situated than the movies; before the movies can develop, and profit hugely, from the entire audience, a change in the highly organized system of distributing pictures is essential; but network radio can continue to exist profitably, in spite of the inroads of television, without altering its structural relation with either the sponsors or the affiliated stations. Both are complicated, and I note only the elements that directly influence the kind of programs the public gets to hear.

I have mentioned the skepticism about radio as an advertising medium, expressed by a Republican capitalist who later became President and by the founder of the great RCA dynasty. Coming from them, it is more significant than opposition which is simply anti-capitalist. The early broadcasters who believed that a public service should not be given over to advertising eventually yielded to "the inevitable"; nothing in the atmosphere of American life in the 1920's favored the development of an institution separated from aggressive capitalist enterprise; we had regulatory bodies like the Interstate Commerce Commission, but the corporations and authorities that came into being, on the British model, during the New Deal, would have been considered Red socialism of the most virulent type under Harding and Coolidge and Hoover himself. The advertisers swarmed into radio because the statesmen allowed a power-vacuum to exist.

But not at all inevitable was the particular way in which the sponsor's power came to be exercised. The original entrance of the advertiser was through a side door; and, although we are so accustomed to "Lucky Strike presents . . ." that we don't notice variations, the older system still persists in some of the most profitable areas of sponsored radio. It is the foundation of the disk-jockey and other record-playing programs, upon which hundreds of small stations thrive, and it is used by the phenomenally successful WNEW, which covers the New York area, is totally unaffiliated, and enjoys a gross income greater than that of all but five or six other stations. This method of sponsorship leaves the creation of the program to the station or network; the sponsor prepares only his commercial, which is read before, during, or after the entertainment. Trifling as a series of records may seem as compared with the elaborate programs directly offered by sponsors, the principle is sound; it is, in fact, the principle upon which broadcasting was founded, and one of the few regrets of a business without unhappy memories is that the job of actually creating entertainment was allowed to slip out of its hands.

In the loud boom of the late 1920's radio was making itself

heard and felt; the demand for entertainment passed beyond the capacity of the broadcasters to provide. The sponsor took over, through his advertising agency, which up to that time had been a buyer of time alone, getting a percentage of whatever the sponsor paid; obviously the next step was for the agency to create the program and take a percentage of whatever it cost. Since the entertainment was primarily intended to carry advertising, it was safe in the hands of those most interested in advertising. Competition sprang up: talent agents, earning ten per cent of the artist's fee, also began to build their own programs; and a new profession grew up, the independent inventor who made his own program, hired talent, recorded a sample or two, prepared a budget, and offered the entire package to any buyer. The discomfited networks saw the most interesting part of their business taken away from them, but they were in a period of intensive growth at the time. They have never entirely given up trying to create programs, and NBC and CBS each had a subsidiary talent agency until the propriety of such combinations was questioned by the FCC. One excellent result of the entire operation was that after they sold their birthright as creators of entertainment, the networks with time to fill spent their energies on sustaining programs.

The original premise of the broadcasters was this: "We are sending out programs that people like; tell them about your product while they are listening and they will buy." This is psychologically different from the basic approach of the new system as the sponsor might express it to his agency: "Put on the kind of program that will be liked by the people to whom I want to sell my product." It placed selling in the dominant position; more than that, it led inevitably to thinking of the audience as "a kind of people" and, presently, to thinking of the audience as a mass. It led to the encouragement of the mass qualities of the audience and to the dulling of those appetites that cannot be mass-fed; and insofar as the audience was not a solid malleable mass, it became the business of radio to turn it into one.

The relations between sponsors, advertising agencies, and networks are intricate but not very interesting. A number of individuals, with different interests, are involved in the making of programs, and pure creative energy sifts through as many filters as it does in Hollywood. The effects of agency and sponsor influence go beyond financial pressure, but the figures themselves are impressive. The four largest agencies have in some years given the networks as much as a third of their total income; and ninety per cent of network revenue has come from as few as a hundred and fifty sponsors. On the management side, network broadcasting is not a minority operation: it is a limited oligarchy. And through their affiliates networks dominate radio.

The essential agreement between affiliates and the network consists of two parts. First, the affiliates agree to hold at the disposal of the network certain desirable periods; these are sold to sponsors and the affiliated station receives payment. Second, the network agrees to send to the affiliates unsponsored programs which they can use or not, as they see fit. The first arrangement makes it possible for several hundred stations to carry the great popular programs at the same time; the second makes it probable that some of the most serious and noteworthy programs created at network headquarters will be carried by only a fraction of all the stations affiliated. Station owners reserve some of their time for sale to local advertisers, and this may be the very time chosen for a prestige broadcast from New York; and even if a station is not carrying a commercial at a specified hour, it may prefer to transmit an entertainment program instead of the documentary on race prejudice offered.

The FCC Blue Book supplies some figures. "Invitation to Learning" (CBS) was taken by thirty-nine stations, rejected by ninety-seven; "Labor for Victory" (NBC, produced by the AFL and the CIO) was taken by thirty-five stations, not taken by one hundred and four; of two hundred and sixteen Mutual affiliates, fifty carried a program by the Marine Corps, forty a round-table discussion of current problems, and thirteen a religious program. A breakdown of station operations indicates that in nine cases out of ten, sustaining programs are rejected in favor of local commercial shows, and there is no indication that the stations create any sustaining programs of their own.

Printed criticism and defense of radio have both been largely beside the point because they refer to network programs and to metropolitan areas where listeners have a choice of six or more stations. The quality of local programs naturally varies; but even key stations in big cities fall below network standards. The listener accustomed to the mature handling of news in the New York area can hardly believe his ears when the big Boston stations (owned by or affiliated with the networks) launch into a morning news program with ten or fifteen items of New England news, all petty crimes or small fires and accidents, leaving a few moments for national and international affairs. The tradition that news, especially in the morning, shall be transmitted without bias was steadily violated by major stations in the Los Angeles area a few years ago, and still may be. The equally important tradition that radio shall not be used to foster prejudice of any kind has not been ignored on a national scale since the Coughlin broadcasts ended, but local zealots come perilously close to it. The time limitation on advertising is respected only by network stations, even in big cities; in small communities the bulk and the sour subject matter of the commercials are appalling. Fragile as the code of the broadcasters may be, it imposes at least superficial good manners; but no network code can be forced upon affiliates, and stations independent of the chains are content to stay within the bounds of common decency as construed by the FCC. Deprived of the occasional superior program by the whim of local station owners, listeners outside the range of multiple transmission find that their own regional interests are scantily served except for news items and sports. Even the charitable institutions of the region have a hard time getting anything but routine announcements, and the main currents of community life are either noted in an unimaginative and perfunctory way or totally neglected.

There are exceptions—among two thousand stations there must be. Stations exist in which a strong feeling for the life of the region makes itself felt beyond the broadcast of traffic conditions and warnings to orange growers to set out their smudgepots. No one who has not lived a fairly long time in a community can assess the quality of the services such exceptional stations render; they are outstanding in a field where the average is extremely low. The reasons are both economic and social: affiliated stations have to carry a certain number of network broadcasts and enrich their income by selling time locally for programs of little merit; hardly any pressure is brought to bear upon them to improve their service, and serious community interests tend to bore those not directly concerned; the stations live in an atmosphere of no-protest, the audiences are satisfied. But if all the stations are blameless, the fact remains that this is what radio is in small communities. As the networks and the metropolitan stations go deeper into television, the situation of the smaller units grows serious; they can survive only if they satisfy interests left untouched by the networks, and in the past they have shown little inclination to discover what these interests are and how to serve them. It has been predicted that the small independent station will be all that's left of radio within a few years; up to now they have been serving small percentages of the local population and not in a way to rouse enthusiasm at the prospect that presently they will have the field to themselves.

## "THEY CAN TURN IT OFF, CAN'T THEY?"

When broadcasters are thoroughly exasperated by criticism, they are likely to blurt out the home truth that no one compels any citizen to keep tuned to a program he doesn't like; something like compulsory listening was reported in Nazi Germany, but to us the mere suggestion of a device that could turn radios on, without the consent of the listener, sounds like a threat to the social sanctity of the home, an invasion of our private lives—and a grim prediction of life under bureaucracy. Sometimes the critic is coyly reminded that there is a little button on his radio by which he can change from station to station or (the unthinkable in broadcasting circles) satisfy a morbid appetite for silence. In more stately terms, when the argument is presented before the FCC, broadcasters note that the number and variety of radio programs offered make criticism of any single program pointless. As far back as 1928 the predecessor of the present FCC "gave short shrift to this argument" on the peculiar ground that "listeners . . . are powerless to prevent the ether waves carrying the unwelcome messages from entering the walls of their homes," which is physically true—the waves do penetrate walls; but the owner of a receiver has the power to keep them silent unless he tunes them in. The reasoning at this point was dubious; the social concept was valid. By implication, the Commission asserted the right of the citizen to inoffensive and to useful programs, saying that when a station is used for undesirable ends, "the listening public is deprived of the use of a station . . . in the public interest." So, since its first decade, radio has been recognized as such a necessity of life that the listener is entitled to services of a specified quality. In recent years the same attitude of mind has been reflected in an FCC decision on giveaways as lotteries: one of the legal specifications of a lottery is that the participant gives a "consideration" in return for his chance to win. The FCC held that giving one's time, during the act of listening, was such a consideration. As Jack Gould said in the *New York Times:* ". . . the FCC would appear to have opened up the provocative line of thought that what radio stations sell is not their own time, but the time of their listeners." The value of that time was implied in the earlier decision: in return for listening, the individual can ask for programs that serve the public.[1] The definition is broad enough to cover a multitude of comedians; the principle is strict enough to prevent comedians from polluting the air.

[1] If he looks as well as listens, he should be entitled to more satisfactions. Unlike listening to radio, looking at television is a full-time occupation.

It is a principle flattering to the power of radio and much more impressive than the mean concept of a frivolous entertainment implied in "they can turn it off, can't they?" Because no one can escape the effect of a broadcast by refusing to hear it. A million sensitive people, capable of judgment, may tune out a demagogue, but if twenty million others listen to him, the minority will be swept away in whatever whirlwind of passion follows. *Not what one person can avoid hearing, but what everyone else does hear, is the heart of radio's power and the core of its responsibility.*

This principle, unformulated but vaguely felt, underlies some of the attempts to restrict the freedom of radio, as surely as it is the foundation of radio's commercial success. No grand moral law gives it majesty; it conforms only to the way broadcasting works. The fraction of the population that does listen is sufficient to support the advertisers; the non-listeners buy the same goods. If the listeners are moved to elect a candidate to office, he will govern equally those who never heard his voice. The circumstance that people listen by ones and twos, and not in large groups, does not make radio less of a mass medium; and since radio offers itself as a mass medium to the sponsors it cannot pretend that its audience has no mass, but is composed entirely of discrete particles, when it faces its social responsibility.

The broadcasters themselves often say that their commercial and their public service functions are closely related; to increase the consumption of good soaps and food is a service to the community, and it is supremely important to the economy as a whole that industry should flourish and have jobs to give. To this end, commercial radio creates an atmosphere of acceptance; the listener is hospitable to the suggestions of the announcer; to be successful a program must lower the threshold of doubt so that simple assertions, without proof, will be accepted without criticism. Of the millions who listen simultaneously to broadcasts, only a negligible fraction has been trained to assess and criticize what they read or see or hear, and radio itself steadily lowers the level of healthy doubt. All the techniques of the entertainment program are used to dull the critical faculties, and when this has been done, the parallel techniques of the commercial message enter, the repetition of an unsupported assertion taking the place of argument or demonstration or proof.

It is simply not possible for radio to break the mood of acceptance and, at a given moment, start to create a skeptical audience, attentive, neither overreceptive nor hostile, but critical. The little devices that distinguish a news analysis from a mystery or a comedy program are legitimate, but in the end the program requiring thought and attention is assimilated to the general tone of broadcasting: the air is still friendly, the voices intimate, humor and human interest are allowed to seep in; the mood of consent is unshaken. No broadcast is an island, complete in itself; all that came before, all that is expected to follow, contribute to the color and tone and warmth and light in which any program is heard. We are familiar with the same thing elsewhere: a band in bright uniforms plays patriotic marches before the candidate speaks; the preacher denounces sin between hymns by the choir; and our modern oracle is heard in the intervals of a three-ring circus.

From the contagion of the slow stain that colors the mood of the audience, the non-listener cannot be immune. Radio is playing its part in the creation of our common character, and even the indifferent or hostile individual is affected by whatever touches his fellow men. There has been only one radio-induced panic, and its lesson was grave enough; but it is half learned if we think only that we must be careful what we say to suggestible people. We have to remember that in part radio created this suggestibility; it was a bit of irony that broadcasts of literal fact —the war scare at Munich—gave the atmosphere of credibility to the fiction of the "Invasion from Mars"; in general it is the other way round—radio's fiction develops the mood of belief. We have also to remember that not only the listeners were involved. The panic spread to those who were tuned in to Charlie

McCarthy on another network; they were called by telephone and heard strange news; and if hysteria had spread a little further, no amount of non-cooperation with the radio audience would have saved a skeptic walking along the street from being trampled by hordes of listeners evacuating New York.

We have erected safeguards against panic, but not against persuasion. What radio can do to start a sudden fire has been discovered and precautions have been taken. But the slow daily and weekly creation of a climate favorable to certain ideas, the unnoticed gentle nudges and pressures that turn people in one direction rather than another, the constant supply of images to populate our subconscious minds—these are not watched, and cannot be, so long as we think we are safe—because we can turn it off, can't we?

### MIXED FORMULA

Lying between radio as pure entertainment and radio as transmitter of news and opinion is an area in which the two functions overlap. Broadcasters allude to this area whenever they banish a public service program to a bad listening hour and say that there is plenty of education in commercial programs. A political writer who is rather given to discovering conspiracies against his party once assured me that every comedy program was under instructions to deliver propaganda in the form of gags, saying that the atmosphere of a joke about the United Nations (favorable or unfavorable) could influence people more than a long lecture; and in that he was probably right.[1]

Strict moralists dislike the trick by which ideas are put over on people while they are being distracted by comedy. They may concede that wherever there is entertainment there is influence, but they hold that the deliberate use of a play or a quiz show

---

[1] During the summer of 1950, while the extension of the Marshall Plan was being debated, the following was heard on a hill-billy program:

"Money talks."

"Yeah. An' all it sez nowadays is 'Good-by, America. Hello, Europe.'"

or a symphony concert as a matrix for political ideas is a decep-
tion. In this their attitude is like that of the movie executives,
who add to this that people resent the appearance of any ideas in
their entertainment. Throughout the first depression and the New
Deal the movies were fairly successful in their effort to divorce
themselves from the currents of contemporary life; in radio the
exact place for drawing the line was harder to determine. The
great debate between isolationists and interventionists was carried
on with scrupulous regard for equal opportunity and was separated from the entertainment which came before and after—
entertainment which, in effect, delivered a large portion of the
audience to the debate. But it was never practical to censor every
newscast for a colorful adjective, an appealing abstraction, or a
sneer in the voice. Even a set policy of refusing to sell time for
the discussion of controversial issues did not guarantee immunity.
The intermission talks of W. J. Cameron during the Ford musical
hour were expressions of his own, or Mr. Ford's, attitude toward
labor, government, and the right structure of society; they remained on CBS long after that network had issued its decree of
separation, perhaps because no change in the contract was possible. During two of Roosevelt's campaigns a parallel issue came
up. A long program featuring many famous people, including
Hollywood stars, was criticized because it dramatized, rather than
presented, the issues; the prevalence of New Deal sentiment in
Hollywood irked the Republican managers. On their side, they
had recordings of the President's speeches which they proposed
to put on the air with such juxtapositions and questions and answers as would reduce them to absurdity; this was also unacceptable since it was dramatic. Also rejected were efforts by political
parties and labor unions to produce daytime serials slanted to
their purposes. The rule eventually broke down without any
basic principle being established. This happens often. It happened
conspicuously in the case of Father Coughlin, who had been
conducting a religious broadcast for children and gradually
turned it into a disputatious social and political program. The

network carrying Father Coughlin was not driven to a clean decision; it merely asked that the sermons be submitted in advance for routine examination; Father Coughlin refused and set up an *ad hoc* network of his own. The propriety of giving or selling time for a religious broadcast which had turned political was not determined.

On a Sunday night in 1949 the listener to two successive broadcasts would have heard Walter Winchell transmit a warning to the American people not to lend money to a moribund England and Louella Parsons threaten a young actress with professional ostracism unless she became more amenable to the desires of her studio. For all their difference in specific gravity, these two highly personal utterances had much in common. Miss Parsons and Mr. Winchell possess oracular authority for many of their listeners; neither the British Empire nor Miss Shelley Winters commanded any effective means for answering; and both attacks came on programs associated in some way with entertainment. Winchell has established himself not as an expert on international economic affairs but as an unabashed gossip with a keen sense of news values, a staccato delivery, and a rather enigmatic personality. His "feud" with the late Ben Bernie was a straight comedy routine. His political side developed as the conflict over the New Deal and the impending war prepared his audience to be interested; he was dogmatic, opinionated, and perhaps reckless, but he acquired a sense of the significance of world events which many people whose advantages and responsibilities were greater failed to do. The feud with Ben Bernie gave way to Winchell's war on Hitler. He brought to it his own temperament, he tended to treat it and all other world affairs as a personal crusade, and professionally he could say that his influence could be only personal, that what he said was effective only—or chiefly—because he said it. When he added exhortations to Mr. and Mrs. America he assumed many obligations, but he never gave up the freedom which came to him because he was not in the same category as newscasters or analysts; his news was, in theory at least, his own, private, the reward of his initiative and persistence. Was he qualified to advise congressmen and denounce ministers of state? The question disturbed a number of people who were quite willing to let other broadcasters, with whom they agreed, do exactly the same thing. The vital question was actually concerned with the code under which he worked. Was it a code of fair play? Was an answer possible? His victims could complain that they were beaten by an entertainer, and entertainers are bound by no code of social ethics to be impartial and to give equal time for a reply. Errors could be corrected, but who could correct the dubious "hmm?" with which Winchell ended many quotations from people he disliked? If time were made available, it would be empty time unless the Winchell audience was present and was as receptive to a stranger as to Winchell himself. He was largely a radio-built personality and in the time it took to build him, no ethics, no etiquette governing radio, had been developed.

Among the ifs of history, one might consider seriously what would have happened to Winchell and to America if he had been a reactionary and an isolationist from 1939 to Pearl Harbor—if Pearl Harbor had come. It is imaginable that a clamor against lend-lease and for appeasing Japan might have brought a strong isolationist candidate into the field instead of Wendell Willkie. It is conceivable that a radio broadcaster with millions of believers, attracted to him originally because he was entertaining, might have thrown the balance toward such a candidate. In the summer of 1941 a single vote in Congress prevented the disbanding of American military training; in the fall of that year one powerful voice added to those already on the other side might have turned the trick.

Winchell is an example of the imbalance of forces in this particular area of radio broadcasting: there is no immovable object to meet the irresistible force. The newscasters, commentators, and analysts have a written code which has not been able to prevent gross malpractice in their own field. When we come upon news being used as a background for propaganda by people whose experience is in other fields, the code of entertainment rather than the code of news seems to operate. It can be nonetheless disastrous to its victims. I do not know whether Miss Winters bowed to the stern command of Louella Parsons (she did become a valuable movie property); I know that a few months later Miss Parsons said (as I wrote down the words immediately after she said them), "A word to Hollywood personalities: don't go to the Paul Robeson concert unless you want to be suspected of sympathy for the Reds." Here was a threat that affected the livelihood of a single individual, and there was no satisfactory reply possible. Even if by some unimaginable pressure Mr. Robeson had been able to commandeer the Parsons time on the air, his concert would have been over before he could undo the mischief done him. The network and the sponsor had permitted Miss Parsons to use her position to attack an individual on political grounds as freely as she had criticized the personal conduct of an actress or, on frequent occasions, given advice with a strong overtone of menace to those about to marry or divorce. So far as I know, there was no protest. The public was not sensitive to the ethical problem.

The borderline cases between entertainment and discussion must be considered before coming to the central problem of radio as a medium of information precisely because they illustrate, better than the news programs, the responsibility of the public as compared to the responsibility of the broadcasters. The evolution of a code of ethics governing the "personality programs" cannot occur in a vacuum; it demands the activity, the disagreements and compromises, the fanaticism and the sober judgment of the citizens, and these things cannot be had if the citizens are unaware of the situation, if they do not know that they are being influenced while they are being entertained. Without a code of ethics to which the public subscribes (even if the code is never written down, never explicit) the rules of conduct set up by the broadcasters themselves cannot be effective. Such a subconscious code exists for the press; we get proof of its existence whenever it is flagrantly violated because violations bring protests. It is, for instance, permissible for newspapers to be party organs, and they are allowed a greater latitude of misrepresentation during a political campaign than they are in the years between; it is not, on the other hand, generally acceptable for a newspaper to attack any religious belief. Pamphlets directed against a single individual are accepted without protest, newspapers are permitted to attack principles through personalities (there has been a marked degradation of this sense of difference during the past ten years). Certain words appear freely in books but are not good form in daily papers; pictures can be shown in textbooks which are not tolerated in magazines. In all these distinctions an ethical code is at work; it developed during centuries of experience, and while it constantly changes, it is crystallized at any given moment, so that the public has a standard of judgment. The most superficial observation shows that this code is based to a degree on a sense of justice and to a degree on a feeling for the physics of the media—the number of copies circulated, where they are read, by whom, how frequently—and these are basic materials in building our instinctive feeling of what is allowable and what should be forbidden. The habit of protest has declined in America—protest has been shrewdly maneuvered into a false position because it was for long the only weapon of extreme radicals; the mayor of an eastern city once declared that whenever he hears the words "civil liberty" he knows they come from a Red. But in the case of the press, the influential and intelligent citizens are aware of indirect effects; they know that you cannot escape the corruption of society merely by refusing to read a corrupting newspaper. In the new media this principle has not been understood.

The demagogue who waves a flag when he cannot answer a question is proof that the uneducated man is as susceptible to abstractions as the intellectual, even if he cannot deal with them in words and prefers to deal with instances. The average human being speaks of his rights, an extremely complex thought in itself, of fair play, and of truth. He is unlikely to give up his pleasures for a remote principle, but he has made decisions in the past that prepare him for handling his present problems. Would it be interference with free speech if Miss Parsons were prevented from injuring the professional careers of Miss Winters and Mr. Robeson? Have her victims any prompt and effective means of replying to her? Is there a body of law that protects people, and can they use the law? Is law too expensive, too tardy? Does common experience show that the weak can prevent the abuse of power by the strong? If a syndicated newspaper columnist says that a man evaded the draft and the man has documentary evidence that he registered, and if the estimated cost of bringing this evidence before a jury and fighting the case through various courts lies between ten and fifty thousand dollars—and the man's work is such that he cannot break it off—what is to be done? (The example given is not for illustration only; it is the outline of an actual situation.) Unless our moral sense has atrophied, we can answer these questions; the answers will not all be the same, but out of them some principles of conduct will evolve.

These have to be general principles, because the instinct to solve a particular problem by prejudice is as strong, at least, as the instinct for justice. The principle governing Miss Parsons must be the same as the one governing Mrs. Roosevelt; the light chatter of a husband-and-wife team in the early morning must observe the same rules as the "Chicago Round Table" discussing atomic energy. And although the rules need never be written, they must come from the people, and when the rules are violated, the people must react as they do to the violation of any other rule of decent conduct.

## THE VOICE FROM THE CAVE

We are now at the center of radio's special relation to the public, and the natural approach is through the programs of news and comment. The subject matter is familiar; a standard of comparison, the daily newspaper, gives some perspective; the broadcasters have themselves focused attention on the field by demanding, and in part getting, the right to editorialize.

The critics of radio who used to ask for "equal time for both sides" and the defenders who asserted a commentator's right to be as one-sided as an editor, both appealed to formulas which had been worked up into moral principles long before Marconi sent the letter S across the ocean at the speed of light. The idealists will resist any attempt to revise moral law by mathematics; but they are not entitled to overlook the prime fact, the essential dynamics, of broadcasting: what enters the studio microphone at the speed of sound is relayed to the home at the rate of one hundred and eighty-six thousand miles a second. Words spoken into a microphone in a large auditorium can reach the entire population of the United States before they are heard by people in the back seats of the hall. For all practical purposes space and time have been annihilated; the broadcasters publicize this when they are comparing their effectiveness with that of the newspaper or magazine, but they pretend to be ignorant of it when they ask for the privileges of these slow-moving media. No broadcaster would submit to the actual conditions of print: the rate at which the printed word is taken in, the repetitions in headlines and subheads and leads in a newspaper story, the editorial page usually hidden away so that the reader is always aware of the fact that he is absorbing personal opinion; all these are against the rhythm and tempo of radio; yet all of them had their part in the long, slow process of building newspaper ethics and establishing the freedom of the press. Writing to prevent thought does occur in print, but even there the actual effect differs from that of the broadcast word, because the rate of absorption is different, because the newspaper's influence is localized, and its authority limited.

Both the laws of libel and the unwritten standards of fair play came into being over a long period of time; they represent an interplay of abstract ideals and practical considerations, and the ideals and the realities are both human in their origin. The noblest declaration of faith in a free press and in the triumph of truth over error was written by John Milton, and the freedom he wanted was to publish political pamphlets for the critical minority; on the practical side, the right to defame has always been coupled with the right to sue, and the law has recognized the difference between published and spoken defamation. Even the development of newspaper chains has been recognized in practice, since the victim of a libel can sue for damage done by each separate publication. The illustrated periodical brought new problems and new interpretations of the law—to publish a photograph may be an invasion of privacy. At every point, law and custom keep step with change in the actual conditions of publication. I submit that it is unreasonable to retrace our steps all the way back to abstractions, in dealing with the realities of radio.

One reality is that fact is delivered in connection or in competition with fiction, with radio's vast quantity of entertainment; one daytime serial leads off with an actual news broadcast, from which a reporter proceeds to her daily quota of fictional crime and mystification; the singing of Bob Crosby led into the news analysis of Edward R. Murrow, for the same sponsor; on other programs the news is sometimes apologetically introduced as an interruption in entertainment; sometimes it is given with amusing sidelights; as often as possible it is sponsored, and the atmosphere of the commercial is the same as on a comedy show. In the psychological state of friendliness created by entertainment, with the critical faculties not active, the listener accepts the news. It is, for the most part, admirably condensed, and up to the time it reaches the newscaster, balanced and impartial. Thereafter it may be distorted by omissions, by suppressions, by exaggerated emphasis, by the use of charged words, by the tone of voice; and it may be, and often is, delivered with complete respect for truth. The listener cannot tell, until he has had long experience, what kind of news he is getting; the audiences of certain stations in Detroit, Hollywood, and Cleveland did not know if the owner of these stations had instructed his newscasters to slant the news or not; if the news was slanted, listeners probably would not have been aware of it even if they listened to other stations as well; they would have accepted one version of the news as willingly as another, believing that differences were merely a matter of emphasis.

The next stage is the presentation of news with commentary or analysis. This is the real oracle of radio, the voice of authority. The commentator is a lineal descendant of the star reporter and the political writer of the newspaper, with a touch, but only a touch, of the sob-sister. Giving the news a highly personal tone was popular as far back as the days of Floyd Gibbons, who artificially created for himself a machine-gun delivery that distinguished him from all other reporters; the mellifluous tones of Gabriel Heatter became famous during his reports on the Lindbergh case. As the economic crisis in America moved into the world crisis, the need for something more than descriptive reporting was felt; radio became the primary source of news for more and more people who wanted analysis and guidance through world affairs, which were growing more intricate and threatening each day. The spectacular vigil of H. V. Kaltenborn during the Munich crisis established the profession of commentator in public esteem, and later international developments brought William Shirer, Ed Murrow, and Elmer Davis into prominence— and incidentally established the CBS news department under Paul White as virtually the creative genius of the profession. All of these news analysts were members of the network staff and worked for a long time on sustaining programs. The most distinguished commentator outside of CBS was Raymond Swing, who had for several years broadcast to Britain a weekly report on America; presently his grave and concerned outlook on the world was heard here too; he soon was sponsored, and he has been credited with the suppression of commercials in the middle of news commentary. (It was fairly simple; on May 10, 1940, he refused to let his account of Germany's violation of neutral territory be interrupted by a sales talk; "it seemed hideous," he afterward said. The middle commercial never returned to his newscasts.)

The sense that news differs from all other program material has colored the theory of broadcasting and even part of its practice; the code in force for many years permitted fifteen seconds less for commercials on newscasts than on other programs, and even staunch supporters of free enterprise in Congress have suggested that news should be withheld from sponsorship entirely. The Association of Radio News Analysts rigorously excludes from membership all commentators who read the commercial for their sponsor. Each of the networks has a news department in which the news is sifted, edited, and often written, for newscasters; many of the sponsored news programs of CBS carry a special identification indicating the responsibility of the network.

For all its skill in analyzing its problems, the radio industry has been less than completely successful in its approach to news programs, commentary, and discussion of controversial subjects. Here the FCC recognized "problems of a complex and sometimes delicate nature," and in the Blue Book it set down no less than nineteen separate questions, to which it appended the notice that "the Commission has never laid down, and does not now propose to lay down, any categorical answers. . . ." Primary responsibility, under the Communications Act, rests upon the broadcasters; the FCC felt empowered only to serve notice that it must review the operations of every licensee and that "the establishment of sound station policy [on these matters] is a major factor in operation in the public interest"; the implied threat is that stations whose policies are not sound would not get renewals of license to broadcast. Justin Miller, President of the National Association of Broadcasters, promptly replied that this left them "completely in the dark," since it asked broadcasters to conform to unspecified standards. He did not say that the questions asked were irrelevant; they do, in fact, reflect awareness of the difficulties involved and are a better guide than a series of accusations and defenses would be. The five relating directly to news are:

How can an unbiased presentation of the news be achieved?

Should news be sponsored, and if so, to what extent should the advertiser influence or control the presentation of the news?

How and by whom should commentators be selected?

Should commentators be forbidden, permitted, or encouraged to express their own personal opinions?

Is a denial of free speech involved when a commentator is discharged or his program discontinued because something which he has said has offended (a) the advertiser, (b) the station, (c) a minority of his listeners, or (d) a majority of his listeners?

It is wrong to say that these questions have been long in the public mind; no evidence exists that the majority of listeners to radio have ever given them a moment's thought. They have been in the minds of a small number of people, including those broadcasters who have honorably tried to discharge a public duty and who recognize in news and opinion a special character.

Certain events have, indeed, come to the attention of the larger public, and individual cases have occasionally brought the question of free speech into focus. Among them:

*Upton Close:* he was frankly isolationist before Pearl Harbor; on the day of the attack he had a broadcast in favor of peace with Japan. He was considered reactionary by liberals. His is one of the few cases in which open pressure by liberal and labor groups, approaching a boycott, caused the removal of a commentator. His comments were later offered by transcription.

*Raymond Swing:* a vehement enemy himself of opinionated commentary, Swing seemed entirely dispassionate in dealing with domestic affairs; his broadcasts were somewhat somber essays, beautifully formed and delivered, chiefly on the trend of European politics and our relation to them. After the war ended he lost his sponsor and presently was dropped by ABC. I have it on excellent authority that no question of political or social theory was involved. That the same network offered for sponsorship

George Sokolsky, an enemy of the New Deal and "spokesman for big business," was purely coincidental.

*William L. Shirer:* after an impressive job in Berlin, Shirer returned to America as part of the CBS news staff. Publication of his *Berlin Diary* further enhanced his value as an analyst. His delivery lacked the shine and brilliance of more successful rivals, but he had a respectable audience for his painstaking and thoughtful reports. He avoided sides in direct political controversy but was liberal in temper. The immediate cause of his being dropped was a disagreement on how his work should be done, but he left CBS at a time when several other liberals had gone from the air. Rather than remain on the CBS staff as a sustainer, he went, after an interval, to Mutual and a sponsored program once a week.

*Edward R. Murrow:* as head of the foreign staff of CBS, Murrow can be credited with its general excellence, which was overshadowed by the illuminated passion of his own broadcasts from London, particularly during the first blitz. He returned to become a vice-president of CBS, but resigned this position to resume broadcasting of news and analysis for a sponsor. In deference to policy, he began by placing a definite caesura between the news he reported and "one reporter's reaction"; but presently he dropped this device. He stays above the political battle, and his most marked prejudice is against communism, but without any blanket defense of capitalism.

*Fulton Lewis, Jr.:* the significance of this case is almost entirely negative. In spite of violent attacks on Lewis as a prejudiced reporter and his open espousal of the Republican cause, he has not been dislodged.

*H. V. Kaltenborn:* after declaring that the function of an analyst was to interpret, but not to edit, the news, Kaltenborn became a defender of more personal commentary. A veteran at the business, he became famous when he correctly predicted that the Munich crisis would not end in war; unfortunately for him, he was on the high seas when war broke out, and Elmer Davis took his place at CBS; Kaltenborn never quite recovered momentum; he went over, with a sponsor, to NBC.

In various degrees, these cases illustrate both prejudice and pressures. There have been others; on smaller stations in large cities a commentator may be heard giving, and acknowledging, an interpretation of the news as it appears to organized labor. Since men who hold all varieties of opinion can be found, it is not necessary to bribe an oracle; one merely goes to the oracle that says the right things. Networks and stations tend to put on the air those whose words have a chance of being sponsored, and liberals generally feel that they have less than adequate representation. The balance has never been so lopsided as in the press, where almost all of the newspapers regularly supported the presidental candidate whom less than half of the population voted for. The principle of newspaper partisanship is, however, of long standing; listeners to prejudice on the air hardly know what they are getting.

The case of Cecil Brown stands out because through him the principles of good conduct in radio nearly came to definition. In 1943, Brown broadcast some impressions gathered on a trip through the nation; they were essentially personal and were so offered, but Paul White, then in charge of news for CBS, doubted their validity, and as they might possibly be harmful to civilian morale, he instructed Brown to omit them. Brown refused and left the network. When the news reached the press, CBS prepared a full-page advertisement giving its position in regard to the sanctity of the news, in the course of which it was stated that analysts of the news should not communicate their opinions. As "opinion" comes close to "judgment" on one side and is connected with "opinionated" on the other, it was an ill-chosen word; staff analysts felt the cold finger of authority pressed against their lips and did not relish living under the threat of losing their jobs because someone else decided that they were giving opinion rather than interpretation. Since I helped to frame a later declaration of policy, I can testify that what CBS wanted to keep off the air at that time was personal prejudice; without passing on the merits of Mr. Brown's case, the principle was that an analyst of news can and must keep his private feelings to himself, that the most ardent supporter or the bitterest enemy of the New Deal was capable of intelligent interpretation of the financial effects of the Social Security tax and that a violent prejudice in favor of first beating Germany need not color the facts about the war in Japan.

The controversy ended without a decision. Mr. Brown went to ABC, Mr. White later left CBS; partisan commentators attracted sponsors, but for a time CBS held off. It is still less likely than any other network to permit outrageous partisanship, but it is said to have cast a longing look toward Walter Winchell's distinctly personal opinions in 1949, which it would not have done in 1945. The issue of impartiality in discussion of the news sank out of sight because a more serious problem had come up.

In 1941 the FCC had been asked to renew the license of Station WAAB (of the Mayflower Broadcasting Corporation). The editor-in-chief of the station's news service had previously broadcast editorials specifically urging the election of certain candidates and support of policies favored by the owner of the station. There was nothing underhanded in this: the station was entering into controversy in its own name. The FCC had been assured that this policy had been dropped and would not recur and had granted the renewal.

In its decision the Commission said: "This licensee . . . has revealed a serious misconception of its duties and functions under the law. . . . A truly free radio cannot be used to advocate the causes of the licensee. It cannot be used to support the candidacies of his friends. It cannot be devoted to the support of principles he happens to regard most favorably. In brief, the broadcaster cannot be an advocate."

For eight years the broadcasters fought this ruling; they were occasionally opposed by liberal and labor organizations; the public, as usual, was not interested.

The NAB called the Mayflower decision a gross example of the FCC's encroachment upon free speech. Frank Stanton, president of CBS, argued that the owners and managers of broadcasting stations were the only people barred from the microphone—"except perhaps convicts confined in prison." (He must have known that the argument is a little disingenuous; nothing prevented him, as an individual, from appearing on a quiz show or from commenting on the news; and Mr. Murrow, had he chosen, could have been sponsored in his news analysis while remaining a vice-president of the company; the decision prevented Mr. Stanton from representing his network only if he appeared as advocate of candidates or causes.)

The argument against the Mayflower decision is that

it abridges free speech (of the two thousand and more station owners and managers);

radio should have all the rights of other media;

suppression of the broadcasters' rights limits public discussion, and "if they are given the opportunity to express their opinion on the issues of the day, we are bound to have a stimulation and invigoration of public discussion which cannot fail to be in the public interest."

The quotation is from Mr. Stanton; the use of the word "opinion" may not be significant, although it is odd coming from an executive of CBS.

The intention of the broadcasters—if they use the rights which have been granted—is to take sides in controversial issues. For a long time some stations and networks held that public controversy was too important to be at the mercy of any single individual or corporation; they would not sell time for such discussion and rigorously deleted controversial issues from the commercials on entertainment programs. The principle was obvious, although it was expressed in "public relations language." *When time is given, it is given to both sides, for discussion; if it is bought, it is bought by one side, for propaganda.* If time could be bought, those with the most money could buy the most time. They could buy this time to destroy those with less money, and eventually they would have all the money—and the power and the glory of running the country. A network holding to the principle of fairness therefore set aside time for public discussion, giving it, free, to both sides (and to more than two sides, so long as something more than a splinter group was represented). In 1941 Niles Trammell, president of NBC, listed "discussions of political principles and other controversial issues" among the types of programs that must be sustaining because they are not suited to advertising sponsorship; a few years later the code of the NAB specified that "the presentation of controversial issues (except forums) should be exclusively in sustaining programs," although the FCC itself had not taken this extreme position.

One of the original reasons for refusing to sell time for propaganda (to use the right word) was the comparatively small number of radio stations and the difficulties of starting a new one. This was called the "scarcity theory" of radio (as compared with the number of newspapers and the low cost of setting up a printing press to propagandize for one's ideas). In 1948 Mr. Stanton noted that conditions had changed. "Originally we [CBS] supported the contention . . . that the expression of editorial opinions by a radio station would constitute taking advantage of a scarcity. Today we recognize the changed condition, and that the past policy has been outgrown." The changed condition is that there are now more radio stations (operating or authorized) than there are newspapers. In theory each station can editorialize to its heart's content because so many others will do the same that all points of view will be represented.

Does the changed condition also affect the principle of selling time for propaganda? Does the existence of many stations make it easier for the poor propagandist to buy as much time as the rich one?

The supporters of the Mayflower ruling candidly rested their case on a guess. Charles Siepmann, a sharp critic of radio whose views had influenced the FCC at the time the Blue Book was issued, wrote: ". . . editorials on the air will approximate in character those of the contemporary press. The group interests of the press barons are reflected in the overwhelmingly conservative if not reactionary tone of their editorial columns. . . . We can expect a similar trend in radio."

Mr. Stanton was on high ground when he replied that the FCC could not deny free speech to the broadcasters because they might use their freedom in a certain way ("without admitting for a moment that editorials on the air will follow a generally reactionary line"). This, he felt, would be saying, "I am afraid that I will not agree with what you are about to say, so I will do what I can to keep you from saying it."

In practice, Mr. Siepmann's position is not so weak; labor, liberal, and radical groups have long protested that they do not get a fair representation of their views on the air; to add the enormous authority of a station or network would throw the presentation of opinion even more out of balance; and while the Constitution declares for free speech, the FCC is bound by law to prevent unfair use of freedom. The Commission might well have said that the appearance of a network, with all its authority, as a special pleader is like giving one side a Sherman tank in a battle of infantrymen and, moreover, withholding armor from the other side. It is not realistic to suggest that minority groups can construct an authoritative network for themselves, and the argument that "the citizen is under no obligation . . . to listen to the programs of a particular station or network" is merely a pretense that broadcasting affects only the individual listener, not the people as a whole. The pretense is carried further when broadcasters imply that their editorials would be a single voice among many and that (as CBS announced) equal time would be afforded for opposing views. "This would amount to a radio counterpart of a 'letters-to-the-editor' column in a newspaper." To compare the specific gravity of a featured, or page one, editorial with that of a letter to the editor gives the show away; the amount of space may be the same, but the drive and force and effect are totally different. Simple people, baffled by the fact that a pound of feathers weighs as much as a pound of nails, may believe that any fifteen minutes of time equals any other; but no intelligent man imagines that a cubic foot of iron has the same weight as a cubic foot of feathers and that is, in effect, what we are asked to accept in the argument that John Smith's reply will counterbalance the special pleading of a radio network because it takes up as much time.

One of the most skillful propagandists for radio editorials has said privately that the owners and managers of the business are abysmally ignorant of current affairs and that the right to issue editorials would compel them to study, to think, and to act in the public interest. Officially the broadcasters have insisted that a change in the rules would not in any way compromise their stand on a fair presentation of opposing views. This did not cause the hearts of all minority groups to rejoice, since they felt they had been getting something less than a fair shake; and they were supported by one member of the FCC who was in favor of letting stations editorialize because it would bring unfairness into the open. Holders of licenses, said Mr. Robert Jones, have in the past "selected commentators to do their work for them," and he added that the files of the FCC are "filled with legitimate complaints of unfairness" practiced by these "alter egos of licensees." The Commission had never demanded fairness from commentators, denying itself the right to penetrate so far into the contents of programs; but Mr. Jones asserted that the FCC had both the right and the duty to do so.

The Mayflower decision was modified June 2, 1949. Broadcasters were authorized to advocate causes, to take sides on controversial issues, "but the opportunity . . . to present such views as they may have on matters of controversy may not be utilized to achieve a partisan or one-sided presentation of issues."

The broadcasters were chary of using their freedom to editorialize, and it was not until April 13, 1950, that the FCC had an opportunity to reassert and clarify its position. WLIB, an unaffiliated New York station, had editorialized in support of the Fair Employment Practices Commission and had not taken "affirmative steps to seek out and present" opposing views. In modifying the Mayflower decision, the FCC had asked broadcasters to "encourage and implement the broadcast of all sides of controversial public issues . . . over and beyond their obligations to make available . . . opportunities for the expression of opposing views" when such opportunities were demanded. In the case of WLIB, the FCC asserted that broadcasters have "an affirmative duty to seek out . . . opposing views." As in the original Mayflower case, the Commission noted an erroneous interpretation and asked the offender for a statement of future policy.

Whatever joy the broadcasters had in their victory was perceptibly diminished by this categorical imperative; their gift of free time, a point of prestige, now becomes a legal obligation. The FCC had not tackled the problem of equalizing the authority of a broadcaster on one side and his adversary on the other; it had assumed that time for reply would be equivalent to the time taken for the original broadcast. The Commission had also passed in silence an important change of policy that had taken place.

One month after the right to editorialize was granted, CBS announced that it was reversing its rule against the sale of time for propaganda, "the expression of opinion on public issues." Since the network now could, and presumably would, take sides, it would sell time to others for the same purpose. There would, of course, still be free time also.

A tremendous power play had been pulled off, a new gusher had been brought in; the great principle that money cannot buy time to influence the public vanished. A few weeks later George Rosen wrote in *Variety:* "The lid is off in radio and practically everything and anything goes. The exacting standards by which broadcasters were guided ten years ago have practically disappeared."

He mentioned "laxative commercials getting a meal-time airing," attempts to get both whisky advertising and religious programs, acceptance of the deodorant business as sponsors by networks which had previously banned them, the prevalence of telephonic giveaways, and the sale of time for propaganda (under the name of discussion of controversial subjects). Business was dropping off, there were good time periods for sale, and standards had to be sacrificed. "Consensus is that 'radio scares easily,'" he continued. "A reappraisal of the fall outlook indicates that business won't be as bad as was originally feared. . . . Thus, in the face of the current retreat [from earlier standards] a lot of people are asking, 'What will radio do when things really do get tough?'"

There is a chance that before things get too tough, radio may be compelled to redraw the picture of the audience it has made for itself. Until that is done, the basic concept of public interest will be blurred over; and unless it is done promptly, radio may lose the interest of the public in the shift to television, where the same problems will occur, but more acutely than ever.

# Pandora's Box: Television

|||

## FOUNDATION OF EMPIRE

Without a moment's hesitation, the American people have given over control of television to the networks, the stations, and the sponsors who have established the standards of radio broadcasting. It is a remarkable vote of confidence, and the masters of this new instrument have every right to be proud. Nothing the intellectuals, the bureaucrats, or the anti-capitalists have said against radio has had the slightest effect; television has a free hand.

If television were developing as the movies did half a century ago, spottily, without a sense of direction, pushed now one way, now another, by a hundred separate exploiters, all criticism of its present state and all guesses about the future would be premature. It is, on the contrary, being directed chiefly by the big broadcasters, who have analyzed their past experience and know precisely what they want; they are building television from a blueprint, eliminating the structural weaknesses of early radio; they are working from a master plan, the grand outlines of which are already visible. The economics of television, as the chronological child-and-destroyer of radio, are paradoxical, but one thing is certain: in the early days of movies and of radio a program style could be tried and thrown away without much loss; in television the cost of any operation is so great that from the start broadcasters have a vested interest to protect. The chances for experiment are slimmer; whatever succeeds now will set the standards for the next ten years. If the direction now taken is in any way unsatisfactory, the moment to call a halt, to reconsider, and to change cannot be postponed.

That television would be used substantially for the same purposes as AM broadcasting became inevitable years ago, perhaps as far back as 1929, when Vladimir Zworykin went to work for the Radio Corporation of America, developed the iconoscope in their research laboratories, and automatically delivered modern television into the broadcasters' hands. If he had been working for any part of the movie industry, the control of television might have been rooted in Hollywood; if he had been a researcher for the Navy, the course of television again would have been altered. Considering the enormous RCA investment in radio, as manufacturer of equipment and the parent company of two radio networks, its enterprise in pushing television is extraordinary. Some competition, especially in Great Britain, has existed, but RCA was for a long time in a position to slow up the growth of television, and did not do so. By using NBC as an experimental station, it has forced CBS and eventually all other broadcasters to take the first steps, and so set in motion the forces which are making television a part of the radio industry, leaving the movies far behind.

Given that situation, and the capacity of television to act as a universal transmitter of virtually all forms of communication and entertainment, the development now taking definite shape is this:

Television will be used as the primary force in the creation of a unified entertainment industry which will include sports, the theater and the movies, newsreels, radio, night clubs, vaudeville, as well as any minor activities, and will profoundly affect newspapers, magazines, books, the fine arts, and ultimately education. Co-existing within this pyramid of entertainment there will be a highly unified communications industry affecting political life.

Under our present laws we are not likely to get a single monolithic entertainment industry; but each network will be, in effect, a vertical trust, creating or subsidizing its own sports events, its own movies, investing in plays; and all the TV broadcasters together will profoundly influence the outlying independents in many fields, just as the movies now influence the production of plays and books and, to an extent, the writing of short stories.

It was commonly said, when television was beginning, that the great problem was not the size of the screen or the cost of production or the reluctance of sponsors; the essential thing was to get into Madison Square Garden; without access to the great fights and other events held there, a broadcaster would not be able to compete for an audience. The Garden is not now the exclusive property of a single broadcaster; but each one can make exclusive contracts with the management of individual events. Before television could demonstrate that it did, or did not, hurt attendance, several new ways of handling sports were worked out. To compete with the NBC monopoly on the fights arranged by the Twentieth Century Club, CBS invested in the Tournament of Champions, becoming in effect a sports promoter.[1] Even more illuminating was the progress of the Roller Derby. The spectacle of young women with long and powerful legs, skating around an arena, jockeying for position, and eventually mauling and tearing at one another, had attracted moderate attention in its native habitat; transferred to television it became a sensation. The ABC network put the Roller Derby under a five-year contract, and the owner could count on such a large income from sponsorship that his primary economic interest veered to television; the techniques of the sport were adapted at least as much to the requirements of the cameras as to those of the arena audience. The major baseball clubs have not yet been affected, but they are receiving substantial sums for telecasts of their games, and one predictable result is that there will be more night games, which come over brilliantly on the TV screen, because the available audience is greater, and this will in turn affect movies, theaters, and restaurants, especially if baseball as a spectator sport is carefully promoted for women, following the precedent set by the cigarette industry. To a degree,

[1] CBS has since retired from this activity.

the pattern set by baseball will apply to other sports; after two years of television the Garden was asking, according to the *New York Times*, sixty thousand dollars for a series of professional basketball or hockey, and as much as a hundred and fifty thousand for a somewhat longer series of college basketball games. (As neither networks nor colleges seem to have a strong historical sense, it may be worth noting that in 1930 the president of NBC said, "We have refused to permit on our system the sponsoring of football games by commercial institutions. . . . With all these youngsters, . . . I just did not quite like to see the Yale-Harvard game announced 'through the courtesy of so-and-so.'" Most colleges and most so-and-sos have not been permanently barred by the scruples of Merlin Aylseworth.)

The telecasting of sports was a turning point in the first phase of TV history. It shocked the idealists who saw a great instrument of imagination and social significance turned to the mean estate of reporting not only a World's Series, but phony wrestling matches and third-rate prize fights as well; and it shook the practical men, because for a moment it seemed that television was moving from the atmosphere of the home (an ideal place for selling clothes, soap, cars, and the other commodities supporting radio) to the saloon, where, according to persistent rumor, it didn't even increase the sale of beer, the spectators being so attentive to the sport that they forgot to order. A few commodities are naturals for sports broadcasts, whether they are received at home or in public places: cigarettes, beer, razor blades, and so on. But these events present their own special difficulties: they cannot be reduced to the specific durations of other programs scheduled for the same time each week; and most of them are long enough to become automatically the feature of an entire evening, so that the rest of the schedule has to be built around them. They are nevertheless ideal material for television, fulfilling some of its essential requirements, giving it a chance to do what no other medium can do; in sports, television transmits instantaneously and completely an actual event the outcome of which cannot be foretold. The condensed movie version of a prize fight, cutting out the dull moments, splicing in slow motion for the knockout, pausing to call attention in advance to the unexpected blow or the disputed foul, is in every way a superior document; but no one (except perhaps Fred Allen's Titus Moody) ever bet on a newsreel prize fight. The intellectual dislike for spectator sports will make no headway against the combination of their inherent attraction and the still miraculous opportunity of seeing them happen, the moment they happen, fifty or a thousand or eventually three thousand miles away. When the coaxial cable and relay systems extend to all parts of the country, citizens in the eastern time zone will be able to watch sports from the first game of a doubleheader at one o'clock in the afternoon to the last round of a prize fight at Gilmore Field in Los Angeles at one the next morning, by his own watch. The God-favored Californian will be able to start watching sports as early as eleven a.m. When network television is complete, the added interest may lead to an extension of the Major Leagues to the Coast; the jump from St. Louis to Los Angeles by plane will take no longer than did the trip from New York to Chicago in the days when the Leagues were founded. The obstacle at present is that, except for World's Series games, transmission is local, not national.

If the sports promoters prove uncooperative, the path of the broadcasters has already been mapped by CBS and ABC: they can create their own events, and the engines of publicity at their disposal will go into high gear to make the sports created by broadcasters more popular than those withheld from transmission. They will not need to create rivals to the National and American Leagues, the chances being that baseball will be happy to increase its paying audience by telecasting the games; but the TV broadcasters will always have it in their power to undermine any uncooperative sport by filling the air with other entertainments calculated to keep the customers looking at the screen instead of going to the field or the arena.

The interaction of sports and television is significant. In the past twenty years Americans have enormously increased their outlay as spectators; professional baseball quadrupled its take in that period; pro football went up a thousand per cent; hockey and college football did not rise so far, but their increase was two to four times as great as the rise in movie receipts; and the relative newcomer, dog-racing, went up nearly two thousand per cent, and did as well as the old established horse-racing. (The figures were given by Charles Sawyer, Secretary of Commerce, in an address to the Theatre Owners of America, whom he tried to console for their humiliating increase of a mere hundred per cent in the same years by reflecting that their take was still three times as great as the combined receipts of all other spectator amusements.) There has also been an increase in active sports, and bowling and basketball are among the leading diversions of the entire country. A medium which can deliver an event as completely as television does is bound to exploit all its capacities to the full, and while fights and wrestling may go down for a while, the only possible effect on sports as a whole must be to multiply its attractions.

They are magnetic enough as it is. In one of its more abstract and lofty essays, the magazine *Life* analyzed the American pursuit of happiness; as a prelude to the discussion, *Life* went through its files and published twenty-five separate pictures showing how we use our inalienable right. The pictures ranged from religious dedication to beauty contests; one-fifth were specifically connected with sport; three-fifths were pre-adult, and only four of the twenty-five were pictures of mature men and women. The number of columns of text devoted to sport in such a sober journal as the *New York Times* is often greater than that assigned to all the arts and sciences, education, the special interests of women, editorials, and human-interest stories put together; in Boston, morning papers make mid-season baseball the lead story on the front page although the actual results of games have been known for twelve hours, and West Coast papers often do the same for stories about the Major League baseball teams which their readers have never seen.

The irritated intellectual knows that all this sitting around and watching other people hit or kick or throw a ball isn't "good"; he knows that professional sport is dubiously linked with large-scale gambling, with corruption and crime; he feels something artificial in the passion of the Dodger fan and suspects that shrewd promotion lies behind it. From critics in the Soviet Union he hears that the build-up of spectator sports is only another device to keep the American people in a state of perpetual adolescence, and he may recall the remark of Thorstein Veblen that, unlike the proletariat of ancient Rome, who got in free, the Americans have to pay for their circuses. All this may be true; but in relation to mass entertainment the critic has standing only in one limited way. If television is not only to satisfy, but actively to exploit and exaggerate, the appetite for looking at sports, the general level of its entertainment will not rise in any marked degree above the sports-lovers' limitations. There will be exceptions; but a mass medium creates its audience by its average. It was great fun to read that the saloon audience shouted "turn on the fights" when the first grand opera was transmitted from the Metropolitan; but one who likes grand opera even less than second-rate fights may wonder whether television intends to build up a mass-minority audience at the sports level, satisfying only one ruling passion, and leaving untouched all the other interests and curiosities and appetites that human beings, including sports-lovers, enjoy. The ready-made (and in part radio-made) audience, eager for baseball and prize fights in television, is not a moronic fringe of the population; if it shows symptoms of delayed maturity when it throws bottles at an umpire, it may be retreating into adolescence for a holiday; and the same people that sit in the grandstands and bleachers are responsible craftsmen and husbands and citizens at other times.[1] But the audience that television will

[1] There is, in fact, another aspect of sports that is vitally important. It is mentioned on page 245.

create if it excites and feeds only one group of appetites will be lower in the scale of human values simply because so many natural human wants will go unsatisfied and so many capacities will atrophy from disuse.

For if the television audience is conceived and created in the image of the robot man, all the other entertainments absorbed into television will be squeezed into the same zone of interest. The process by which the movies reduce Dumas to farce or Flaubert to melodrama, and radio reduces relativity to a series of puns, will continue; the reluctance of producers to stage a play that has no chance in Hollywood will find a parallel wherever the "television angle" will be the decisive factor. (A woman with a pleasing voice was supplanted on the TV version of a radio program by a singer not nearly so good; the radio singer was fat, the other slender.) The area of effect will depend on what is popular at any moment. Night clubs and resurgent vaudeville will come under the influence of television at once, since they depend on personalities, on flash popularity, which television can build; from there the effects will radiate to musical shows. If television goes in for a series of short dramatizations, the writers of short stories will be touched; if methods are found to visualize fantasy, Superman and Batman and the rest will be written with television in mind.

The decisive influence of television has already been manifest in two areas: radio and newsreel. Quite apart from the complexity of financing an increasingly expensive TV operation from the proceeds of a diminishing pool of radio income, networks and agencies alike must now see to it that any program for radio, unless it is very cheap, can be handily translated into television, since a sponsor is naturally reluctant to associate his product with a program he may have to drop in a few months. Another direct effect is the appearance of new program types during the daylight hours, adaptations of night-time techniques with "name stars" familiar to night-time audiences; this may be transitional until television solves its special problems of daytime programs, but there is a fair chance that a brightened daytime radio will hold its own for a considerable time. It is even possible that radio will become experimental again if it has to fill much unsold time.

Out of the nettle danger the newsreel companies may yet pluck a golden rose. When television began to broadcast newsclips within ten hours of the event, the slow-moving newsreel, released once every three or four days, was doomed, and with it the newsreel theater. The late Fred Ullman, when he was head of Pathé News, had foreseen this and planned a major change in the character of his service; he intended to eliminate entirely the tediously recurrent clips of motorcyclists climbing hills, slow-motion reversed film shots of shapely young women leaping from pool to diving board, parades, and the like; the newsreel was to become a brief documented report on important subjects, with a strong editorial stand. Parts of this plan are still under discussion, and action must follow as soon as the feature-movie audience begins to fret at seeing the older kind of newsclips which no longer have any news value. Television will carry fashion shots, on film or with live models, and will pick up important news events on the spot when the coaxial cable is completed; the newsreel, feebly functioning for years, will have small excuse to continue. The makers can sell newsreels to TV stations (some of which have organized their own supply); but salvation in the present is not to be looked for. It lies in the past. Millions of feet of film made during the past fifty years lie in the vaults of the major newsreel companies, and these are useful in a variety of ways, in documentaries and quizzes, as background shots, giving the period for dramatic shows, and purely for their own inherent value as history and as comedy. They are already bringing a sizable income to the newsreel companies and will bring more when the relations between Hollywood and the networks are stabilized. The newsreel companies are subsidiaries of the great motion-picture studios, and these studios have not yet decided whether they want to cooperate with television or—

But they know they cannot destroy it.

For three years after the end of World War II the management of the Hollywood studios walked about in a somnambulistic
trance, muttering, "Three years from now will be time enough";
toward the end of 1948 they woke to the dreadful truth, that last
year was already too late. Paramount alone had an experimental
studio in operation; the other companies had vague affiliations or
none, and the general assumption was, "We know how to make
pictures; they'll have to come to us." What the bankers were
doing while the studios worked up this apathetic fallacy is hard
to imagine; if the managers of the country's railroads had said,
when Henry Ford was going into business, "We know about
wheels and axles; he'll have to come to us," they would have
been equally intelligent. Radio-trained TV executives did not
underestimate the usefulness of a movie connection; but when the
first tentative proposals were met with a combination of arrogance and indifference they turned to the development of the
non-fictional side of television, and when television ran away
with them in 1948-49, they did not have to add worry about the
movies to their problems. The movies, hat in hand and with
millions in the hat, came to them.

A natural move was to "buy a position" in the industry; the
bid made by Twentieth Century-Fox for the entire American
Broadcasting Company was rejected; as ABC had been formed
out of the Blue network when cohabitation with the Red (NBC)
was forbidden, it came late into the broadcasting field and had
not yet built its fortunes, but it was the only network that might
be bought, and the movie company offered several million dollars, writing off the radio past of ABC for a chance at its television future. The offer was a confession: Hollywood was scared.
Small units went into the business of making half-hour series
(dramatic or Western) for sponsors; independent executives
flirted with the thought of becoming vice-presidents in charge
of television for the networks; the major studios refused to let
stations rent or buy recent pictures. At the end of several years
of masterly inaction, the position of the broadcasters was im-

proved, kinescopic recordings of Eastern TV programs were shown in Hollywood, Milton Berle, re-created as a star by television, was starred in a major studio production, and the real-estate side of the movie business was looking over the possibilities of large-screen projection of televised sports and other events to supplant the B picture. But the zest and enterprise of the days when the movie empire was threatened by the coming of sound are not in evidence. Warner Brothers, the leader in that earlier and more courageous approach to danger, put a bid in for a station with a TV license; but the failure of the industry as a whole to go energetically into the business was a public confession that the movies were reconciled to playing a supporting role; they might supply pictures to television, but the great enterprise of creating a unified entertainment industry was beyond their power.

The relation between television and the movies may work out in several different ways. The essential factor is that until now the audience for television is substantially the same as the movie audience. Nothing in the quality of the product stands in the way of a merger of interests; and if no agreement is reached, each will be the mortal enemy of the other.

In Hollywood are huge studios, magnificent equipment, trained technicians, and the most popular of all entertainers; also a backlog of several thousand feature films. Owned by Hollywood, and not necessarily on the credit side at this moment, are theater buildings all over the country. The studios can use what they have to make pictures for the theaters; or they can, after some revolutionary adjustments, make pictures for the television industry and bring into the theaters both their own pictures and certain types of TV studio programs.

Or they can compromise. They can act as a manufacturing unit for television, preparing pictures to the specifications of broadcasting, and at the same time reach out for the audience neither Hollywood nor television attracts. This would follow the pattern set by the theater after the movies came to Broadway; the melodrama of the 1890's disappeared, and the parlor comedy followed when the movies offered their own version; some plays were put on in the hope of sale to the movies, but for a generation the theater survived by attracting a non-movie-going audience. It was not done without bankruptcies and heartbreak; but the theater survived long enough for new talent to come into it. Whether the movies with their enormous overhead can afford anything like this purging experience is doubtful; but if they get a substantial income out of the pictures made for television, they may have time to reorient themselves.

The movies may, however, take their bearings and go off into a wilderness of Westerns and musical extravaganzas. In these departments television cannot compete. Networks and sponsors may commission short films or cheaply made longer ones; if they cannot get them from the major studios, they will find independents to make them, or they will go into the business themselves. But the spectacular film, well made, in color (which will not be generally available to television for several years) is too costly. It may be a risky thing, but if Hollywood chooses to fight television, competing for the same audience, these noisy and infantile productions are available; and local theaters may make a deal with independent television stations to pipe in sporting events and quizzes so they will have some form of television to offer. The audiences attracted by this combination of the least significant elements in the two media would not tolerate the best of Hollywood's current product, and the net result would be a further lowering of movie standards.

Through the movies, television will affect the theater and fiction writing, so the direction Hollywood takes has general significance. Although pious statements about "better pictures" have been made and the facts about the dwindling audience have finally become a commonplace in speeches by executives, no decisive change in the Hollywood atmosphere is visible. No one can say how long the movies will go on pretending that television never happened. The halt in TV building operations after the

FCC stopped issuing licenses in 1948 gave the movies a breathing spell; a shock to the economy at any time in the next few years would help them even more, especially if it came before the large metropolitan markets were well equipped with receivers; but even a slight depression *after* television has come into common use would be fatal to the movie theaters and ultimately to the studios. The advantage five years from now is even more marked on the television side, since it will have a new selling point to exploit—color; whereas the movies have nothing but stereoscopic depth to promise, and it isn't enough.

In theory the movies should be able to beat off the invasion. To the average man television is something like the movies and something like radio; whenever television tries to create the kind of entertainment familiar in the movies, it subtracts—it loses color and size and technical perfection and the spaciousness of motion pictures; it can afford to spend on an hour-long dramatization little more than the movies spend for each minute of a first-class film (in recent years the average cost of A pictures has ranged from fifteen thousand to twenty-five thousand dollars for each minute of finished film). On the other side, whenever television uses the materials of radio, it adds the priceless ingredient of sight. The cost goes up, but the non-dramatic programs of radio remain relatively inexpensive when they are made visible; costly settings and long rehearsals are brought down to a minimum, and the spontaneous program, the vaudeville acts perfected for the stage or night club, the sport events, can be produced within a reasonable budget. Since television has been developed by radio as its own successor, it might concentrate on the programs best suited to its nature, leaving to the movies the exploitation of fiction as well as musical extravaganzas and spectacles. As a formula this is logical; but the rivalry between the two media will not be governed by a plan. Television will learn, as radio did, how to tell a story, and the sheer voracity of the medium, using up as many stories in a month as the movies use in a year, will force the broadcasters to adapt all kinds of fiction and probably to evolve a system of repeating their productions so as to cut down the cost. To the movies will be left the costly spectacular entertainments which are disastrous when they don't pay off and which are entirely useless for the creation of an audience new to the movies and not tempted by the average fare of television.

## THE POLITICS OF COLOR

Without prejudice, one thing can be said of the harassed men and women who have tried to make television an entertainment while it was running away with them as an industry: television has undermined the confidence of the movies, revolutionized the structure of broadcasting, and seriously affected half a dozen other types of mass diversion without creating a single significant entertainment of its own. The natural question is: what will television do when its capacities are fully exploited? And the question behind that question is whether we will ever be permitted to discover just how great its capacities are.

The great successes of television have been triumphs of transmission, not of invention: rather bad vaudeville and night-club acts, spectator sports, old Westerns and some good British pictures, and plays about which the critics say, in highest praise, that they seemed almost like movies; after these in popularity are musical events and some attractive programs for children, but no program outside of the four major categories has a large following. In a survey made by *Variety* it was discovered that nearly half of those who had been using a television set for more than six months, for whom the novelty had vanished, preferred variety programs, and nearly a quarter gave sports as their favorites; live dramas and feature films (most of them old or Westerns or both) were about even, ranking high with nearly a fifth of the audience; no other type of entertainment got as much as one-twentieth of the vote. More significant still was the low level of interest shown in the broader possibilities of television: the same owners, asked what they would want to see, plumped for new and better movies, Broadway plays, and first-rate vaudeville; they were apparently getting as many fights and games as they wanted and considered these first-rate in quality too; of some twenty other kinds of programs, ranging from homemaking through quiz shows to opera and magicians and news, the audience wanted virtually none—the highest in the list, homemaking, attracted less than one viewer in twenty-five. It seems a rather pathetic lack of curiosity, and it testifies to the satisfaction given by the popular programs, since the audience wanted more of them; even the suggestion that they could be improved is not a serious criticism of the kind of program, only of individual examples. Actually, the "wantlessness" of the audience is a constant phenomenon in mass entertainment; the audience did not ask for giveaways or serials; but the moment an attractive program of a new type is discovered, the audience will find that it wanted that type all along. The significant element in the list of favorite programs and in the list of desired programs is that they are both led by entertainments of the same general quality; with the exception of some of the dramatic productions, they all lie within a single zone of interest.

Before television could discover its own powers and learn to do well what it does better than any other form of entertainment, it was committed to some of the basic, and not necessarily the best, formulas of radio. The preferred time periods are quarters, halves, or full hours, although it is quite possible that the dramatized incident which fills a half-hour in radio could best be told in twenty minutes when sight is added to sound. The weekly recurrence of events is well established, and only economic pressure forces certain programs to try the rhythm of alternate weeks to relieve the pressure of work and the staleness of material. Discussion programs of no particular visual interest are used as inexpensive fillers, and many other radio programs, including the chatter of married couples and the daytime serial, have been tested. With a few respectable exceptions, the commercial messages are as insistent, and almost as false-seeming, as those of radio.

These factors in the growth of television can be traced to

certain decisions of the FCC in the past, and each may have a profound influence in the future. At the moment television is more an instrument in the forging of a gigantic entertainment industry than a creative medium of entertainment itself, because the two most decisive powers, CBS and RCA, have diametrically opposite interests in the business (neither one has any difficulty in reconciling its interest to that of the public in general).

As the parent company of NBC (which at the time was composed of two networks), RCA was from the start interested in the stability of radio broadcasting; so was CBS. As a great research-and-manufacturing company, RCA allowed itself additional, and conflicting, interests. It held patents on the most successful equipment for studios, transmitters, and receivers of television and proposed to market these at the earliest time that coincided with the public interest, convenience, and necessity. This date CBS attempted to set as far in the future as possible. Except for its subsidiary recording company, CBS was not a manufacturer; it had always been a seller of time and of programs; it foresaw no substantial income from television until long after RCA had recouped its investment by sale of equipment; and for several years it allowed its prestige as a pioneering and alert network to be jeopardized by doing nothing at all in the new field.

In 1940 Dr. Peter Goldmark, the head of the CBS television engineering department, informed the executives of the company that he had solved some of the problems of transmitting in color and received from them enthusiastic encouragement to proceed with his work. The possibility of color TV gave CBS its first opportunity to defend the public from premature investment in television receivers; within the next few years it spent, according to report, some three million dollars in support of its position. In that period RCA appeared as often as necessary before the FCC to press the claims of commercial television in black and white and continued its work in research and manufacture as well as TV broadcasting over the NBC transmitter.

The argument of CBS was based on the technical requirements of color, which could be transmitted only on much higher frequencies than had been allotted to television; consequently receivers adapted to black and white would become obsolete the moment color was introduced. The public would be deceived into buying sets which would serve only during the halting early days of television; only the manufacturers and the retailers would profit. Since color was inevitable, why not wait a short time and launch television in all its brilliance? Supporting the argument was the suggestion that color was not only inevitable, it was essential; without it the spectator could not tell one team from another or follow a chemical demonstration or enjoy a work of art. Most of the known deficiencies of the television machinery would be forgotten if the picture was seen in color. When it was suggested that waiting for full development before launching an invention would have kept the United States without railroads until the streamliner and the Diesel engine had been perfected, CBS retorted that if the FCC established standards and hundreds of millions of dollars were invested, television would be frozen at about the level of the Puffing Billy; there would be no progress for a generation or more.

The preliminary decision to allow television in black and white was made during the period when virtually all economists, federal or private, expected a recession directly after the war. It was recalled that radio had been a sort of ladder industry in the past, and the FCC would not forbid manufacturers to branch out into a new field which was, moreover, closely tied to the sale of many commodities. The rapid acceptance of television destroyed the argument that color was indispensable; for a time CBS fought on for concessions which would have kept alive the threat of obsolescence, but in March 1947 the FCC finally gave unreserved approval to the opposition, opening the way for network operations of commercial television on a grand scale. This was what RCA and some other manufacturers wanted. They had argued that black and white would be acceptable, that no practical color system could be marketed in less than five years, that eventually a color system would be developed which would be compatible with the black-and-white system, requiring little or no adaptation of the receiver, and that the public should be allowed to buy television at every stage of its development without being scared by threats.

The frequencies assigned to television were all taken up by licensees within eighteen months; by the end of 1949 the FCC was again listening to argument. In order to satisfy the clamor for more stations, the FCC was considering the very move CBS had hoped for earlier, that is, opening the ultra-high frequencies to commercial stations; and since color is at home there, the demand was again made that color should be given at least equal rights. It is still the position of RCA that a color system can be perfected, in good time, and there is no need to hurry. It is the position of CBS that a color system, its own or another, should be approved. The debate on technical points obscures the real issue: Should the public be notified that a superior television system will presently be available? Should the public receive a guarantee that sets now bought will be adaptable to the new transmissions? It is obvious that even with guarantees an announcement of radical changes in television sets is bound to slow up sales, with serious repercussions among sponsors, and that the erection of new sending stations will also be delayed, so that the runaway phase of television would finally be check-reined. If this is the objective, some of the events during the first boom may explain it.

The powerful trinity of business, government, and research worked together to accelerate the progress of television. The decision of the FCC not only encouraged the manufacturers; it actually disturbed a calendar of events in which Frequency Modulation was to come after the postwar demand for conventional AM sets had been satisfied, and, when FM had been exploited, television in black and white would follow, with color as a third phase. The FCC relegated FM to a low priority, and a surprisingly large number of smaller manufacturers joined the big companies in making TV receivers. They were helped by the technological advances made during the war in the entire field of electronics; a fairly good image was now to be seen on a table-model set, and the price broke below one hundred dollars toward the end of 1948. At the same time large screens and magnifying devices made the saloon-and-sports phase possible; an important prize fight and the presidential campaign in the same year were additional spurs to activity, and the radiation of the coaxial cable, from New York, soon took in Washington, Boston, Philadelphia, Chicago, and St. Louis, creating a substantial audience for national advertisers; the audience was only five per cent of the AM and TV total at the beginning of 1949, but it doubled within a year—exactly as radio had doubled in its first year. (By spring of 1950, nine of the fifteen most popular broadcasts in New York City were on television.) Local advertising, which was expected to finance television for a long time, became relatively unimportant; the popular programs were on the networks and sold brand-name products. By the end of 1949 the trade estimated that network and "spot" sales amounted to some twenty million dollars, local sales to six million.

No one pretended that the programs offered in this period had any great quality, but television proved that it was an excellent medium for "putting across a personality," the chief beneficiaries being Milton Berle and Hopalong Cassidy (whose old films were transmitted, making him so popular that he enjoyed a new lease of life in the Westerns). Berle's case was an exact parallel in one respect to that of Amos an' Andy in radio; like them, he became news; church sociables had been delayed and movie programs suspended to let patrons hear Amos an' Andy, and now movie houses and restaurants began to expect a fall in business on Tuesday nights, and many shopkeepers closed their doors that evening, not expecting the television audience to come out even after Berle was finished. Unlike Amos an' Andy, Berle was a second-rate performer and his style was peculiarly unsuited to the medium; but his popularity and the publicity it generated were positive factors in the television boom.

It seemed through most of 1949 that the rate of growth would continue, signifying a loss of twenty per cent at least of the radio audience by the end of 1950 and a respectable TV coverage of the entire country by the end of 1952. Radio sponsors were discovering how vulnerable their programs were, since the set owners reported, without reservation, that they habitually gave up their own favorite radio shows in order to enjoy *any* program whatever on television. This argued a superior power in the medium itself, and although ninety per cent of the people still had radios, a number of advertisers dropped off the air or took their first steps in television. There were not enough of the latter; TV stations carried sustaining programs, offering them for sale; on one dramatic half-hour a week, ABC spent nearly half a million dollars and then dropped it for want of a sponsor; by the beginning of 1950 drastic cuts in production costs were made.

The dilemma of the broadcasters had been foreseen; every expansion of television was financed by profits from radio and at the same time cut into those profits; a moment would come when television began to pay and might, in turn, finance the deficits of the parent enterprises. But no one could be sure of the stages of development, and a sudden swoop in costs for the TV department, accompanied by a dip in radio revenues, might undermine the whole structure of the business, leaving the broadcaster with a double deficit, since he would have to pay for too many sustaining programs in radio while he failed to break even in television.

It seemed at first that television would parallel the first days of the movies, when it was virtually impossible to make a reel of film without a huge profit; the year of the saloon was also the cartoon year, when the accidents and the foibles of the new medium were illustrated in *The New Yorker* and in Webster's "Unseen Audience" series, and the country had reached that state known to advertising agencies as being TV conscious. But the increase of the audience was not matched by new stations; there was a delay in building so great that the FCC had to warn holders of permits to start construction or surrender their licenses. In 1948 the FCC further checked advances by holding up all activity until the problems of the ultra-high frequencies (and color) had been settled.

The summer of 1949 in which nothing spectacular was offered by the program departments was followed by a winter in which only a few shows were remarkable; within two years television had landed in the doldrums. (In 1926 an RCA executive had noted that radio programs were in a rut and suggested that "novelties and revolutionary additions" were required to prevent the public from losing all interest in the medium. He thought rebroadcasts from abroad would turn the trick; actually the job was done by Amos an' Andy, Rudy Vallee, and other home-grown talent.)

The overhead of television is staggering by radio standards; the returns, by the same standards, are small if the broadcaster makes his profit only on the sale of time. The major studios have established various rules under which their income should be more satisfactory. In addition to paying for his time on the air, the sponsor pays for all rehearsal time during which the equipment is used; in many cases the stations build the scenery in their own shops and make a profit by selling it to the advertiser; some studios require the sponsor to engage a member of the staff as director of the program. But the most rewarding income has come from the creation of programs themselves. The error made in radio during the 1920's has not been repeated; in television the stations propose to be the prime creators of entertainment. They do not refuse to accept programs put together by package merchants outside, but they have the stronger position: most television programs have to be seen before they will be bought; many of them need several weeks of a shakedown run before they are right. The stations naturally give preference to their own programs, broadcasting as many as ten at a time, and the outsider has little competitive opportunity. In the radio business, a packager could put together a show and record it for very little; the kinescope of a TV program is costly, and no independent studios for kinescoping were in existence in the first years of television. For a time, the operating stations enjoyed a physical monopoly and their use of it was tempered by their own good sense: they needed salable programs, and often, as in the case of ABC noted above, kept an outsider's package on the air for a long time; but their first interest was their own product. On a package of its own a station could make two or three times as much as it got from the sale of time alone; in the early stages of investment in studio space and equipment, of increasing staffs and unpredictable overhead, it was imperative for the broadcasters of television to go into the business of selling programs to sponsors.

The consequence is that there is no counterweight to the commercial program, that no regular series of programs is produced to explore the public interest outside of salable entertainment. The long years in which radio developed its sustaining programs, to fulfill its duty to the public or merely to fill the blank spaces between sponsors, brought out new techniques and used a variety of materials which ultimately enriched the commercial side; these sustainers account for the broader scope of radio as compared to the movies. It may have been bad business for networks to set up sustaining program departments remote from the ruder noises of the market place; but at least the existence of many interests was acknowledged and the possibilities of the medium were explored; programs were produced at low cost and were held on the air for years if they satisfied a sufficient body of listeners; they were not quickly withdrawn because they failed to acquire a sponsor. Their ultimate fate was none too happy; news and symphonic music entered the charmed circle of commercial programs and were lucky; cultural programs in general were kicked around, losing their place on the schedule when sponsored programs needed the time, and many of them vanished entirely. But they had contributed to the unfolding of radio's powers. In television experimentation is hedged in by the motive of profit, which is exactly right for the agencies and the packagers and should always be a part of the broadcasters' business also; but if the program not specifically built for sale is left undeveloped, television may be well housed and brilliantly clothed, but it will be ill nourished during the critical years of growth.

The doctrinaire and the defeatist both hold that nothing can be done: in a capitalistic economy everything must eventually be submitted to the test of profit, and this is considered either the surest way to satisfy the public interest or the surest way to deceive it. A network reporting a profitable year in radio and an over-all deficit of several millions because of its television operations will not be seduced by noble words into putting unsalable programs on the air; and no non-profit organization exists to take over the work. Miss Frieda Hennock, a member of the FCC, has declared in favor of assigning some of the new TV channels to educational institutions, but the history of radio is against her, educators being as obstinate in their suspicion of mass media as sponsors are of education. For purely technical purposes, special channels may be exceptionally useful: a single experiment in a laboratory can be piped to a hundred schools; the arts and sciences can be demonstrated, if not taught. But this does nothing to solve the major problem of how to integrate *all* the elements of our culture, all our interests, into the widely accepted programs. If they are kept separate, if a special channel is assigned to them, the commercial channels will be more justified than ever in concentrating on the lowest forms of entertainment and constantly reducing that entertainment to lower levels.

### *"WHAT HATH GOD WROUGHT?"*

The amount of unimaginative and tasteless entertainment already offered by television seems to justify the dour prediction of one of the most astute critics of the communication arts, Charles A. Siepmann, who says that television will probably "conform rapidly to a few . . . stereotyped conventions. It will be technically ingenious and inventive but artistically poor. Except on rare occasions, and for some time to come, its true scope as a medium of expression will not be fully realized." As the foundation of a vast entertainment empire, which it is now becoming, television may never have a chance to exploit its own essential character; but in my opinion its character is so powerful that it may, in the end, prevail.

It is not for aesthetic reasons but for plain profit that the managers of television should be searching out its prime qualities; they must continue to use it as a transmitter of anything that can be brought before the cameras to entertain people, just as they must continue to show whatever movies are made available; but in the long run a medium of entertainment succeeds by using its particular techniques, by doing what it can do better than any other medium can. The movies proved this when they began to tell their stories not as photographed plays but as something totally new; and radio proved it when it developed its own mixture of vaudeville and personality shows into the basic comedy pattern, when it struck off into fresh fields and created the daytime serial. The essential nature of television is obscured by the apparently limitless number of things it can do, and what is expedient at the moment is to keep television forging ahead and to give it time to grow; what is expedient now is, however, fatal if it forces television to grow out of its natural shape.

I have noted some of the patterns imposed on television by radio; the movies have not yet exerted their influence directly, but already television producers, eager for the accolade of the critics, have accepted certain cinematic techniques, as, for instance, in shifting from one camera to another. The almost undetected rhythm of the movies, which appeals to the pulse of the spectator while the eye and ear are held by images and sound, is created by cutting, by the shifts from one angle to another, the insertion of a close-up, the duration of one shot relative to the duration of those that came before and those that follow; and it happens that this ground swell has become standardized in

Hollywood so that the rhythm of nearly all pictures—comedy, melodrama, or tragedy—is virtually the same. The public has been conditioned to choppy cutting, and if a shot is held beyond forty-five seconds the picture seems odd; foreign pictures, in a different tempo of cutting, seem slow-moving. There is no proof that the Hollywood tempo of cutting is right for telling a dramatic story in the medium of television; there isn't even sufficient ground for believing that the kind of stories Hollywood tells is the kind that television can tell most effectively.

In 1949 the alert Mr. Goldwyn foretold (in the magazine section of the *New York Times*) what Hollywood may try to do to television, in a discussion of the changes the movies must make in themselves if they are to be good television fare. Of his three major principles, one surely meets with universal approval: he said the movies must be better. He then proceeded to details of this improvement. The movies, he said, must go in for a broader style of acting because the subtle and delicate points now brought out on the screen would be lost on the small home receiver. It will not do to inquire what these subtleties are, and it isn't even too important to note that a spectator sitting within eight feet of a sixteen-inch television screen sees as much as one in the far reaches of a balcony at a big Broadway picture house. His argument reverses the truth; Mr. Goldwyn is like Mayor La Guardia—when he makes a mistake, it's a beaut. The style of acting in television is determined by the conditions of reception; there is simply no room for the florid gesture, the overprojection of emotion, the exaggeration of voice or grimace or movement, inside the average American living room. The television camera is merciless in detecting fraudulent appeals; in a play or a quiz show or a bit of vaudeville the individual who presses and fakes is instantly shown up. And even an audience fed for years on synthetic and substitute emotions can spot the imposture at close range. The level of projection in the movies has happily gone down, and good directors keep it down; there is no need to return to hamming in order to put a story over for the television audience.

The style of television acting (it could as well be called the level of self-presentation) is determined by a unique capacity of the entire system, from camera through control room to the receiver in the home: the capacity to transmit and deliver a completely rounded human character. This is the source of its special power, this is what it must exploit to become totally successful. It is not what the movies attempt to do, even when they adapt novels of considerable complexity of character. Mr. Goldwyn suggests that what the movies now do to novels is only a beginning, because when movies are made for home television they must pay much more attention to "plot structure." It is apparently sound advice, for it implies that the family group watching television needs to be kept interested.[1]

In practice, plot development for the movies is fatally involved with the concept of the twist, which I have already described. In virtually every case the word is accurate and descriptive because to accomplish what is desired, either the plot or the character is twisted out of shape; it is not always serious because the material is made and meant to be twisted. The five pictures which collected the important Academy Awards in 1947 were *Gentlemen's Agreement* (a man pretends that he is a Jew to get data on anti-Semitism), *A Double Life* (an actor confuses his roles with his private life), *The Farmer's Daughter* (Cinderella as a smarter politician than the Prince), *Miracle on Thirty-fourth Street* (there *is* a Santa Claus, as proved in Court), and *The Bachelor and the Bobby-Soxer* (Myrna Loy gets Cary Grant in spite of Shirley Temple). None of these is either important or contemptible; in every one the twist is palpable. In the course of making

---

[1] Mr. Goldwyn's explanation is also illuminating: at the movies, he says, the patron will sit through a dull part of the feature because it is too much trouble to go out; he waits until the picture becomes interesting again. At home he has only to turn a switch and he escapes boredom. The implication is that the movies hold their audiences in a trap; this I cannot accept.

even a respectable and faithful adaptation of a novel or play, the twist may appear at intervals, a new character appears or a minor character is changed so that a bit of comedy or an additional charge of excitement is injected; in important deviations from the theme and atmosphere of an original, the twist supplies the motives for violence, for sensation, for the murder and the chase and the jury trial. These elements of thrill, which keep the movie audience reasonably satisfied, must now be multiplied, we must have no quiet moments, because the spectator of television isn't trapped by people sitting next to him, he can get up and leave—he has only to change to another channel.

That television drama needs careful plotting is true enough; but if the twist becomes standard, if it spreads beyond the mystery drama in which it is acceptable, television will not only be distorted—it will be stunted. For, going back to its unique power to convey the fullness and the truth of human beings, it possesses an endless source of material in the drama that rises out of the relation and the conflict of character, a source so natural that everyone must respond to it and so unfailing that it has supplied the theater and the other arts of fiction from the first day when men invented stories about men and women. The plot that develops naturally and logically from character has its own complexities, its own surprising turns; it needs no artifice of twisting, because human beings are unpredictable, and it will keep the audience of television contented because "people are interested in people"—perhaps even more than in plots. Great skill is required to render character so that the audience becomes interested and concerned, without which they will be impatient, but the medium is capable of communicating character far more complicated than the movies have, so far, proved they could. I note [1] this comparative weakness in discussing the power of the daytime serial to make its remote and phony characters seem to live as friends of the audience; the techniques of television are not the same, but so long as they do not subvert themselves and become

[1] On page 240.

mere counterparts of the techniques of the movies, they are miraculously effective. The movie which is planned for an hour and a half of sensation, for which the audience has gone out of its homes and has paid at the box-office, appears in the trappings of luxury and presents a confused image, half-character and half-personality, the product of publicity as much as of the imagination, and to project this image, to keep it constantly in motion that attracts the eye, all sorts of twists may be necessary. The drama in television is carried into the home, the whole construction of glamour and personality is out of place, because these are public attributes and television is fundamentally private; there is sensation enough, but it is of a different kind: it is that "shock of recognition" which comes to us when we encounter our fellow beings in moments of stress and revelation, when they are being frankly and completely themselves.

That is the atmosphere in which television lives; within its incomparable mechanical illusion it is incomparably the conveyor of truth. No high degree of sophistication is needed to spot and discard what is false; but perhaps some innocence of the spirit is needed; perhaps the audience for whom television is being prepared has been so steeped in the corruptions of movie fiction that it will, for some time to come, accept base metal for genuine. But if the creators of television in the East do not fall under the movie spell, if they set in motion across the little screen a flow of images that are natural and true, the audience will at least have a standard of comparison. And—more pressing at this moment— the radio managers who now have their investment jeopardized will be creating a kind of television that will fend off the illusions of Hollywood, a television they can afford to produce over many years, until the movies reluctantly learn that their twisted plots and thrills for adolescents will not capture the great audience at home any more than they captured and held the audiences in the movie theaters.

Nine-tenths of what one sees in television today is aimed at the drifting movie audience, it is true. But even within that limitation the extraordinary power of the medium asserts itself. The programs that have impressed people (outside of sports and special events and Hopalong Cassidy) have again and again been triumphs of character. All the TV serials based on the radio formula (artificial characters in unbelievable adventures) have failed, while pure character-comedy has succeeded, with "The Goldbergs," the "Mama" series, and their several imitators. With no admiration for the techniques of Milton Berle, I perceive his attraction, because in his way he presents the unvarnished, the aggressively brash truth about one human being, himself, subduing to it all the other elements of entertainment his vaudeville should supply; it took longer for a milder, and more intricate, personality to arrive, but Garroway illustrates the same golden rule, that what a person *is* counts inordinately. The puppets in Kukla, Fran, and Ollie are characters, and all the ingenuity of rival groups cannot shake the special hold on the audience of these character-puppets. Even the extravagances of the personality program, the exploitation of handsome women with a lot of friends who "drop in," testifies to the essential soundness of building programs around what people are more than around what they do. (I pass without comment a number of programs which have gone Hollywood, giving themselves the bends in an effort to find new twists; these are personalities, in the gossip-column sense of the word, whose character either does not come over or is unattractive, and the efforts to promote them are deplorable.) Of the dramatic series, particularly on CBS and NBC, this can be said: they vary from good television to feeble imitations of the movies, but the best individual programs, those approaching closest to what television can accomplish, have consistently been well received; and, at the other extreme, those commercial announcements which have tried manfully to catch the accent of true character have also been successful. It is too early to make final judgments about popular taste, but the significant minimum of hope remains—good television has not been driven out by bad.

I repeat that this is important to the managers of the business because their situation is serious. They have already lowered the standards of radio broadcasting perceptibly, and the temptation to do anything that makes money in television is understandable. It is gratifying that those programs which rise above the expected level have held their own, because a persistent loyal adherence to sound principles now will give television a chance to develop normally, not merely as a supplanter of radio, but as a going concern, a genuinely popular entertainment.

The public interest is greater still. Television can drain off all that is popular in both radio and the movies, the trivial and the important at the same time; if it becomes the medium for mass entertainment only, as that is now conceived, radio and the movies may survive as substantial elements, radio living on its daytime and other special services, the movies attracting the vast audience they have neglected, the audience that mass television will not permanently hold. The danger is that neither of the older entertainments will survive through a longish period of reorientation, that radio will become insignificant and the movies will become feeders for television. If this happens before television itself discovers the range and diversity of an art that is both popular and democratic, it will be disastrous. All the pressure is in that direction, and the good omen I have emphasized—that interesting and experimental work in television has captured both sponsors and public approval—is in itself not enough. Some form of public counterpressure is needed.

It is justifiable because of the dual nature of television, its function as a means of communication that marches with its function as a medium of entertainment. That television news and analysis may drop below radio standards has been foreseen; in a sober memorandum Edward R. Murrow has looked into the possibility that a man with a face and voice and personality peculiarly suited to the medium may become a national sensation, though he is without competence to assay the news and has no sense of responsibility to the audience. The misuse of television in semi-

faking of news has already occurred; [1] the abuse of confidence
by bearing false witness will be all the more serious if the channels of information become limited, if radio dies out and television stations remain expensive. The pull toward the truth will,
however, be strong; again, the nature of television itself favors
a certain honesty; the impulse to fake will have to be very strong
before the risk of self-exposure is taken.

The sense of existing in the present which marks radio off from
the movies is even more strongly felt in television. This, we feel, is
happening now, it is the real thing, it is the truth. On that quick,
instinctive response from the audience a good director in television will base his entire style, the rhythm of movement, the
frequency of close-up shots, the intensity of facial expression,
the level of projection for the voice; on it the sponsor will build
his advertising, the balancing of adjectives and proof, the incidence of slogans, the substitution of the handshake for the hammer blow of radio. Nothing essential is foreign to this concept
of television; so long as we feel that we are in the presence of
something truly created, we will accept fantasy as soon as we
accept fact; we will understand *Macbeth* and *Private Lives* and
*Alice in Wonderland* if their characters are presented boldly,
with emphasis, without counterfeit emotions.

The golden opportunity of television is in the hands of the
people as much as it is in the hands of the producers of programs.
For every hour the individual citizen gives to television, the
producers owe him something: diversion, entertainment, enlightenment. Only the individual can decide whether he is being
sufficiently repaid for the time he gives. I suggest that he does
what I have done—suspend whatever he is doing and look for an
hour or two at the best that is now offered.

In television, entertainment and communication can reach their
highest point; for all practical purposes, presentation is complete:
we have sight and sound and immediacy, color is coming, and
three-dimensional presence is not impossible. In a staggered and

[1] An instance is noted on page 207.

illogical way, we have approached a sort of platonic ideal of communication. And the probability that this undreamed-of technically perfectible instrument should be put to the service of base and mean purposes is enough to make us question everything we have done in the past to make the popular arts serve the people.

# False Witness

There is a chance that by pushing the older media around, television can bring about a reorientation of all the popular arts. The extraordinary sense of actuality given off by live television programs can show up the fictitious quality of the movies, the artifice which has become their art. And the mere fact of visibility can impose limitations on the deceptions practiced by radio. The danger is that television itself, so persuasive, so seemingly real, can be more effective in falsehood than either of its forerunners.

I have noted the turn the movies took, away from story to myth, from imaginative fiction based on truth to the distortion that is properly called fictive. The atmosphere of falsehood that pervades a part of radio is more subtly contrived; it rises out of the obligation of broadcasting to sell commodities, but the commercial message is, in itself, less important than the methods used to give the message its effective setting. The present form of radio advertising is not the only possible one; the atmosphere in which it is presented could be changed if the style and character of the messages were changed. As television will inherit and can alter both of these elements, I propose to examine each one briefly.

## THE VOCABULARY OF ADVERTISING

The mischief done by persistent attacks on the radio commercial was considerable. So far as the devoted listener knew of these attacks, he put them down as another instance of the crankiness of the intellectuals, that strange section of the community which could always be trusted to find some reason for being against anything the average man liked. The networks and a few independent stations were sensitive to criticism even if they were not sensitive to the bad taste of some advertising they carried, and in prosperous times standards of "commercial acceptance" were set. Before they had been imposed on sponsors, the campaign against the commercial petered out, leaving the broadcasters in a stronger position than ever; the critics had failed to rouse the people against the most vulnerable part of the business, and the implication was that everything else was immune to attack. Researchers, indeed, discovered that antagonism to advertising was insignificant and that when commercials were dropped, as in programs rebroadcast to the services during the war, they were actively missed.

In a serious sense, I believe the nature of the commercial itself is important only because it affects the content and the style and the atmosphere of the programs. In the mind of many sponsors, the program has no specific function of entertainment: it is only a vehicle for the message. "We have no right to spend the stockholders' money on entertainment," one of the most lavish of radio advertisers said. "Taking a hundred per cent as the total radio value, we give ninety per cent to commercials, to what's said about the product, and ten per cent to the show." This feeling is common; the consequence is that all the other possible values of a program must be subordinated to its suitability to the product advertised. Institutional advertising with no peremptory command to rush right down to the drugstore and buy a bottle right away may be carried on a program of symphonic music or an hour-long drama; where the listener must be prodded or cajoled into immediate action, the program type must be shorter and snappier.

The basic styles of the radio commercial were set by people accustomed to billboards, magazines, and newspapers, and at first they attached their messages to the rudimentary entertainments developed by radio stations for the single purpose of promoting radio. These programs were not suited to sales talks, and the writers of the commercials, with their background of print and illustration, felt keenly the perishable nature of the spoken word with no picture to catch the eye. The overcharged adjectives became a substitute, creating an image for the mind's eye, and the repetition of the same words at the beginning, in the middle, and at the end of a program were designed to take the place of the second and third look a reader gave to an ad when he turned the pages of a magazine.

The devices special to radio are used in support of principles common to all advertising, chiefly the principle of association, the principle of repetition, and the dual principle of promise-and-threat.

The association technique, which flowered in the 1920's with queens and duchesses writing testimonials, is not an American invention: in 1889 the Duchess of Plaza-Toro confessed (in *The Gondoliers*):

> "*I write letters blatant*
> *On medicines patent*
> *And use any other you mustn't*
> *And vow my complexion*
> *Derives its perfection*
> *From somebody's soap*
> *—which it doesn't.*"

In essentials, association is always made with something the customer admires or aspires to; an inexpensive coffee is shown being poured from a silver coffee urn held by a beautiful woman who sits at a table shining with damask and crystal. In another form, we have association with people like ourselves. The old personal testimonial, which was popular for patent medicines generations ago, has been brought up to date; while men of distinction drink Lord Calvert, plain John Smith has switched to plain Calvert (the commodity dictating the kind of advertisement).

The method of repetition, used in billboard advertising, with the same bull appearing at regular intervals along the railroad tracks to sell tobacco, was carried to its most maddening point under George Washington Hill, who mystified and irritated great numbers of radio listeners by announcing two or three times on each program that "Lucky Strike Green has gone to war"; each shouted statement was itself repeated three times with a loud affirmative "yes" to connect them. The meaning was that the Lucky Strike package would no longer be green, as the pigment was not available because of war needs. Throughout the life of Hill, who sat for the principal portrait in Frederic Wakeman's novel, *The Hucksters*, the rule of three was inviolable, on the royal principle that "if I say it three times, it's so."

Aggressive repetition is calculated to prevent the listener from wondering whether the original statement is true or has any relevance. On the West Coast a manufacturer of gasoline announced that "more SUPR-X[1] gasoline is sold in California than anywhere else in the United States." The whim of the sponsor led him to repeat the statement, with the reassuring "Yes." As one of a series of burlesque messages it was entirely legitimate; that this gas was sold only in California was the only fact omitted. The parody had in fact achieved the perfection of the commercial slogan: it said nothing emphatically; it silenced all questions, raised no doubts, and sold gas.

The principle of the threat became prominent in the halitosis ads for Listerine in magazines and was used brutally at first and later rather humorously by Lifebuoy soap. It is of course the reverse of the promise, and both are actually variations of the testimonial and association ads. The special feature is that commodities are not sold on their merits alone but on the social success they will bring if used, on the social miseries bound to follow if not used.

This is the form of advertising that provides the best clue to one of the strongest motives in mass-commodity selling. It is not merely to sell a large quantity of the product and to keep the patron well disposed toward the cereal or soap he is in the habit of using; for that purpose a milder attack would be sufficient.

[1] The name is invented, the commercial is otherwise textually accurate.

The stronger motive is to persuade customers of other brands to switch. Manufacturers of mass commodities like cigarettes or gas or soaps know that at the end of ten days of using another brand the customer is just as happy as he was before. Something more than the quality of the product must therefore be sold to the customer; something must at least be promised which no competitor has thought of promising. The confirmed user of the right hair fix, the whisky of distinguished men, the soap that ensures social acceptance, may come to doubt their magical properties; but the insecure man or woman may be tempted to try these wonder workers, especially since these are obviously as palatable or handy or attractive as any others. Putting over this "social plus" requires the energetic pounding, the oleate caress, the sweet reasonableness that is totally unreasoned, in the commercials. And programs must be adapted to them.

This brings us back to the eminent sponsor who attached ninety per cent of the total value of radio to the commercial message and only ten per cent to the program that delivered it. If the sponsor is right in his allocations, any program that attracts listeners should be as effective as any other, and this was, in truth, accepted in the early days of broadcasting, when the station or network sold time before and after one of its programs for naming a sponsor and for a few words about his product. In 1930, according to William S. Hedges, who was then president of the National Association of Broadcasters, one minute out of thirty was a satisfactory limit for commercials, and on his own station, WMAQ, very few sponsors used more; at the same time William S. Paley reported that "of all the time used on the air [CBS] during a particular week, the actual time taken for advertising mention was seven-tenths of one per cent. . . ." Since in those days three-fourths of all CBS programs were sustaining, the figure does not indicate how much of each sponsored program went to the commercial, but all the evidence shows that the established standard held this time to a minimum. Moreover, the early style of commercial was not aggressive; by the criteria of 1950

it wasn't "selling" at all. In 1925 the total advertising, direct or
indirect, of a very popular and successful program appeared in
exactly thirteen words, the ones set off in the following "opening announcement":

> *"Tuesday evening means* The Ever-Ready Hour, *for it is on this
> day and at this time each week that the* National Carbon Com-
> pany, makers of Ever-Ready flashlights and radio batteries, *en-
> gages the facilities of these fourteen radio stations to present its
> artists in original radio creations. Tonight the sponsors of the
> hour have included in the program . . ."*

An executive of the company explained: "The statement of the
name of your company or the sponsorship of the program must
be delicately handled so that the listener will not feel that he
is having advertising pushed over to him. . . ." And the rest of
the program, he said, was "entirely for the pleasure of the listeners."

Four years later the National Association of Broadcasters (one
hundred and forty-seven stations at that time) wrote into its
code of practice: "Commercial announcements, as the term is
generally understood, shall not be broadcast between seven and
eleven p.m."

These echoes of a far-off, possibly happier time are significant
only because broadcasting was actually a commercial operation
in those days; it did not follow the idealistic objectives of David
Sarnoff, who conceived of the business as a public service supported by a tax on the makers of radio receivers and, when that
proved insufficient, hoped for an endowment, like that of librar-
ies, or a generous group of patrons. It was already giving the lie
to Mr. Hoover's optimistic statement that "It is inconceivable
that we should allow so great a possibility for service, for news,
for entertainment, for education, and for vital commercial purposes to be drowned in advertising chatter." Radio was adapting itself to a capitalist economy, sometimes abusing its privileges,
but holding in the main to rigid professional standards. It was

inevitable that the number of sponsored hours would increase as the networks grew and hundreds of small stations sprang up to serve local needs; it was not inevitable that under the spur of competition, standards should have been lowered as far as they were and that the commercial message should, in the end, take precedence over the program itself. The fact that commercial broadcasting existed, was satisfactory to sponsors, and gave every indication of growth and profit before these standards were altered is of prime importance; it knocks into a cocked hat the notion, delicately advanced from time to time, that any interference with the commercial is in itself an attack on free enterprise.

Open to criticism are these features of the commercial: its length, frequency, placing, and taste. The reader is familiar with criticism on all of these points even if he is not a confirmed listener to radio; if he lives in a metropolitan area he may not know that small stations are more generous in their allotment of time for commercials than the networks are and that as many as six spot announcements, covering nearly five minutes, could have been heard a few years ago "without program interruption." Some advertising agencies insist that their program ratings go up when they pile in more announcements; on the other hand, one of the programs most effective in selling the sponsor's product carries no commercial at all, merely the announcement, "The Goodyear Rubber Company presents 'The Greatest Story Ever Told.' " The most serious question of taste does not concern deodorants: it came up during the war when manufacturers gave the impression that their shoes or cigarettes or cosmetics were prime contributions to victory—and they were promptly rebuked by the Advertising Council. It is one of the few occasions on which considerable public disapproval of advertising has made itself felt. By and large the public has little to say against the radio commercial in detail and has not protested against the atmosphere in which the commercial is presented.

It is an atmosphere of pressing urgency and gross exaggeration.

The laws against misbranding are ineffectual. The Federal Trade Commission, which can enforce a cease-and-desist order against a false statement on a label and in print, cannot touch an announcer's worked-up enthusiasm; it cannot say three times is out because the pounding of a commercial prevents listeners from understanding that it is meaningless or fraudulent in intent if not in words. The wild outcry against the singing commercial—a brilliant stroke, a "natural" for radio—rose from irritation at the degradation to commercial use of songs for which people have sentimental attachments; but the singing commercial actually reduces the pressure, the stale voice of the announcer has given way to agreeable variations of solo and group singing, and it isn't easy to be peremptory or oily while sticking to the tune. The singing commercial, with all its subsequent foolishness, should be welcomed, because it gives a simple, almost neutral, air in which the atmosphere of insinuated fraud is modified.

It is this atmosphere that works back on the program itself and makes the representation of the simple truth so rare in commercial broadcasts. One sees the commercial as a microcosm of the whole: in a familiar type an entire drama is produced in ninety seconds when girl meets boy, an obstacle comes between them (his mussy hair, his failure to be promoted because of his mussy hair, or her bad complexion, her nervousness caused by her bad complexion), the obstacle is removed (*deus ex machina*), and girl gets boy. This is the contour of a three-act play and as satisfying as many romantic dramas. In other ways, too, the commercial imitates or influences the program. The short commercial requires the program to be short, few of them running beyond half an hour; the commercial is punched so the play is punched; the commercial is superficially true and leads in a false direction, the program likewise, for it would be unfair to expose the program to any touch of reality. The separate elements add together into the golden rule that to protect the commercial the program must induce the temper of unquestioning acceptance.

The adaptation of radio commercials to television is proceeding by trial and error and has already turned up some interesting tricks. Sponsors with an established slogan, accustomed to repetition, have understood that they must offer visual counterparts to the spoken word and have discovered that if you change the picture you can say the words over and over again, as many times as in radio. Animated drawings of cigarettes dancing or a combination of people dancing among stylized columns that later turn into cigarettes, have been used; by having two animations of about ninety seconds each, you can keep the announcer out of sight and pound your message home hard. Anything that attracts the eye—geometrical forms taking shape, bubbles floating upward—is sufficient as background. On the other hand, when an announcer is shown, the style tends toward the candid, simple approach, the seller reasoning with the buyer, praising his goods, but not shouting, not begging. The commercial is integrated into the program in many ways: a detective stops at a tobacco store and buys his favorite brand (the sponsor manufactures three kinds of smoking tobacco so the store front seems to have the usual variety of stock on hand); the flower outside Mrs. Goldberg's window is growing in a Sanka tin, and Mrs. Goldberg, as a good neighbor, is genuinely concerned because her friend next door hasn't tried Sanka. (Mrs. Goldberg, completely out of character, is compelled to speak the exact words about the coffee from which "ninety-seven per cent of the caffeine has been extracted," and if her creator weren't an astoundingly capable person, the commercial and the program would both be irretrievably lost at that moment.) A number of sponsors use the method of demonstration for washing machines and television sets; motorcars are sold by film inserts showing them in action. In general, no one has given up those devices which were imposed on radio because it lacked a video channel; but the tendency seems to be toward a more natural style, to something less than total pressure.

It is interesting to note that on a dramatic program television often sets off the commercial by fading out the play. The fadeout in the vocabulary of the movies implies a lapse of time, perhaps involving a change of place. Fading a play to bring on the commercial is a satisfactory technique because it transfers the audience from one psychological atmosphere to another. On comedy and personality shows the star almost always introduces the commercial, which is then taken over by someone else. Comic commercials, which appeared in radio in the time of Ed Wynn, have already been tried, and it is gratifying to note that Ed Wynn himself is doing some of them.

If television develops a genial, humanly acceptable commercial it will be because the excesses of radio are not required and would, in fact, be intolerable. No visual parallel to the triple adjective is needed, and television is so forthright a communicator of truth that it exposes the false note mercilessly. An early commercial for Lucky Strike cigarettes used a theme familiar in its other advertising: a woman drops a cup, she tells her husband she is "edgy," he gives her a cigarette, she puffs and says, "You're right, I feel better already." It provoked hoots of laughter from average audiences, although the time given for the soothing cigarette to take effect was at least as long as it was in radio; no one in the audience doubted that cigarettes could be soothing, but the spurious air of the entire episode, the maneuvered little accident, the acted concern of the husband, the phrasing and intonation of the commercial announcer, were all incredible. An air of sincerity and candor is required, and if it becomes standard in television one pull toward faking will slacken; and if commercials can be delivered honestly, programs may also draw away from the atmosphere of unreality. The more reasonable practices and standards of broadcasting of the 1920's may reassert themselves. It is a slender hope, but at least it is a hope. Without it we face an aggravation of the persistent tendency in the popular arts to debase the moral currency by passing counterfeit so constantly that even the sharpest eye is deceived.

## *"A COUNTERFEIT PRESENTMENT"*

The creation of popular "personalities" is one of the triumphs of the broadcasting business; a Kate Smith, a Mary Margaret Mc-Bride, an Arthur Godfrey becomes known to the public, not as a movie star is known, but completely; a peculiar intimacy is established between the audience and the human being behind the microphone. The approach is friendly, less intense than the high-strung dramas with which these programs compete. A sense of candor and simplicity rises from the casual way in which little personal anecdotes are told, opinions are offered, commercials are kidded, and products endorsed. The genuine honesty of the character is felt, and it does no harm if the speaker seems silly or ignorant at times. Everything is familiar, folksy, and true.

Many of these radio personalities employ ghost writers as well as reporters and researchers; some do not. The effective and successful ones translate what is handed to them into their own vernacular; they discuss atomic energy or the art of Picasso in terms they themselves, and the audience, understand. They are like those comedians who, without wit of their own, manage to impress their own sense of the comic on the material the gag writers supply, throwing out what is wrong for them, working over what is right until it comes naturally to them to use it.

Among the most pervasive of the radio personalities is Galen Drake, who broadcasts on one network five times a week and over the local New York outlet of another network twelve times a week. His counterpart in Chicago is Paul Gibson, and in Los Angeles, Knox Manning; and Paul West, Lee Adams, John Trent, Lewis Martin, Mark Evans, and Roger Bennett follow his pattern in Seattle, St. Louis, Philadelphia, and other parts of the country. There is something simple and manly about all these names; they are short, easy to remember, and have no peculiarities; they are a sort of basic English in names, and with two exceptions they are trade names, like Prudence Penny or Aunt Jemima. Moreover, these commentators' voices are "grooved" so that they sound very much alike; when Galen Drake was ill, many listeners refused to believe that it wasn't his own voice saying, "This is Roger Bennett substituting for Galen Drake." Knox Manning, who established a considerable reputation as a newscaster, an interviewer, and something of a personality in his own right, has kept his name but "regrooved his voice and style" when he began to do the "homely philosopher" programs similar to those of the others. These men not only sound alike but for the most part say the same things; they tell the same stories and they chuckle in the same places; it is either a monumental coincidence or the triumph of mass production.

Writing in the *New York Times*, Val Adams has described the process which began when McIntyre de Pencier transformed himself not only into Fletcher Wiley, but into the Housewives Protective League as well, though no one knows definitely against what the Housewives are actually protected. Fletcher Wiley sold the League to CBS "for approximately a million dollars," and with it the idea of manufacturing commentators by the traditional American system of identical parts, particularly the larynx. "Each commentator gets the same batch of material every day and turns out the allotted amount of whimsy and reflection." Something of a maverick in this stable, Galen Drake "insists that he uses very little, if any, of the script material ground out by [the League's] mimeograph machines. His programs, he points out, are ad libbed from notes." Moreover, he has committed an act of "insubordination" by having his picture published. The League is opposed to this exploitation of personality; just as all thoroughbred horses have their official birthdays on January first, so the members of the League stable are all supposed to have the same face—which is never seen.

In an age of prodigious faking this is surely the easiest to forgive; most of what these commentators say in their identically grooved voices is innocuous, without bite or character or personal style. Who cares whether they say their own words, utter their own thoughts? Who can be sure that their profoundest

private convictions might not be even less interesting? Perhaps
we are entitled to a faint quiver of distaste when we discover the
amiable imposture, nothing more. Not for the moment, at any
rate.

But as we follow the thread supplied by this trivial fraud we
become aware of a constant, deliberate deceit practiced not only
in the popular arts but in all the media of communication. Events
are re-enacted for the newsreel camera and presented as the
original; and the great American handshake that used to puzzle
Europeans because it was so hearty and emotional has become
a sideways thing, performed with one eye on the camera. The
faces of human beings are no longer permitted to appear as they
are, and the sounds that people make when they talk have been
"upgraded" to compete with the tremulous excitement or the
oily smoothness of the commercial announcer, so that the simple
accent of truth is now the rarest sound on the air. On "We the
People," men and women in the stress of unusual emotion read
copy prepared for them by hackwriters who know what they
want the public to hear. The results sometimes are startling, even
to the speakers. The first man on whom a new drug was tried
reported, "The next day my temperature was down to normal,
one hundred and five degrees," then stopped—you could almost
see him looking at the text prepared for him—and repeated, "My
temperature was down to normal, one hundred and five degrees."
This error was obvious; the errors that falsify the entire program
are not so obvious, and they destroy the truth of human emotion, washing out the expressive features of the individual, making men and women dummies wired for someone else's sound.

John Crosby, who has exposed the fraudulent as often as any
writer on broadcasting and who is especially sensitive to faking
in television, has had a lot of indulgent fun with the popular
sportscaster Bill Stern who makes a specialty of anecdotes, little
episodes told about anonymous people until the punch line comes
in—"and that boy was . . ." John Barrymore, for instance, was
catcher for one inning and advised the young pitcher to go into

professional baseball, "and that boy was Lefty Gomez." Mr.
Stern has little objection to using actual anecdotes and none
whatever to inventing; a number of his stories may be inaccurate
but are so blandly offered that no one cares, not even the
people mentioned. This indifference is apparently universal. Publicity men send out bright remarks on current topics, attaching
them to the names of their clients; writers of gossip columns
print these and they also attach well-known names to stories they
hear from their friends. Professor Irwin Edman once told Bennett
Cerf that he enjoyed all the stories Cerf attached to his name,
especially those he had never told. And the trivial lies of radio
are matched in many other fields. No single one is of the slightest
significance; together they add to the general impression that no
one cares or needs to care about the simple truth—not even people who have become famous for the angular sharpness of their
characters. In the early days of "Information Please" one of the
great delights was the eruption of Oscar Levant, harsh-voiced,
belligerent, touchy, unmistakably himself. His natural rudeness
fell in with the current mode of radio, the comedy of insult, and
presently Levant was co-starred with Al Jolson, condemned to
make endless jokes about Jolson's age and ignorance; immediately
Levant lost all his character, his voice no longer grated, his "attack" was no longer clean and brilliant, he read without conviction parodies of his own spontaneous and caustic wit, and he
became for two or three dolorous years the poor man's Oscar
Levant, a conspicuous example of downgrading which came
close to degradation.

The guest appearances of stars are another variation of the
process. During one of Arthur Godfrey's programs a distinguished man of science, speaking on atomic energy, faced a studio audience, largely adolescent, which did not want to listen
and was apparently incited to create a disturbance in favor of a
crooner on the program. Godfrey rebuked the audience. It was
a remarkable occurrence in more ways than one, for radio personalities flatter the studio audience, and men and women of

standing in the world of art or science habitually lower themselves to gain favor with the present audience as well as the listener at home. Operatic stars pretend ignorance of music, critics use a word like "definitive" and apologetically say "whatever that means," and the universal practice of belittling education and intelligence is enthusiastically accepted by the educated and the intelligent. It is their common fate, in the end, to demonstrate that Charlie McCarthy is not only better company than they are, but a wiser guide to the life of reason.

All this happens to people who are presented as themselves, in their own right, not as characters in a work of fiction. The rule of radio seems to establish a schedule of alterations: first the human voice and the tonality of an individual are changed, then the words, then the ideas and emotions, until an entirely unreal personality, lacking all the character of the original, is projected. The great success of quiz and giveaway shows, the persistence of some discussion programs and genuine interviews, the popularity of a few men and women who have resisted the smoothening process, are partly due to the relief one feels at hearing again the simple accents of a human being, no matter what he may be saying. Many of the MCs on participation programs reduce the average contestant to nullity by using the questions, the jokes, and the mild insults that have become standard, provoking the standard replies; the good ones still try to let the peculiar virtues of their guests come through, and on occasion they are rewarded by a stubborn character or a wit more quick than their own. These programs have escaped radio's morbid fear of an impropriety on the air and take a chance on the decency of the average citizen; they run the risk of dullness, but if dullness comes it is at least natural and spontaneous, it is not the calculated insipidity of the prepared program.

There are some technological reasons for the way both the movies and radio have tended to present patterns rather than people; the movie face was built up before sound came in; radio's voice, with its stock intonations, was worked over because the speaker was invisible. Between them, two of the essential features by which we identify human beings have been reduced to standard formulas, and presently the only way to distinguish one person from another will be by individual gait or posture. Even horses have more characteristics of their own.

Improvement of the TV camera tube will make heavy make-up unnecessary, and the appearance of hundreds of non-professionals will work against standardization of the human face and voice. A little faking has already appeared; the most dramatic moment of the Democratic Convention in 1948, as covered by *Life*-NBC, was the exit of the Southern delegates; before the TV camera they tore off their badges and flung them on a table, and a close-up of the mounting pile dramatized their emotion. It was not, however, a spontaneous gesture; after the interviews were over the delegates returned and put their badges on again. The director who suggested the piece of business was not false to the meaning of the event, but he had illustrated the way in which the great instrument for conveying the simple truth can be subdued to the uses of accepted faking.

# AFTER SUCH PLEASURES

This book is based on two kinds of experience. From the time I was ten, or thereabouts, I have enjoyed the lively arts in one form or another; and after having written about them, I worked for many years in three of the major fields: radio, the movies, and television. It goes against the grain for me to say anything derogatory about them. I do not want to give aid and comfort to their enemies, and when I began this book I did not know how damaging to the popular arts, *in their present phase,* my conclusions would be. I suspect that certain portions of the book may betray some resistance on my part to accepting these conclusions.

It would be easy to reconcile the pleasures I have had with the judgment I have had to make by saying that whatever I enjoyed was exceptional; but this is simply not so in the sense that I enjoyed only such pictures and programs as the majority of people did not. Quite the reverse; a great many of the movies that gave me satisfaction were box-office successes, and among my favorite radio programs at least a third have always been high in rating. I have always been slightly unsympathetic to movies made for the few, and one of the criticisms I have of certain types of radio documentaries is that they were presented snobbishly, as if the producers didn't want the average man to listen. The exceptional picture that becomes popular, the intelligent program that holds a large audience, are more interesting; and the important thing is that the bulk of the product in these and the other areas of the popular arts should constantly approach the quality

211

of the successful exceptions, while the singular and unusual things move ahead another step. The entertainment industry has lived either on a small minority, as in the case of the movies, or by satisfying only some of the needs of a much larger minority in the case of radio. Nothing in the essential nature of either of these media prevents them from becoming better servants of the public, nothing prevents the lowest grade of their product from being steadily assimilated to the next higher grade, and the higher from approaching the next one in the pyramid of quality. It is the way they are made and the way they are sold that stands in the way.

I have been so long an enthusiast of these arts, and have so often built up a corporate defense against other critics, that I can anticipate the rebuttal to my own arguments. One point, affecting my central theme, I have often made myself, and I now think it invalid: the point that each of the popular arts produces so many "finer things." If we were discussing aesthetics, the exceptions would count heavily; when we talk about effects, the general average alone counts. It alone has sufficient mass and velocity to become a creative force. The climate in which we live is not affected by a hundred superior movies each seen by a small number of people; it is affected by the pictures of Cecil B. de Mille, seen by over three billion people, pictures exceptional only in their vulgarity and outstanding because none of them has ever contributed anything important to the art of the screen or enriched in any way the lives of the spectators; and the essential quality of none of these pictures has been affected by the superior products of Hollywood during the almost forty years of Mr. de Mille's ascendancy. The three hundred features turned out each year in Hollywood show a technical advance. Today's B picture is often as well made as the A picture of 1930. But the essential quality of the average picture has not shown any remarkable change, and the striking effect of a successful exception is usually that its superficial attractions are imitated and debased. The bulk of radio is measured in astronomical figures; using the time of each individual listener as a unit, we have some three hundred million hours per day, and the average program of 1950, which occupies most of these hours, has not been deeply touched by the occasional prestige program or the arrival of a fresh comic spirit; the most popular programs of 1950 are, in fact, precisely the same as those of ten years ago.

The argument based on exceptions stands the principle of guilt-by-association on its head and asks us to believe that the average program or picture can acquire excellence by propinquity, as if some of the merit of an unusual piece of work brushed off on the others. Unless the exception actually raises the general level, unless the exception is produced so often that the public demand for it is steadily greater, it serves no purpose; it is merely a demonstration of what can be done. It is also a demonstration of what is not being done.

The exception cannot be effective in a hostile atmosphere. When radio is criticized for the quality of its entertainment programs, its defenders reply with praise for its handling of news, because in relation to the rest of the total program content, news programs are exceptional. No one has said that the American people have developed a critical faculty by listening to news analyses, but the networks are proud of the statistics that nearly half the people get most of their news from radio and that among these listeners the quality of radio news is considered very good. However, four years after the United Nations was established, with enormous radio coverage, it could not be identified by as many as a third of the citizens of Cincinnati. This is not flattering to the newspapers either, but, matching their circulation with the audience of radio, the papers can justifiably put a large part of the blame on the broadcasters. Intelligent news about the United Nations has never been lacking on the air; there have been discussions and debates about it and its day-to-day decisions; but the fatality of being off the central beam of radio cannot be escaped: in the atmosphere of entertainment *at a single level* news programs are the exception, and the simplest information has not been conveyed. In the atmosphere of the Lincoln-Douglas debates, ideas could be communicated; if all our present modes of communication do not succeed in distributing mere information, it is not the fault of the mechanisms at our disposal but of the use we make of them.

The exception can do very little to counteract the effect of the average product. The destructive effect of television on all other activities may be mitigated somewhat when the new medium becomes familiar (but as it will also provide better entertainment within its limits, there is a chance that people will spend even more time on it). Not only competing forms of entertainment suffer; those who read books and magazines stop reading; children stop studying. (Children even stop buying comic books, saying that television is comic books with moving pictures.) If the three major media are going to occupy so much of our time, they cannot prove their worth, their right to continue in their present direction, by citing their few exceptional offerings. They can justify themselves only if they offer a balanced entertainment in their average product, if they interest the individual in as many ways as he is capable of being interested, and serve all significant groups instead of the single large section which they can excite by setting off firecrackers or amuse by verbal hotfoots or frighten with ghosts in bedsheets.

Since I am unwilling to accept anyone else's standards for my private entertainment, I do not care to see mine imposed on other people. But I think that in keeping with the spirit of our life, a true variety of choice should be available, not merely a variety of packages for identical goods. The pleasures I have had have been many, and although I have written and broadcast my gratitude for them, I regret that I cannot list all of the attractive talents, the creative people, the expert technicians, whose work I have enjoyed. There was a time for that, and there may be again; but not before the people know what the popular arts are doing to them.

# The
# Great
# Audience

# Measure for Measure

For many years neither the movies nor radio had to worry about the characteristics of the audience; mechanically these media were available to everybody, and for a long time this purely quantitative approach to the audience was justified. As all movie studios were producing substantially the same pictures, no one cared about the income, education, or living habits of the audience; the same kind of people went to see a Famous Players picture as went to see a Selznick or a Laemmle. The broadcasters were also turning out identical products, but their situation was different: their audiences were delivered to sponsors and they could ask so much per head; they began to count.

In the early years the size of the radio audience was estimated by the sale of sets; when a single station's share of the total had to be measured, more reliable methods were developed, but all the elaborations and refinements have not shifted the center of interest, which is the size of the delivered segment of an audience; analysis may discover how much the audience remembers, what parts of a program it likes best, how far it is influenced by the comedian and how far by the commercial—but size remains the dominant. This is natural enough for any popular entertainment, and the complaints from people in the business, like Fred Allen, that radio is a slave to its ratings, fall on deaf ears because this slavery is precisely what the sponsors want. A purely numerical standard can be as deceptive as the batting average of a team on a single day; hits have to be made at the right moment to bring in runs, and pennants are won by runs, not by averages;

the broadcasters and the sponsors remain convinced that if you have enough hits, you'll get enough runs, and they are absolutely sure that you can't win games any other way. If the audience is big enough, it will pay off. The concept of the audience as a unit begins to crystallize at this point, and the emergence of half a dozen industries as the dominant users of radio becomes inevitable. If a sponsor is satisfied with fifteen per cent of the listening audience, he must believe that the people in the audience are pretty much alike and he must have a product that virtually everyone can be persuaded to buy even if it is not indispensable. The audience must be large [1] because the sponsor can count on selling his product only to a share of it; it must be homogeneous and in the mood to be persuaded, because the sponsor cannot afford to argue with eccentrics and doubters; and since radio is repetitive, the act of buying must also repeat itself—hence soaps, soups, cereals, drugs, cosmetics, cigarettes, confectionery, gas, commodities that do not last, are the mainstay of radio advertising. Sponsors of these products have contributed seventy-five per cent of the total network income.

If the mass media merely serve their audiences, the measurement of size is a sound business practice; if they go further and create audiences for themselves, the conclusions they draw from their statistics become important to society at large. In practice, the managers of the two most important media arrived at the same ends by different routes, the movies retreating from the consequences of their researches and the broadcasters embracing them. Without the spur of competition for sponsors, the movies decided to let the audience vanish and to play for the adolescents

[1] Absolutely large, not relatively. An eminent news analyst, with a satisfactory rating as compared with his colleagues, was not an effective salesman for a canned food product. The sponsor admired the analyst, but careful research proved that he "didn't sell" to women. Neither he nor the distressing news he analyzed before the Korean War broke out could induce the mood of consent in more than a fraction of his listeners, and a fraction of his small audience was insufficient. The same fraction of a comedian's audience would pay off.

they could hold rather than make any change in the quality of pictures or the system of distribution; radio went into a deeper analysis of the audience, determined to factor out all the complex equations of listening until it isolated the prime ingredients on which ever larger audiences could be built. The broadcasters' concept of the audience is the more interesting; before they arrived at it, they had left enumeration far behind and were launched on a genuinely creative enterprise, in accordance with their lights.

They began to sample the audience, to submit programs to carefully selected groups before putting them on the air. It seemed a natural way to ensure against failure; it was harmless and necessary. But the very act of sampling indicated that the broadcasters already had a definite picture of the audience in their minds, and that this picture was colored by their own statistics on the size of the audience. The figures were so impressive that broadcasters began to believe they were serving the majority of the people. As one of them said, "There is a lunatic fringe that doesn't listen to radio." He meant, it seems, that only very few people never listen at all, but he expressed graphically the conviction upon which broadcasters act: that there is a vast heartland of listeners, around which, like a glacial fringe, are dotted the insignificant, inattentive few. If the broadcasters are right, they can be criticized only insofar as they have failed to meet their obligations to their majority; if they are wrong, the serious charge against them is that they have had the privileges of a true mass medium and have served only a large minority.

It is probably true that more than half of the people in the United States are frequent-to-habitual listeners; it is true that next to sleeping and working, listening to the radio takes up more of the listeners' time than any other single activity. And it is also true that, except for rare moments, between fifty and ninety per cent of the people are not listening to the radio, not even in the golden hours when the most popular comedians are on the air.

The explanation that radio is a mass medium is offered as a

general clue to its character and as a specific defense of any portion of the program schedule. A good exhibit in this connection is the daytime serial. In its behalf is offered the fact of its popularity, and statistics are available showing that women of all degrees of wealth and poverty, ignorance and intelligence, are among its listeners. (A few years ago it was understood that no other kind of program would attract women in the mass; it has since been demonstrated that they will also listen in sufficient numbers to programs of chatter and to giveaways.) Not offered in evidence is the simple fact that more than three-quarters of all the women who are at home and have radios may not have turned them on at all during the morning hours. The size of the morning audience varies. In one survey in Boston it was found that seventy-six per cent of women in homes with radios were not listening. In one of the few surveys of non-listening ever made, a dozen good reasons for leaving the radio silent were discovered, but these reasons left the original fact untouched. At these hours radio was not serving a majority, it had not become habitual. Even if the number of listeners rises considerably, the basic situation remains: the listeners may still be a mass, but the mass has shrunk to a fraction of its potential size; it is a minority. United in the glorious bond of suffering with their heroines, the women who follow the serials are the only group for which radio has found a common denominator; there are enough of them to support the programs; according to the philosophy of the broadcasters, there are enough of them to justify total neglect of three times as many others.

The daytime serial is too extreme a case for anything except illustration; but remembering that networks defend the serial as energetically as any other program type, we can observe the principles involved. The obvious fact is that three-fourths of all the women who have radios are getting no program service they consider worth their time; the second is that neither broadcasters nor sponsors have tried to attract three-fourths of their potential customers. The concept of the mass, in this case, relieves the broadcaster of any obligation to the majority and at the same time deprives the sponsor of most of his customers. The abstention of the great majority of the public is not enough to force a change in program policy. The producers of other types of programs also have failed to attract audiences—and in this the special case of the serial is most illuminating. The reason is that *the nonserials compete for the serial audience;* they are programs of bright, inane chatter or of sentimental recordings, far below the serial in skill of presentation, innocuous, and directed to women of the same level of experience, intelligence, and emotional maturity. The final point to notice is that no audience for the serial existed before the serial began—obviously. No proof exists that radio could not have created an audience for other kinds of service. The daytime serial reaches all of one group; half of the others would make a respectably larger audience.

## PROOF BY NUMBERS

With their firm conviction that the audience is a mass, the broadcasters could proceed to sample its preferences in advance. Refinements in technique now tell a sponsor whether his program or his commercial is remembered the day after a broadcast; the Nielsen system, which attaches a tape to the radio receiver, on which every use of the instrument is recorded, offers data on the flow of audiences from one program to another; the Radox method, using an electronic device to report instantaneously every turn of the knob, every press of a button, enables a sponsor to start changing his program almost as soon as it is off the air. But the important thing is to know what the public will not want before you try to give it to them.

The first significant step beyond statistics was the invention of the Program Analyzer in 1940. It was the work of Frank Stanton, now president of CBS, and Dr. Paul F. Lazarsfeld, of the Bureau of Applied Research at Columbia University. A selected group of listeners push buttons to record their responses, in terms of pleasure, distaste, or indifference, to any program; ample checks and controls are used, and when the composite register of likes and dislikes is studied, allowance can be made for any nervous excitement of the listener who may have pressed the red button instead of the green one. The Analyzer is used to ferret out any unsatisfactory items in a program that is losing custom; it can also be used on several versions of a program in the process of being assembled.

Another analytical service has been provided by Horace Schwerin, who has expressed a large skepticism about the effectiveness of unanalyzed programs and commercials and has data to prove that so small a point as shifting the relative positions of a gay and a sentimental song may affect the holding power of a program by as much as ten per cent.

The most completely integrated research into programs and audience is conducted by Albert E. Sindlinger and his New Entertainment Workshop. In addition to Radox, which I have mentioned, he has Teldox, an intricate refinement of the Program Analyzer, which permits the respondent to draw a flowing curve of likes and dislikes, and Recordox, a wire-recording apparatus, which takes down the remembered likes and dislikes of the Teldox panels a month later.

In an article in *Politics*, Harvey Swados describes the flowering of Mr. Sindlinger's method. Plays and novels are tested at various stages of writing by submitting them to selected groups. Out of eight plays voted likely to succeed, seven were actually successful on Broadway; whereas sixteen out of seventeen which failed to pass the test were also failures when produced. Sterling North's novel, *So Dear to My Heart*, was put through the mill and, according to Mr. Swados, other writers are preparing to test successive drafts of works of fiction by the Sindlinger method. (It is interesting to note that Mr. Sindlinger himself thinks of his pretesting system as a way for genuinely creative artists to escape from the pressure of publishers and studio executives.)

The poll which began by counting noses has thus developed into a scientific method for guaranteeing the popularity of works of fiction. The movies have not been as thorough as radio; they have tried out only titles, and from time to time have sampled audiences about their likes and dislikes, inquiring whether they were more likely to go to a picture with a happy ending or an unhappy one, whether they wanted to see certain stars in comedy or Westerns, and so on. The consequences of polling and pretesting are fairly obvious. Even without the pretest, a sponsor is likely to favor a program based on elements that have proved popular; studios follow the leader and go into cycles of film production using any theme, plot, or character, new or old, that has captured the public; there is a premium on material that is safe and on gimmicks to make them appear fresh. With pretesting, the manufacturers of the popular arts find justification for repeating their formulas, and an independent creative mind will have little chance unless a Sindlinger test group gives him a vote of confidence. Clifford Odets, returning from Hollywood, reported in the New York Times: ". . . a private Gallup poll, calling itself 'Audience Research, Inc.,' . . . told one studio to whisk away from my desk four months' work on . . . Sister Carrie, because as a film it could end only in financial disaster.[1] When I reported this piece of commercial prescience to the old but yet magnificent Dreiser, he growled, 'But they're really cocaine sellers out here. Are you surprised?'" Audience Research, Inc., to which Mr. Odets refers, is the same organization which provided the statistics on the age levels of the movie audiences.

The sheer mass of duplicated material will increase, and with it will increase the number of those who like the mass product. This is precisely what the manufacturers of packaged foods, of soaps, gas, and oil look forward to, but the remarkable thing is that in some of these fields independent manufacturers, working on a smaller scale, do manage to survive; there are packaged breads with a flavor of their own, and unusual soaps, and tooth

[1] A picture based on Sister Carrie was announced a year later. Perhaps a way was found to "lick" the disastrous elements; perhaps someone took a chance and turned his back on pretesting.

powders, and razors, all sold to sizable minorities; it seems to be only in the arts that room for diversity and independence is shrinking to the danger point.

The defense of pretesting—apart from the assurance it gives to the sponsor or the studio—is that the people have the right to get what they like. It seems illogical to go to all the expense of creating an entertainment intended to be popular without finding out in advance that it will be. The sample groups whose judgment is accepted are not asked whether a work is good or artistic; they are asked whether they like it. The democratic assumption is that they are entitled to get what they like. "A mass medium," says Mr. Stanton, "can only achieve its great audience by practicing . . . cultural democracy, . . . by giving the majority of people what they want."

I believe this concept of democracy is faulty and that its consequences are extremely dangerous. It is right to let people have the chance to get what they want. To talk of *giving* them what they want is nonsense unless we know the capacity of the giver to satisfy wants and—the essential question—how people come to want what they want.

### NINE P.M. TUESDAY

I have used the words "the public." I mean by that a large number of people. Like "the majority" and "the mass," this word is unstable, and since all of them are used in connection with the tricky word "democracy," it is desirable to be specific. In the passage I have quoted from Mr. Stanton, what does the phrase "giving the majority of people what they want" actually signify? Does it mean giving fifty-one per cent of the men, women, and children in the country what they want in the way of entertainment on Tuesday night at nine o'clock? Or does it mean offering them something similar several hours a night all week long? In part Mr. Stanton answers this question by saying, "We find that most of the people most of the time want entertainment from their mass media." But what kind of entertainment and why it is wanted are not stated. If the argument is valid, the manufacturer of a murderous comic book can adapt it to his purpose and say, "We find that most of the people most of the time want horror in their comic books," and thus be relieved of any obligation to publish any other kind.

Behind this concept of the public there stands a picture of the mass of the people. In this picture people are not only all alike, but they have a limited number of identical interests, the chief of which is their desire for entertainment. We may be bringing such a mass into existence, but I don't believe the picture is accurate. Our common experience is different. We meet people and instantly sort them out, placing them in groups that we know—they are tall or short, blond or dark, active or lethargic. Presently we know them by their business affiliations, their religion or lack of it, their marital status, their incomes; we may not find a pencil maker who reads Sanskrit and writes poetry, but we can discover a broker who composes music and a taxi driver who collects butterflies. All of them share certain common appetites and interests, but each one has a point of distinction, and the baseball fan may be deeply concerned with the politics of his labor union, the education of his children, and the War Department's attitude toward paraplegia, whereas the successful lawyer may be an enthusiast for hockey, and like to cook, and read little except mystery stories. The average man lives at many emotional and intellectual levels in the course of his day. He can discuss baseball statistics and abstract justice in half an hour's conversation; he is curious about a great many things. He has an appetite for fact, and unless his mental processes have been dulled, he looks for entertainment of many kinds. This is true of those people who make up the mass to which radio and movie executives refer. When they say that the majority of people want entertainment or movies of escape, they appear to be justified because it is true that at nine o'clock on Tuesday evening a sufficient number of people want to satisfy that particular appetite, and the same thing is true at seven o'clock on Sunday, and at four o'clock every day of the week. But it is not true that these same people have no other interests and would reject other kinds of diversion if it were presented to them in understandable terms.

The broadcasting business has been more energetic than the movies in hunting up new kinds of entertainment. In the early days the head start of NBC gave it such a commanding advantage that competitors had virtually no audiences on certain nights of the week. They tried then to discover new kinds of programs to interest a sufficiently large number of people, and by their own testimony they failed. People were interested in comedians, in popular music, in plays (especially comedies), in personality shows, and a few other types. They wanted entertainment. The unhappy competitors fell back on doing the same thing that NBC was doing, and a generation later had the satisfaction of seeing the situation reversed when CBS bought or attracted the most popular programs and NBC, searching for competitive material, announced a dozen new programs, every one of which was already stale with repetition.

There was a fallacy in the concept of the audience. The search began with an attempt to find a substitute for milk and meat and bread—there is none. It should have begun by offering stable commodities in a variety of new forms, by baking a better loaf, by finding a substitute for the milk bottle or different sauces for the meat. The searchers for new material fell back into being imitators of the old because they believed that all audiences wanted not only entertainment, but entertainment of the same quality.

In any discussion of the audience, both radio and the movies point to the great variety of interests they serve. The movies supply musical shows and Westerns and comedy-dramas and historical pictures and mysteries; radio has symphonic music and hit parades and quizzes and serials and drama and news. On the face of it, they seem to have something for everybody, and the only criticism should be that the proportions are not right. But a closer look at the actual product shows that the variety is superficial; ninety per cent of our movies are made according to formula, and with the exception of classical music and news in radio, the total offering all lies within one zone of interest, requiring the same kind of attention, giving virtually the same kind of pleasure, and, more than anything else, creating the same kind of acceptance.

The two exceptions are important. Both appeared first as sustaining programs. News on a large scale, with broadcasts from abroad and studious commentary, was not considered salable, and a few early attempts to sponsor the Boston Symphony did not make a definite mark, so that the great orchestras were placed in the sustaining category, for prestige. When the best hours were crowded, during the war, a sponsor with no product to sell bought the Philharmonic to keep a corporate name before the public, and this orchestra stayed on the sponsored list for many years. The size of its audience grew respectably, giving ample proof that the audiences for the Hit Parade or André Kostelanetz were not the only possible ones; actually, Kostelanetz followed the Philharmonic, and part of the audience stayed with the station, finding pleasure at two musical levels in succession. News and commentary became a salable commodity during the war and have remained so, to an extent, ever since; they are not offered as substitutes for the comedy and quiz shows, but they find their audiences and keep them loyally.

These exceptions indicate that radio broadcasting is not merely a process of spooning food into open mouths; it is creative. It takes people and makes them into audiences, and this creativeness, which is its highest honor, is what radio has chosen to neglect. The difficulties are great, but the broadcasters have multiplied them because until now it has never been necessary to find out how an audience is made. A local New York station has tried to play for fractional audiences: those interested in the theater, in stamp collecting, in photography, and so on; the assumption is that special programs will attract a fairly large portion of those interested and that at least some of these listeners will get into the habit of tuning in a station that recognizes their special interests for other programs as well. For a network this fractionization is impractical. Facing the uncomfortable fact that certain nights each week "belong" to their competitors, networks have tried to find program material of sufficient general interest, anything that will scoop together a reasonably large group of listeners, to compete with the established types of program. Except for news and serious music, they have not succeeded; they have retreated to the position that the only audience that pays, the only group large enough to justify serving, is the one radio has already brought together; and therefore that all the stations in a single area must compete for sections of this same fragment of the whole. At its lowest extreme, this argument means that ten stations may all be broadcasting to a fourth of the available listeners, while none tries for the other three-fourths; at best, the broadcasters confess a weakness in creative power.

It is quite possible that radio does answer all the simple requirements: it delivers a laugh and a thrill, dramatic works of the imagination to take people out of themselves, mystery and a touch of the morbid to fret the nerves, sentiment and adventure, now and again a moment of wonder at the strangeness of human life—a balanced ration altogether. From time to time a cycle of Shakespeare has been produced or dramatizations of the world's great novels, and radio has not been wanting in tribute to science and such arts as it could present. The fatality has been that these things have appeared sporadically and for prestige, without any conviction that they could become normal parts of the schedule of programs. Even when they came under sponsorship (U.S. Steel and the Theatre Guild, for instance) the atmosphere was rather lofty until the prestige value was established, after which the programs tended to run down to the average level; when a sponsor's enthusiasm begins to wane, programs get a "hypo"— by becoming more like their successful, straight commercial rivals.

The way to a democratic radio is not through serving the

interests of small fractions of the community. It is through attracting the largest possible public at every point. The broadcasters have aggravated the fallacy of the mass with the fallacy of
the single level of interest. They have produced the Weeping
Woman by day, taking care to give her five or ten consecutive
programs all of the same kind, and at night they have done their
best to make things agreeable for the Laughing Man, going to
great trouble to eliminate a news program that comes between
two comedy shows, convinced that the listener will not tolerate
interruption, that he lives for nothing but laughs. They have figures to prove that people who like drama prefer two or three
dramatic programs in succession, and that music lovers listen to
music until they fall asleep. They have no figures to prove that
the average man has to have all his comedy and all his drama at
one level of intelligence. They have been looking for new materials; they need a new approach. Just as the movies can enlarge
their audience by more intelligent handling of comedy and melodrama, the radio can use its present materials for programs that
will attract a large part of the audience they have and steadily
add to it the people they have missed.

## "A PLURALISTIC UNIVERSE"

Opposed to the idea of the audience as a mass is the most familiar, perhaps the most fundamental, principle of American life.
Like most principles that work out in practice, it is not absolute,
it is not always respected, it involves compromises and reconciles
contradictions. It is the principle of the diversity of human
beings, the variety of their experiences, the value and dignity of
each individual. When people are brought together under this
principle, they can do what the Colonies did when they formed
"a more perfect union" without losing their identity; people belong to one another because they share the same fundamental
appetites and emotions and interests, and they join a dozen
different groups, for business and for the good of their souls, to
play bridge or send poor children to the country, but they

never coagulate into a mass. The quantity system in production and distribution has made it harder to remain an independent person, but our pluralistic mode of life is still dominant and still worth preserving.

It corresponds to our physical geography and to our history. It begins with the variety of people who have made the nation which, from the start, has asserted the revolutionary principle that anyone could *become* an American by an act of will. This meant, psychologically, that every man has in himself a number of qualities; he not only can make something of himself, he can make himself over. When a German became an American in 1848 he became something that half a dozen other nationalities had created and in turn added something, so that the Irish in 1870 and the Slovene in 1900, when they became Americans, were incorporated into an even more complex national character. Everything brought by immigrants, beginning in the seventeenth century, underwent a profound change in America because the country always believed that change was possible and because all barriers against change were broken down. The sense of infinite possibilities within each citizen is the real, if not always acknowledged, philosophy of American life. To allow full expression to these possibilities is the practical aim of our society, and whatever limits and constrains and suppresses goes against the national character.

For a hundred and fifty years this sense that America is always coming into its own was the essence of our laws and customs. While the nation was one, its people were always in a process of change. It was only after we put an end to immigration—and after the emergence of radio and the movies—that we began to think and talk of a fixed, unchanging mass character in America. The stubborn fact is that we cannot destroy the creative past; we are the children of all the peoples of the earth, and we are one people because we have undergone the experience of becoming Americans through our forefathers if not in ourselves.

We have always lived in several time zones, physically and

spiritually, and it is symbolic, perhaps, that network radio for years refused to face this simple fact. A citizen of California, driving home from work, would hear on the air a tense dramatic program suitable to the quiet after-dinner hours, because it was eight or nine o'clock in the East. Some programs were acted out again several hours later for the West Coast, but the simple device of recording the program on its first broadcast and playing the record whenever suitable in the different time zones was fought off by executives who had built up in their minds a mystic philosophy of a network as a unit, a great monolithic structure imposing itself on America.

But Americans are not one huge lump. We are, as we always have been, a pluralistic society; the word comes from William James, the most American of our philosophers, the one most derided for being "practical." If it was never a perfect state, it was always a changing society, and the feeling that change was possible multiplied the interests of every citizen so that his life had variety and he belonged not in a single class but was at home in a dozen different groups at the same time.

This was the America that made us, and if today everything seems to tend toward sharper class lines and huge monopolies and a static society, nothing in our history suggests that we are done for, unless we lose our independence of character and the spontaneous capacity for action—unless we have already been robotized into mass men.

Radio and the movies today correspond closely enough to a society in which financial and industrial power is highly concentrated; they do not correspond to a society in which resistance to concentration is active. They prosper because wealth is widely distributed, but the networks which create the dominant character of radio get the greater part of their income from a small number of large manufacturers through a handful of agencies, and the movies are financed by the big banks to whom they return the money paid in at the box-office. They live in an atmosphere of concentrated power, they deal with companies that have absorbed little competitors and merged and spread. They see no other life possible for them. They are the great engines of democratic entertainment and culture, and they are committed to the destruction of democracy.

## A NATION OF POETS?

To have great poets, said Whitman, we must first have great audiences; to have popular entertainment, say the managers and the sponsors and the measurers, we must have big audiences. It is hard to say which principle is capable of more harm unless the terms are well defined. For the Whitmanite usually means a hundred and fifty million intellectuals, and the broadcasters are trying to create a hundred and fifty million indistinguishable chunks of a single mass. It is the variety of human beings, not their intellectual eminence, that counts; just as it is their variety, their individual character, and not their number that counts. And variety means not only that one person differs from another; variety dwells within each person. We are a pluralistic society because each one of us is more than one, we lead plural lives, in a diversity of climates.

A medium of entertainment that can serve everybody and chooses to serve primarily "the civilized minority" is contradicting its own nature; if it chooses to serve the greater number it is doing well, provided it constantly enlarges the area of its service, constantly encourages the diversity of interests of those it serves. It is doing badly if its ultimate result, intentional or not, is to reduce more and more of its audience to a single level, as an educational system would be doing badly if its end result was to prevent children from growing into adolescents and to erect a firm barrier against maturity.

It is not a nation of poets we ask for, but a nation of men and women.

# A Nation of Teen-Agers

## "THE MENACE OF THE YEARS"

"The faults of radio are the faults of the American people," says a veteran broadcaster, and the same theme was in the mind of the executive who said that to criticize radio is un-American because, in effect, radio is so much a product of the people that we are disloyal to our country if we suggest that radio may have taken the wrong road at times. The movies are defended on the same ground, and so are comic books, which correspond to the age of violence and insecurity in which we live. The generalization is that every country gets the popular arts it deserves.

It was because I found the popular arts so expressive of so many impulses in American life, so uninhibited and energetic a response to the flow of our energies, so bold to the point of brashness, so unaffected by traditional taboos, that I accepted without question the vast amount of entertainment they offered; and when questions were raised, I fell back on the defense that the popular arts corresponded to our general situation. I now think this position is too vulnerable because these arts are themselves among the forces that create our situation. They are not alone. They reflect our economic and political and moral situations, and it isn't sensible to expect popular arts to stand against the spirit of the times. They cannot make themselves eccentric, they cannot and should not exist on the fringe. But just because they are popular and are entertainments, they can also have a certain independence and can be attractive by going cross-currentwise. They can laugh at fads and fanatics because they are close to the enduring spirit of the country. They are happiest in the comic vein, and comedy is as critical as it is kind. The popular arts can perform their great corrective service if they remain true to the people; they cannot do it if they surrender without reservation to any dominant group, political or economic or religious. As soon as the popular arts give up their independent status and place themselves in the hands of the managers of our economy, they lose their corrective function, they help petrify social customs, and they lose the right to say that their faults are the faults of the people. If these arts are trivial and false because the people are trivial and false, the people desperately need arts that are serious; if the people are incapable of accepting serious arts, how far are the popular arts responsible for reducing them to this level? And if the people are capable of enjoying more kinds of entertainment, haven't the popular arts a magnificent opportunity to gain profit and prestige by giving the people all the kinds of entertainment they want?

For an example of the interaction between the people and their arts I return again to the extreme case of the daytime serial. A "symbolic analysis" of this program type was made by W. Lloyd Warner and William E. Henry of the Committee on Human Development at the University of Chicago; it is far removed from the statistical researches and hasty conclusions usually put forth on the subject, and it constitutes, in the main, a reasoned defense: "We found the representative programs we selected functioned very much like a folk tale, expressing the hopes and fears of its female audience, and on the whole contributed to the integration of their lives into the world in which they lived."

For their investigation Warner and Henry chose a group of listeners the great majority of whom named the daytime serial as their favorite kind of program; almost all were married housewives, living in Chicago or Detroit, and all were of the same social level, which the authors call "the Common Man level"— "their way of life constitutes the main stream of American culture." For contrast a small group of women with more education and more skilled professional activities, belonging to a higher social level, was questioned.

The serial used in the test was "Big Sister." I do not quarrel with the choice, but the reader should be warned that this is the best example, among popular serials, for putting the whole type in a favorable light. In "Portia Faces Life," usually one of the top ten favorites, the scenario for eight weeks included a grafting politician, a false accusation of illegitimacy against an unborn child, a stolen chemical formula, blackmail about the theft and the murder of the blackmailer, and blackmail again of the murderer and a bought confession of murder by a man who is having trouble with his mother-in-law. The heroine of another serial, "The Right to Happiness," was described by the knowledgeable Max Wylie, who concocted some of the story, as "an experience in emotional mildew"; she has a past, having killed one husband and divorced another, given birth to a child in the penitentiary, and achieved both respectability and the love of two men; one month of this serial revolves around one of these lovers, a district attorney who is fired by the governor of his state for refusing to ask the indictment of a woman accused of murder; he turns to her defense, unaware of the fact that she is his own mother.

These are the actual stuffs of the daytime serial; they create the atmosphere, and even family serials like "Big Sister" are subject to an injection of violence if the rating falls. And ratings do fall: when Portia's husband stayed home for a few weeks and life was relatively placid, the serial dropped from first to twenty-fourth place in popularity.[1] Knowing this, the reader may return to the researches on the audience of "Big Sister." The listeners were, of course, familiar with the plot and characters:

> "Ruth and John Wayne are happily married . . . but are always entangled in the troubles of relatives and friends. . . . Christine, Billy, and Tom [all get into] compromising situations . . . dangerous situations. . . . Christine is a scheming woman with . . . an interest in John and in John's nephew Billy . . . a young and

[1] Max Wylie, *Radio and Television Writing.*

inexperienced fellow. Tom is rather nervous and undependable.
. . . His questionable behavior . . . exerts a bad influence . . . a
constant source of trouble. . . . They all depend on Ruth and
Ruth helps them. . . ."

With this background, the listeners were asked to continue
several fragments of the plot. In one Tom accuses Billy of
stealing money, and in another Christine tells Ruth that John
is really in love with her, Christine; in all, five typical situations
were offered.

From the listeners' projections of these plots and their responses
to questions, a detailed picture of the group and of its attitude
toward the characters emerged. The listeners admired Ruth's
ability, they liked John but considered him "essentially non-
sexual"; he needed his wife's guidance and support, whereas she
hardly needed him. Christine was condemned when she stepped
between man and wife, but otherwise she was envied for her
physical endowments and denounced for making use of them.

The psychological characteristics of the listeners were noted:

*"Reduced imagination and personal resources* . . . a dulled use of
imaginative power . . . as though they were holding to the past.
. . . Their ideas are routine.

*Impulse suppression* . . . seem to distrust imaginative expression
. . . to fear spontaneity . . . resistance to mentioning sex directly. . . .

*A struggle for personal control and a fear they will not succeed*
. . . feeling that the environment is against them . . . hope of
some solution [by] accident, suddenly becoming world famous
. . . lack active control of one's own fate. . . .

*Interpersonal relations stereotyped* . . . *strained* . . . constantly
some block placed between the man and the woman . . . through
fear of sex, or domination, or separation.

*Sameness and monotony of outer world* . . . a view of the
world as conventional, repetitive, filled with petty detail . . .

lack of richness and vividness (in their view of the world) . . .
the world unrewarding and frequently punishing for moral in-
fractions.

*Apprehension of the unknown* . . . the challenging, the unknown
and the irregular hold no charm . . . uncomfortable and resent-
ful when forced to make new decisions."

"They have been trained . . . to be wives and mothers and, unconsciously, to carry out and maintain the rules, moral beliefs,
and values of their social level. This they do most effectively."
Yet they see life as monotonous drudgery, personal relations as
troubled; they hope to escape by some stroke of magic (or by
magically achieving education), they do not look forward to the
future, their hopes are dim.

The women who did not listen to daytime serials were not
given to stereotyped thinking, they had resources within themselves and imagination, they saw people not as troubling one
another but as cooperating to solve difficulties, in their private
world "people are expected to get along, their lives are not constantly hampered by the terror of losing a husband or by the
irrational fear of infidelity. . . . The atmosphere of disillusion
and frustration that permeated the listener group is not found
here. . . ." These women, professionals of considerable standing,
seemed to feel less than the others that women "really know
best" and should guide the destiny of men; the non-listeners felt
neither the need to dominate men nor much sense that their lives
were tragic; they did not go in for self-pity; they did see "some
disappointment, frustration, and bad fortune in the world about
them," but they did not assume, as the listeners did, that nothing
could be done about these ills; to them the future looked not
"drab and threatening" but "possibly pleasant and challenging,"
and they accepted the challenge because they did not look for a
magical solution to human problems; they believed in personal
effort, they used their imaginations to cope with the unfamiliar.

Unfamiliar with the atmosphere of "Big Sister," these non-listeners found it hard to believe that the characters had any reality; they thought the situations were psychologically false; they did not envy the predatory Christine, they thought she was probably an aging woman, lonely, perhaps afraid, and therefore seeking reassurance by proving she is still attractive to men. They made down-to-earth suggestions for solving the problems, including "Big Sister can pour her husband a Scotch and soda, take one herself, and tell him that she doesn't know anything better to do at the moment," but in general they were "stuck because [the plot] involves such nonsense. . . . No family runs like that." To non-listeners "Big Sister" herself seemed a smug and interfering busybody, a woman who "played God"; they did not admire the passive role taken by the husband (not true to life) and they obviously saw no connection between the problems of the serial and their own.

The writers of this study then proceed to demonstrate the importance of the daytime serial. They paint a picture of the hard, limited, and terribly insecure lives of the women who marry the Common American Man. They grow up as dependents; they have a brief moment of freedom when they are old enough to be courted (which is, I may remind the reader, the time of their going to the movies), and then they become dependent again; the sex theme quickly becomes secondary as they grow into mature wives and mothers; they play a subordinate role in our society, have no money of their own, are unsure of their husbands' fidelity, find social stability in the church and ladies' auxiliaries of fraternal orders. They have reconciled themselves to insignificance but they are not secure, and into their lives comes Big Sister, who has successfully adjusted herself and is clearly the most important person in her own world; during the quarter-hour she is on the air her stage is the kitchen and living room of every listener's home. She brings her troubles with her, but no matter how doubtful the listeners are about solving their own problems, they are sure that Big Sister will come out all right. They are also morally sure that the wicked Christine will be punished; Christine represents sex, which, as in the movies, is associated exclusively with bad women. (As her husband is taken to be passive and sexless, Big Sister herself has presumably outgrown "all that.") The listeners' "petty difficulties . . . are now dramatized and become significant and important; and the women who experience these difficulties feel themselves to be significant people." That is the constructive action of the daytime serial.

Throughout this study the anxiety of women is prominent. In discussing the technique of soap opera, I noted how it broke up the suspense of the movie serial, doling out fragmentary doses of suspense. Since the central character of "Big Sister" is happily married and insecurity is felt through the characters who surround her, it is possible to say that this program "condemns neurotic and non-adaptive anxiety" and "provides moral beliefs, values, and techniques for solving emotional . . . problems." But there is one significant omission.

It was hinted at in the descriptions of the two groups of women who responded to the questions. In brutal terms: women who listen to daytime serials suffer anxiety, frustration, a sense of futility; women who do not listen do not suffer these ills. Obviously two explanations are possible: women who are anxious and frustrated turn to the daytime serial; or women who listen to daytime serials become victims to the anxieties and frustrations exploited in these programs.

No controlled research has been made to answer this question. Fragmentary evidence that serials are to blame for some neurotic manifestations in women has been brought forward, chiefly in angry pamphlets which skilled dialecticians have demolished. Until we have proof on either side, we cannot accept the accusation or the defense; we have only a few facts at our disposal.

The first is that anxiety is exploited by the techniques of the serial as well as by the intent of the writers; the anxieties of the listeners themselves are relatively brief, those of the serial drag endlessly on; as I have indicated, the structure of the serial (as well as the commercial use to which it is put) postpones the triumphant resolution of any discord as long as possible. If a program disparages the neurotic characters, it still concentrates attention upon them, and its lesson in psychological sanity is like the tag "Crime doesn't pay" after fifty episodes of a gangster comic book. The atmosphere of the serial is all tension, the characters are wound up, they are prevented from discovering the simplest facts, they cannot telephone to find out how an invalid is getting on, they cannot open a letter promptly, so they live in a world of shadowy terrors, and when at long last a threat to their security takes definite shape, new obstacles rise to inhibit action. A kind of psychological strip-tease against a tremolo background is the serial's substitute for the catharsis of pity and terror. It is a crafty and calculated exploitation of anxiety.

The serial is effective because its characters become friends of the listeners, members of the social group with whom they live and "visit" several hours a day. La Rochefoucauld's maxim that we are all strong enough to bear the misfortunes of our friends explains the hold of the serial, in part; no misfortunes, except those suffered by friends, can move the majority of people. The movies avoid tragedy because in their brief hour they cannot create the sense of being friends with the characters; they go in for melodrama, the tension of which is brief, acute, and created by external events. The serial deals more largely with character, out of which tragedy can emerge, but by its nature it has to prevent its listeners from experiencing great emotions frequently; the continuing base is worry—worry over detail—on which are mounted fear, hostility, disappointment, frustration.

In this atmosphere we sometimes find a central character who attracts anxiety like an electric magnet, concentrates it and emphasizes and exaggerates it, and solves the difficulties that produce anxiety by interfering with the lives of others; when the nerves have been sufficiently frayed, the lesson in living is brought home that a little Führer shall lead them—and he, of course, leads them not to peace but to another war of nerves. The "techniques for solving emotional . . . problems" come down in the end to praying for help from the outside; at the end of all their listening, the women still lead unimaginative and impoverished lives, without confidence in themselves, afraid of the future, their relations with men "strained" and uncomfortable, their whole existence precarious. This is what the defenders of the serial say, but they do not say what part the serial has had in aggravating these unhappy tendencies of the listeners. I have no data to prove that non-listening women, of the same education and social position as the listeners, are any less afflicted by anxiety. In the past twenty years listeners and non-listeners alike have felt the once solid ground of our way of living shift under their feet. The daytime serial, which began between two wars, has always avoided the economic situation; it took advantage of the loss of confidence during the depression as it takes advantage of the loss of direction in the years of the cold war. Moreover, it exists in the atmosphere of jeopardy induced by much of radio's advertising: cosmetics, laxatives, and other commodities to a degree, constantly threaten women with the loss of their husbands unless they act promptly. This breakdown of confidence is reinforced by ancient wisdom about the wandering affections of middle-aged men and by contemporary statistics on a rising divorce rate; it holds the threat of a lonely future over women whose children have already started families of their own; it has the psychological strength of all glamorization of the past.

## "GOLDEN LADS AND LASSES"

At this point the exploitation of the insecurity of women joins with another powerful theme in American society, of which one aspect is properly called the glorification of youth, the other phase being the prevention of maturity. Again, as in the case of the anxiety of women, the popular arts correspond to a social reality. Again, we do not know how far they are themselves responsible for the situation they exploit. Magazines are published for the young, and books prescribing their special etiquette, and cookbooks; active and spectator sports and motorcars are "angled" for their patronage; hundreds of products are sold through them if not to them. The economics are simple: young people stay alive longer, and if they get the habit of buying a magazine or a lipstick or a shaving cream in their youth, they are profitable customers, theoretically to the end of their lives. "If you get them young they stay with you longer." The overtones are interesting.

First there is the placing of the age line. "Keep that schoolgirl complexion" is a positive marker on one side; so is the magazine *Seventeen; Mademoiselle* is supposed to keep its readers through their first baby, presumably placed in the early twenties; and there are indications, in the magazine field and elsewhere, that thirty is to be considered young, maturity beginning among the "over thirty-fives." Our educational system, our child-labor laws, the fairly consistent rise in the level of take-home pay, all contribute to the prolongation of the period of adolescence. In the time of Pitt and in the time of Lincoln childish things were put away before the age of twenty—there were not so many years one could count on after that. As the life span took a prodigious leap forward in the past two generations, people apparently decided to spend the extra years science had won for them in the pleasant trifles of youth, not in maturity with its burdens. At the same time a shift occurred at the far end: it became dangerous to change jobs after forty, and fifty was beginning to be synonymous with unemployable. The span of productive maturity was shrinking at both ends. The machine age did not need the old to work its machinery. But the society produced by the machine age made some demands for maturity.

The popular arts were not the only forces putting over the notion that maturity means middle-age. Faced with the prospect of being lonely and unemployable at fifty, people naturally guarded themselves against the forties; the simplest method was to prolong the years of adolescence, lopping off as many years as possible from adult life. Our climate and our customs, our quantity production and our holidays, our optimism and our small families, let us replenish our physical vigor; at least two-thirds of the nation had all the material necessities for a long and productive middle period of maturity.

Set in motion against this was a determined effort to perpetuate the adolescent mind. In this the share of the popular arts is one of the dominant factors.

The exploitation of the anxieties of middle-aged women by the daytime serial is matched by the exploitation of youth in the movies. What happens in the movies is chiefly love, and it happens to the young-looking if not to the young. This corresponds to one form of reality, since the subconscious message of a vast amount of advertising reduces all sex attraction to one age level (for women); it is not the consuming fire of grown men and women, but the flash-point of adolescents. This is the promise-and-threat that sells cosmetics and girdles and sweaters. The faintly mustached Ninon de Lenclos who had lovers until she was ninety might have admired the apparatus of attraction; but she would have asked at what point in modern times men became indifferent to the air of excitement that surrounds a woman devoted to love-making and experienced in its arts. And it is not only the courtesan who would question the concentration of sex in the immature. It is a common and humiliating experience to lose a husband to a woman of one's own age (and, in fact, men have lost their wives to their college chums and their partners in business). The attraction of youth is a known quantity, but men and women who make spectacular multiple marriages seem to thrive with the years, the predatory and successful amorist of either sex capitalizes on the same attractions as the roué and the courtesan, not on innocence and youth.

Whenever the "youth movement" does recognize the truth of sexual attraction, it falls back on its great selling point that the mature woman must *seem* to be young; appearance, not reality, counts. This, too, had some relevance in the past; when women worked hard and bore children regularly and were treated as inferiors, they aged faster and lost their attractiveness; leisure and the cosmetic arts were enjoyed by the few. The coming of age of women, their achievement of social equality, their success in the world of affairs, is a prime phenomenon of the past fifty years precisely because it affects women of every class; and the cosmetics industry can take honorable place with the typewriter and the bicycle as one of the energizing forces in this emancipation. It is reflected in the daytime serials' central character, who is a woman of mature age; it is not recognized in the young-love myth of the movies.

The parallel and contrasting descriptions of listeners and non-listeners supplied by the admirers of "Big Sister" throw light on the matter. The listener group, as described, could have existed in the 1850's; the women are not among the seventeen million who earn some twenty billion dollars a year in postwar America; they are dependent on their husbands; they are not among the considerable number of women who do not work for a living but are almost in complete control of the family income, receiving it as a right and spending it largely as they see fit; they are not among the women who have profited largely by general or professional education. They have the psychological marks of the immature and are unwilling or unable to face or understand or cope with the realities of their own fairly simple lives. The contrast group are actually women in professional life, but their characteristics of independence and confidence, their eagerness to meet the future, are found in salesgirls and stenographers; their equilibrium in relation to men can be observed among women who earn their living and among those who do not; and these qualities of twentieth-century women are independent of wealth and education: they come from living in the contemporary world, not the world of the past, from knowing that wealth and education are available to women, and above all that the self-reliant integrated woman is no longer exceptional and is accepted in the world of men.

The daytime serial may allay the anxieties of women, but it

inspires no action on their part to get rid of anxiety; it casts a glory around the weak, the clinging, the submissive; it accepts misery as the natural state of womankind, and by sponging up the fluid, unchanneled emotions of the listeners it renders them passive, perpetuating the very qualities that limit the imagination and stultify emotional life. The movies pick up here and deliver a counsel of despair: the anguish and frustration women have known is all they can hope for; they are too old for anything else. Explicitly or by implication, matureness is presented as the end of possible happiness for women. Between them, the radio and movie myths add up to a cold zero.

Nothing in the popular arts suggests to people of thirty or forty that they can safely read a book, discuss politics, bother about juvenile delinquency, go on a picket line, demonstrate against picket lines, serve on a jury in a civil suit, earn a living, or write a letter to the editor—all of these things and a thousand others are the stigmata of maturity and must be practiced in secret, if at all. The eternal juvenile takes no part in the life of the community and has no resources of his own; to the aging who want to be as like him as they can, he offers other occupations.

## THE BIG GAME

Principally sports. In 1948 the American people spent more money on equipment for fishing than they did at the movie box-offices; on hunting and bowling they spent a billion and a half dollars, almost equally divided, which again is more than they spent to see the movies; the once exclusive pastimes, golf and motor-boating, were so popular that the amount spent on them roughly equaled the movies' take. On these five sports alone Americans spent twenty times as much money as they spent on all the books they bought—and the figure excludes all admission fees at spectator sports. Taking part in sports, looking at others taking part in sports, and talking about sports together constitute a major preoccupation of the American people, and they could of course be more wastefully and mischievously employed.

Sports do, in fact, precisely what the popular arts have failed to do: they supply a counterweight to the uniformity and routines of work in factories and offices and big stores, and a fresh and unpredictable element to balance the sameness of radio and movie programs. But even in spectator sports there has been a gross degradation, which implies a serious loss of sensitiveness in the audience. Wrestling bouts are known to be exhibitions planned in advance, but they are so patently burlesques of sport that they can be tolerated. However, the complete failure to keep college athletics within the liberal limits of the "sanity code," the brassy admission that players are hired, and the growing enthusiasm of the spectators as the games become less and less honest—these are signs that the spirit of sportsmanship is not all it is cracked up to be.

In spite of the influence of gambling on some sports, the spectator sees a contest; the outcome is more uncertain than it is on the average radio mystery show, the surprises are greater than they can possibly be in the formulas of the movies, the reversals of fortune happen more frequently than they do in the dialogues of Rochester and Benny. The people engaged are individuals, they are our prime exemplars of free enterprise when they swing at a pitched ball or hit an opponent on the jaw; they are outside the depressing influence of codes and dictatorships and monopolies. Merely to watch men acting in freedom, under accepted rules, with energy and zeal, is a positive good and a refreshment of the spirit. When people go in for sports themselves, it is a reassertion of human independence miraculous in our time, when the occupations and most of the diversions of men and women have been routined and regularized. The commercialization which has overtaken some sports is distasteful, but on the good side it has taken sports away from the leisure class—except for racquets I can think of no sport that isn't universally practiced; tennis and golf and water sports have been democratized. The forty-hour week, the established Saturday-Sunday week end, as well as vacations with pay, work in with commercial sport to give people a chance at breaking the routine of labor and the almost equally deadening routine of mechanized diversion.

There has grown up around sport, and particularly around the contests that people watch, a whole complex of sentimentalities, ranging from local pride to hero worship, and some of these are manifestly artificial, rigged up by smart publicists and helped along by the color-school of sportswriting.

When sport becomes not a refreshment but an obsession, its real qualities are lost—and its pretenses exposed. Perhaps the Spaniard watching the crisis of a bullfight, when the *espada* is closest to death at the moment of dealing the death blow to the bull, lives vicariously in crisis, perhaps he is suffused at that moment by the tragic sense of life; the last man up with a chance to bring in the winning run in the final inning of the last game of a World Series doesn't pretend to this exalted position; he engages our sensations, our nervous system, and it is a poor diminished kind of man who refuses the tribute of pure excitement at the moment; it is also a man lacking in the full capacities of a human being who can pretend that this is as complete a moment of living as he can experience. That is precisely what the sentimentalists of sport imply; the spasmodic response to the home run or the strikeout becomes an end in itself. It isn't good enough.

*INVESTMENTS IN MATURITY*

We have to ask for more if we are to be mature men and women. The philosopher of the life of reason exhorts us, "Let us be frankly human, let us be content to live in the mind," which is as extreme for most of us as the exhortations of the distractionists who want us to live only by our immediate sensations. Adult life is not the life of an intellectual and it is not the life of instinctive reaction to stimuli: it is the life that the average man can lead if he is not prevented. He is prevented if he is constantly being urged not to put away childish things, to shrink from the awful consequences of a mature and responsible life.

The devices for delaying maturity are heavily capitalized; the enterprises that profit by our coming of age are relatively few. Book publishers, large-scale distributors like the Book-of-the-Month Club, magazines of small circulations and magazines with balanced content like *Life*, live on the accumulated increase of grown-up minds. A magazine may frankly use the lure of sport or sex to gain circulation without lowering its entire tone to the level of the unthinking reader; a publisher may make a small fortune on a historical novel and spend a good part of it on books that do not sell widely. The enemies of mass circulation are critical of these compromises. They challenge the simplifications of science and art in popular magazines and question the cultural value of cheap reprints and book-club choices. They do not see that the popularizers are almost alone among businessmen in having a vested interest in general culture, standing against those mass media which have a vested interest in apathy and ignorance. These popularizers fulfill an essential function; they expose the incurious to new experiences, they set light and serious endeavors side by side, and, if they use sensational effects, they do not actively reduce the range of the average person's interests. Reading and listening to classical music and going to art galleries and getting a smattering of information about science are not in themselves criteria of an intelligent adult life, but the recognition that the arts may be interesting and can enlighten us does counteract the effect of those popular arts which work against enlightenment. The function of the popularizers is not to impose a discipline but to offer attractively more kinds of experience, to extend the range of choice, precisely as *The Atlantic* extends the range of its readers' interests when it publishes Raymond Chandler on mystery stories or Al Capp on the comic strip. The popularizers need a literate, at least partly educated public. They have made their way in the past twenty-five years by a judicious combination of appeals, sometimes answering the same needs as the movies and radio, sometimes gratifying interests neglected by the mass media. They now have to hold their own against television, and they are troubled. They should be.[1] By themselves they may not be powerful enough to counteract this new medium if it turns, like the others, to the exploitation of the infantile. There is no vested interest in maturity, although the maturity of its citizens is the prime interest of the nation. "Preach, dear sir," wrote Jefferson, "a crusade against ignorance." And, he might now add, against immaturity.

[1] In fourteen million homes equipped with radios, *no* magazines are read; families with television sets read fewer magazines than those who do not have them; half the adults in America never buy books.

# The People and the Arts

## THE STANDARD OF LIVING

Sports and the cultural enterprises which do not saturate the mass give us perspective on the popular arts. Certainly the mass media are more interesting than sport, and their exceptional products are prophetic of greatness; the danger in them is that the bulk of their product has none of the range of the popularizers. The tendency is to approach the lower end of the scale of values, to exclude the exceptional. The result is that the popular arts not only convey a flat and limited picture of life, they actually encourage people to limit the range of their emotions and interests. Our standard of living is still considered the highest on earth, but the standard of life is going down. We begin to accept completely the teen-age standard. Nothing in our daily lives must interfere with our having a good time; everything must be attractive to the adolescent. We gain by this a vast improvement in the appearance of our kitchens and living rooms, but the life of charm and leisure (as it appears in advertisements for washing machines) escapes us. Dr. Margaret Mead has suggested that even the young and successful housewife feels this; "she chose wifehood and motherhood, but she did not necessarily choose to 'keep house.'" Perhaps it is because the picture in her mind, as she got it from the movies and radio and from ads in the magazines is not "keeping house" but "playing house." The reluctance to take on the responsibilities of parenthood is in part a refusal to sacrifice the irresponsibility of adolescence and in part a fear that children will interfere with adult pleasures. Marriage itself is not a boundary line between youth and maturity, but having children is; and nothing in the representation of life by the popular arts suggests the intense, complex, and rewarding life of parents; instead we have child worship, which has nothing to do with parenthood, and idolatry for the old mother, which has nothing to do with childhood.

The realities of adult life arrive as a series of shocks. Our psychological systems are unprepared for them, and they are resented because they do not correspond to the promises made to us. Because we reject them, these experiences cannot enrich our emotional life, and we cling to the sensations of youth. We have evolved devices to put off the appearance of maturity and gadgets to entertain us, and we do not feel that our lives lack in variety, that we may become impoverished in our feelings as we become superficial in our thoughts; the gadgets are the most intricate in the world, and they prevent us from facing actuality. But "the contemplation of things as they are, without superstition or imposture, is in itself worth more than a whole harvest of inventions."

It is the function of the popular arts to divert, but not to deceive. When they become the only arts of great numbers of people, they can be held to account for what they do.

Moralists from Plato on down have condemned all the arts because they represent something less than the literal truth; and artists have replied, with some arrogance, that they alone penetrate to the essence of truth below the deceptive surface of facts and figures. To avoid the swampy ground of aesthetic dispute, we can find a reasonable place for the popular arts by putting theories aside and fixing our minds on what these arts actually do to people. Not what their exceptional efforts do, but what they do in bulk, what they are compelled to do by the conditions they have imposed on themselves. If they present a view of life so false that it is dangerous to us, if they prevent the community from raising mature and responsible citizens, their function as entertainment is not fulfilled, and the good they do must be balanced against their failures while we try to discover whether they can change direction without losing their vigor and attractiveness.

So long as the popular arts do not blank out the great arts, comparison between them is useless. When they do, it is worth while examining the qualities ascribed to the great arts to see whether any of them apply to the others. In general it has been assumed that the great arts have these functions:

They give form and meaning to life, which might otherwise seem shapeless and without sense.

They give us a deeper understanding of our own lives and the lives of others.

They express the spirit of an age or people.

By all these things they create a certain unity of feeling.

They provide diversion from the cares of the day and satisfy desires unfulfilled in our common life.

The great arts and the folk arts have in different ways accomplished some or all of these purposes for a great many people. I will presently put down my reasons for not accepting the assertion that the fine arts *alone* represent all that is worth remembering in the life of a nation and for believing that the popular arts have a useful function outside of the one they now perform, which is the last on the list above. As background, I propose to examine some theories about the popular arts and some very practical uses to which they have been put outside of the United States.

## "THE TREASON OF THE INTELLECTUALS"

The popular arts have always worried the moralist and the aesthete.

The true Puritan condemns the pleasures of the people because they are not uplifting, they do not contribute to the glory of God; the aesthete condemns the popular arts because they are

vulgar parodies of the great. In the United States the intellectual
has reflected both of these attitudes, and, perhaps without knowing it, he has reflected also the complex social situation created
by the immigrant and the pioneer. During the early days the
culture and a great part of the wealth of the country was managed by Anglo-Saxons on the Eastern seaboard, while the land
was taken over by westward-moving seekers for security who
were presently reinforced by people of various European stocks.
Even before the Revolution, New England divines denounced
the democratic mob, and the struggle between the coast, the tide-
waters, and the hinterland was on. The strain of radicalism is
one of the few constants in our history, a bright red thread to
follow from the time of Nathaniel Bacon, through Shays and
Jackson, down to our own time. In the great century of expansion, Eastern bankers financed the railroads that opened the West,
but they also took mortgages on farms and controlled the price
of money, so that the wheat grower and the herder felt that they
had to pay back twice as much, in the hard terms of their product, as they had borrowed in currency. In the 1880's the Popu-
lists concentrated fifty years of dissatisfaction into a movement
which colored American political life for generations, as their
useful proposals and their evangelical tone were taken over by
Bryan, Theodore Roosevelt, Wilson, and the New Deal.

There have always been a few writers of radical temperament,
but in the formative century of our growth from a coastal fringe
to a continental nation, the major intellectual movement was
transcendental or communistic or both, and was fatally divorced
from the aspirations of the traditional American radical, whose
chief ambition has always been to correct the unequal distribution
of land or money or power; the average voter, Jacksonian or Populist, Progressive or New Dealer, never turned against private
wealth: he wanted more people to enjoy it. The hapless Alcott
who could not run a farm, the "cranks" who attended reform
conventions, the phalansteries and communities whose sawmills
always burned down, did not impress the westward-moving set-

tler. The intellectuals wanted to make toil agreeable and to share a common wealth; the average man, radical or not, was accustomed to long hours of labor and wanted only a chance to earn as comfortable a living as his neighbor; he did not want to divide his earnings with others. He was not surprised to hear that Charles Fourier, who inspired so many utopian communities, had predicted that the waters of the seven seas would turn into oceans of lemonade; everything the Fourierites suggested seemed equally probable, and nothing they did was any more helpful to the victims of our first era of expansion. Not for the first time or the last, the common man was suspicious of those who loved him.

The writers and the painters longed for European recognition, and many of them went to Europe; the gap between the intellectual and the people widened. The thin and sentimental novels, the stiff pretty paintings, had nothing to say to men who may have been, as Lewis Mumford has said, brutalized by their "rape of a continent"; the men left the arts to the women, and another American tradition took root—that the intellectual life of a community was women's affair. It was an unfortunate division of interest, reducing the area of sympathy between men and women, encouraging men to keep their active life away from their women and women to keep the life of the mind and the spirit away from their husbands; encouraging also the artist to address himself chiefly to women, to be precious and flattering and dandified. Not only did the Hartford Wits and the minor poets of New York divorce themselves from the common life; when the horrors of the degraded mills of Massachusetts were first exposed, and a New England philosopher was asked to help the miserable workers, he answered, "Are they my poor?" Emerson looked back on the era that began scientific studies at the colleges, a time that brought a host of practical inventions as well as the beginnings of a strong labor movement, and coldly remarked that there had not been "a book, a speech, a conversation, or an idea" in the state of Massachusetts. On the day after Lincoln's call for volunteers, the poet-prophet of the common man wrote: "I have this day, this hour, resolved to inaugurate for myself a pure, perfect, sweet, clean-blooded, robust body, by ignoring all drinks but water and pure milk, and all fat meats, late suppers—a great body, a purged, cleansed, spiritualized, invigorated body." Whitman's fellow countrymen ("I utter the word Democracy, the word En Masse") were about to undergo a less dainty regime.

The artists of mid-nineteenth century America set the tradition of escaping to Europe or staying at home and forming coteries of contempt. "Our country is deficient in materials of society most pertinent to the purposes of the novelist," wrote Cooper, and a minor artist like Freneau asked, "How can a poet hope for success in a city where there are not three persons possessed of elegant ideas?" Before he discovered the dense intellectual life that actually surrounded our writers, Van Wyck Brooks accepted this tradition and said that "a vast unconscious conspiracy actuated all America against the creative arts"; at the same time he told us that the world of Longfellow was "a German picture book," that Hawthorne "modeled in mist," that Poe was "sterile and inhuman," and that the heroes and heroines of fiction in their time "lived in a world of moan and moonlight . . . irreparable farewells, dungeons, assassinations, premature burials, hidden treasure . . . gothic castles."

"When one views the nineteenth century in perspective," says Bertrand Russell, "it is clear that Science is its only claim to distinction. Its literary men were second-rate, its philosophers sentimental, its artists inferior to those of other times. Science ruthlessly forced novelties upon it, while men of 'culture' tried to preserve the old picturesque follies by wrapping them in a mist of muddled romanticism." This is the judgment not of a philistine but of a philosopher who is an artist in his own right. If Russell is right, the men who were too busy conquering a wilderness to pay much attention to the arts were less to blame for the isolation of the intellectuals than the intellectuals themselves.

The tradition that America had no place for the artists who

alone could express its inmost soul continued well into our own time. "Suppose I am the national genius," Ludwig Lewisohn suggested in the 1920's, "Dreiser and Mencken and Francis Hackett and I." And Ernest Hemingway wrote that "a country, finally, erodes and the dust blows away, the people die and none of them were of any importance except those who practiced the arts." I cannot accept this elevation of a host of second- and third-rate men for the sake of the merest handful of great artists in any country at any given era; nor do I know any system of values in which the roadbuilder and the research scientist, the saint and the average sinful man who leads a decent life, become of no importance—and along with them Lincoln and Marx, Edison and Freud and Mr. Hemingway's own Belmonte, James J. Hill, Joseph Goldberger and John Humphrey Noyes, in a single universal relegation to non-importance. The idea that only the writer-painter-composer expresses the genius of a nation comes naturally to writers and painters and poets, and a tiny fragment of their work does resist the ravages of time and fashion. But the soul of man manifests itself also in the Declaration of Independence and in a tariff bill, in the song of a stevedore and in the laughter at a clown in the circus.

Both Lewisohn and Hemingway lived for considerable time in Europe during the time of the second great expatriation of American artists. It was natural for those who had a high regard for their sacred mission to go where they thought they would be appreciated, and it was also a little irritating for them to discover that part, at least, of the *avant-garde* abroad was enchanted by the very rudeness and bad taste and bumptiousness from which the Americans had fled. The self-exiles and the debunkers denounced America, shrilly or humorously, their books were bought by the American people, but their total effect on our national culture was not great. They contributed to some refinement of manners, but they did not rescue the country from materialism and they probably helped to bring into existence the anti-intellectual superpatriot who dominated the last years of the 1940's.

It is not an edifying story, and the intellectual can take as little pride in it as the philistine. From the time of James Fenimore Cooper to the day of Sinclair Lewis, writers have found some way to attack the average American, not in loving correction but in contempt. In all that time perhaps two dozen men and women have been artists so great that they were misunderstood; the rest were good, but not good enough to separate themselves from their fellow men; they made little effort to understand what was happening in America, were incapable of helping or guiding or comforting. The theory that the artist was rejected by Americans because he disclosed the emptiness of their lives is only half true; the other half is that the artist had little to give Americans, little that was relevant to their time and situation in the world. "The American intelligentsia," says Eric Bentley, "consists of people isolated from their communities." The isolation is partly self-exile.

Perspective on this long separation between the artist and the people is helpful in understanding the present relation between them. The "misunderstood" artist of the past has given way to the artist who no longer cares whether he is understood or not, since he is not trying to communicate anything in the traditional sense of the word. "All modern art," says Ortega y Gasset, "is unpopular, and it is not so accidentally and by chance, but essentially and by fate." Popular taste has always demanded the recognizable object in a painting, the melody that can be hummed, the order of words that is easy to follow; and the great masters of our time have not been willing to satisfy these demands —nor, indeed, to be romantic or sentimental or particularly moral. Like Stendhal, they are making appointments with posterity.

*FOLK AND "THE FOLKS"*

It is natural that other forms of expression should spring up to serve those whom the lofty arts leave behind. When we meet these forms in the past, we call them folk art; we have been taught to respect them. The ballads of the Scottish border, Negro spirituals, old English songs kept alive in the Appalachians, are among these; they are anonymous, they come down to us changed by generations of singers from their lost original form. As an enemy of "the people," H. L. Mencken vigorously refutes the theory of spontaneous creation, assuming that there must have been an individual who composed a melody or wrote the words, even if nothing was put on paper; but this is political more than aesthetic argument. It is certain that besides the work of professional artists there have been songs and crude drawings and (as in our West) tall tales which gave pleasure to people and were adaptable, so that they ran through many changes and persisted for generations. (The smutty story is a modern example; I do not know of an authoritative study of its origins and transmutations.)

In spite of their obvious differences, folk art and popular art have much in common; they are easy to understand, they are romantic, patriotic, conventionally moral, and they are held in deep affection by those who are suspicious of the great arts. Popular artists can be serious, like Frederic Remington, or trivial, like Charles Dana Gibson; they can be men of genius like Chaplin or men of talent like Harold Lloyd; they can be as universal as Dickens or as parochial as E. P. Roe; one thing common to all of them is the power to communicate directly with everyone.

## ART AND POLITICS

As I am concerned with the practical effects of the popular arts, I am not too interested in theories of their origin. But as most modern theories on the subject are actually extensions of political argument, and as politics may decide whether the popular arts are to continue free, I have made notes on a few interesting points of view, some of them totally opposed to my own. T. S. Eliot's conviction that all culture must be aristocratic and religious reflects his admiration for a churchly and highly classified society; romantic rebels against tradition exalt the primitive, the naive artists; the demagogue sneers at the intellectual minority and calls its art anti-American; and the non-communist Marxian holds that the popular arts are commercialized and corrupted versions of the arts of the people.

The theory that assigns the most important position to the popular arts is held in Moscow; the Soviet Union is the only place in the world where a movie, a comic strip, a comedy, a magazine illustration, must be considered primarily for its effect on the people, and the only place where symphonic composers are rebuked by the government for deviation from true principles. If we are shocked by a composer's unmanly haste to repent, we must remember that even a reprimand from the Politburo is such recognition of the power of the artist as he could never find elsewhere. The principle that the artist must serve the state, following an official aesthetic, is foreign to us, and I am not sure that the reports we have of the merit of Soviet art are altogether unprejudiced.

But if the details of Soviet practice seem ludicrous to us, the basic approach to the arts has to be reckoned with. The artist is believed to have a profound influence, he is as important as the educator, the police spy, or the statesman in the united effort to establish the socialist state and create a new man. With this approach all entertainment must fall under the direction of the state. In the United States the influence of government, whether federal or local, is limited to those artists who voluntarily accept work from the state, and the entertainment arts are, officially, untouched by the hand of authority. The function of the artist is not defined, his activities are not restricted except by the specific laws covering obscenity, slander, and other misdemeanors which he may commit as a citizen. Our general attitude toward the artist is one of tolerant skepticism if he is difficult; it ranges from deep affection to idolatry if he is simple; but he has no position as a revolutionary power; except in wartime he is not an instrument of policy.

It would be remarkable if these two diametrically opposite principles should, in practice, produce identical results. They often do.

The analysis of the entertainment arts offered by non-communist radicals shows how. These critics are enemies of the all-powerful state and of uninhibited capitalism; they are consequently in the traditional line of American radical thought. They differ from Mencken and his followers because they earnestly want the artist to speak to the people; they want him to be aware of his creative power; they want him to reflect in his work the issues of our time. They are, moreover, emancipated from the genteel tradition and do not scorn the comic strip or film or radio, although they are not always successful in using these instruments. Among them, James Farrell and Dwight Mac-Donald are particularly clear in their statements.

"In America," says Mr. Farrell, "a tremendous commercial culture has developed as a kind of substitute for a genuinely popular, a genuinely democratic culture." By his definition, a democratic culture "would re-create and thus communicate how the mass of the people live, how they feel about working, loving, enjoying, suffering, and dying." But, "owing to basic economic causes, something of the most profound significance has happened in American culture: it has been invaded by finance capital. American commercial culture is owned and operated by finance capital." Finance capital is responsible for the conditions of American life which "create alienated and truncated personalities. . . . The conditions of earning one's bread in this society create the lonely modern man." Mr. Farrell sees the movies answering a desperate want of companionship, presenting again and again "the same reveries, the same daydreams, the same childish fables of success and happiness. So much of the inner life of men is dried up that they tend to become filled with yearnings and to need . . . consolation. Tastes are thus conditioned."

The movies serve the finance-capitalistic state because most of them "distract the masses of the people from becoming more clearly aware of their real needs; . . . they distract people from the real and most important problems of life." They do this by the perpetuation of certain myths. "The values generally emphasized are those of rugged individualism. . . . The dominant characteristics . . . are those of the pioneer. The past is re-created in accents of weak nostalgia; the present glorified. The future is promised as no different. . . . What characterizes almost all Hollywood pictures is their inner emptiness. A culture . . . should help to create those states of consciousness, of awareness of one's self, of others, and of the state of the world, which aid in making people better, and in preparing them to make the world better." (Substitute "citizens of the Soviet state" for "people" and the categorical imperative would be accepted in Moscow.) "Hollywood films usually have precisely the opposite effect; most of them make people less aware, or else falsely aware. This, to me, is the sense in which Hollywood films fail to fulfill the real cultural needs of the masses."

Mr. Farrell is a candid moralist; in other passages his contempt for the film as entertainment is made clear. "What serious person in the whole world history of mankind has ever argued that in order to bring light to a darkened world . . . it is necessary to entertain?" he asks, discussing war propaganda films and Hollywood's insistence that films with serious messages must be successful at the box-office. "Did Jesus Christ and the Twelve Apostles believe that in order to spread the Gospel they had to do so with entertainment? . . . When you really teach, you do not need to entertain. . . ." This is an attitude with which I do not sympathize, but I can respect Mr. Farrell's position; in hundreds of films he has seen every element of intelligence, of human reason, of individual character, degraded in the sacred name of entertainment; he feels that when people are entertained by low devices, their status as human beings deteriorates; so he turns against entertainment.

Dwight MacDonald's position strikes me as being somewhat less doctrinaire; T. S. Eliot has said that it is the only position opposed to his own for which he has much respect. In an essay on "High and Popular Culture," MacDonald has developed these points: The old upper-class monopoly of culture has been broken down by political democracy and mass education, and capitalism has found a market for mass-culture products; in order to sell their movies, phonograph records, reprint books, and the like, the dealers in these products manipulate the cultural needs of the people; they do not satisfy popular taste (as Robert Burns did)— they exploit it. On one side, popular culture is a continuation of folk art, but it is also a vulgarized reflection of high culture, and the pressure on artists has become so great that they now must compete with the merchants of popular art—because bad stuff, following Gresham's law, drives out good. A generation or so ago the *avant-garde* did not compete, the theater had not degraded itself into being a feeder for the movies, and the movies themselves had a small coterie of artists, including Griffith and Chaplin. Now the theater and the movies are at the same level, and the movies, though better entertainment, are worse art. Since the popular arts feed foolish myths to the people and at the same time draw down the level of the great arts, the exploitation of popular taste becomes a serious threat to democracy.

I have always found the Marxists' analysis of the past more persuasive than their prophetic vision; and these two non-Stalinist dissections of the present state of popular culture seem to me impressive because they deal with a possible situation: the creation of a democratic art. They also imply the alternative: the development of a popular art which will end with the robotization of humanity. Mr. Eliot's position is irrelevant to my interests because I neither foresee (nor desire to experience) the creation of a highly stratified aristocratic and hierarchic state in America. His own early poetry indicates that he once was influenced by, and perhaps even took pleasure in, one of the popular arts, in his use of the rhythms of jazz to contrast with the stately phrases of the past. But I feel that he is not a useful guide to the politics of democratic culture precisely because he has turned his back on the reasonably possible future.

In the sections devoted to the separate entertainment arts I have tried to sketch the economic background of each and have accepted, as normal and natural, that the popular arts in a capitalist society reflect the ethics and practices and mythology of capitalism. My major ground of criticism has been that we are also in a democratic society which is not totally capitalist, and that the popular arts do not sufficiently reflect the ethics and the aspirations of a democracy; holding no grudge against entertainment, I feel that the failure of the popular arts rises from the low value placed on them by the exploiters who are willing to provide entertainment for a mass minority; they neglect the profit and honor they could win if they cultivated the entire field instead of plowing and harrowing the same lower forty over and over again. I differ from Mr. Farrell because I do not believe as devoutly as he does in the mission of the arts, great or small; I see a place even for entertainment that distracts and limits, provided it does not monopolize the field, provided even those who care for the cheapest kind of diversion are exposed at intervals to other types of entertainment.

My difference with Mr. MacDonald is largely one of approach. He seems to feel that the big battalions cannot be on the side of God and that mass entertainment under capitalism is condemned to operate on a quick turnover of the cheapest and shoddiest goods. Neither he nor Mr. Farrell allows sufficiently for the particular arrangements of the movie industry—for instance, the system of distribution which dominates the methods of production and which is not the only system capable of operating with profit; they seem to assume that the present combinations are not only typically capitalist but unchangeable. They may be right, but I do not believe they are. The manipulators of public taste will change their methods under pressure and give us new kinds of pictures and programs if that is the only way for them to make a profit.

I differ with Mr. MacDonald also in his dark diagnosis of the ills of the superior artist who is compelled to compromise with his inferiors. He appears to believe that expanding capitalism drove between the artist and the people, forcing them apart, and compelled the artist to work for a small, appreciative fringe group; but, as I have noted in the preceding section, it seems equally fair to say that the artist in America took the initiative, rejecting the woes and passions of the average man, and then complained that he was not appreciated.

It is a misfortune that this tradition of hostility between the artist and the people should persist in the age of mass entertainment. As each new medium comes into being, the intellectual shies away. In fifty years of movies, many first-rate novels and plays have been adapted, but few writers of the first order have tried to master the movies as a craft, as a new mode of expression for themselves. In radio's brief span, one American poet, Archibald MacLeish, has been conspicuously represented by a work expressly written to be broadcast; there have been one or two others who halfheartedly tried their hands at the job, without troubling too much to learn the capacities and the limitations of the instrument; I know of no attempt made by broadcasters to enlist poets. The only complete reconciliation between the American artist-intellectual and the average man came between Pearl Harbor and the death of President Roosevelt; we have reverted since to an armed truce, with serious threats of open conflict. The congressional ferret is only a symptom of a sustained effort to make all intellectual activity appear disloyal; modern painting, progressive education, serious fiction, purely theoretical approaches to sexual problems, have been as viciously attacked in Congress or in the press as the Mendelian law in the Soviet Union. We are still able to fight back at encroachments on our civil liberties, but the atmosphere of free activity in which the speculative mind lives is being polluted. The attack is so determined, and the defense so splintered, that Huey Long's prediction of a dictatorship may come true in the realm of the intellect long before our actual political liberty is jeopardized; and as Long suggested, it will be one hundred per cent American.

## THE COMMON OAF

I have emphasized the estrangement between the artists and the audience because a revolutionary change of attitude is urgent. It may even be too late. The manufacturers of commercial entertainment have done their work well, and the audience is conditioned to suspect or despise the thinking man. But it is not too late for the average intelligent man to become aware of the new situation and to do something drastic about it.

The new situation, as I see it, is a persistent, unremitting, successful attack on the reasonable man of intelligence, the balanced man of thought and feeling, the individual who has so far escaped the contagion of mass thinking.

In an extreme and obvious form, this anti-intellectualism appears in both radio and the movies as an attack on education; not only on progressive methods (which would reflect the social attitude of twenty years ago) but on all education, and this goes against the essential American tradition. At a time when the school system of the entire country is woefully understaffed and teachers are forced to menial occupations in order to eke out their sub-standard salaries, both radio and the movies consistently present two images: the angular spinster and the absent-minded professor, the former without sympathy, the latter without respect. Perhaps there have been some favorable presentations of the teacher, but in years of listening at random and in something like eighteen months of scrupulous observation, I have noted not one comedy program in which a teacher was not made into a figure of fun. Then, too, all the programs about adolescents are in the same vein: the sympathetic character is the one that, in a group of semi-intelligent people, knows less than they do. The studious child, the adolescent who reads a book, the young professional man able to discuss his own work, are all foils for the triumphant ape.

The movie version is necessarily drenched in romance. The wise elderly character-actor-professor occasionally appears, and the research laboratory, which is highly pictorial, is used as a setting. The typical figure remains the youngish scholar so engrossed in his work that he forgets about love and is brought down by an adolescent chit. Her wisdom is greater than his. The movies' great tribute to the intellect is in the figure of Mr. Belvedere, a man of vast erudition, possessed of an elaborate vocabulary and a studied rudeness. A novelist working as a baby-sitter, he develops the attributes of the Admirable Crichton, coping with all domestic emergencies, notably disposing of an unruly child by plastering its face with porridge. The novelty of an intellectual who could deal with practical affairs was a nine days' wonder; on the tenth Belvedere was cut down to size and became a figure in a movie series, the old stereotype standing on its head for a change, a loquacious marionette.

The stereotype was invented in the days when the man of learning was rare, a remote and cloistered figure, and even primary education was limited to the few. Since the principle of universal education has been accepted, since heavy industry is founded on scientific research, since higher education is becoming more and more a requirement for good jobs, the attack on the trained mind is a mean anachronism. It flatters and exploits the victims of our educational system, those who have failed to benefit by it, and it calls in question the basic premise of the American political system.

## THE AGE OF CONSENT

The motives for using stock figures to belittle the intelligence are mixed. In general, stock figures possess certain advantages: they are ready-made, requiring no brainwork or imagination to launch them into action; they are familiar to the audience; they correspond to the myths being told. But there are other motives. Radio, perhaps unconsciously, pokes fun at the average intelligent person because he does not fit into the climate of passive acceptance which commercial broadcasting has to induce; the intelligent man is to an extent critical; he asks questions, he is curious. These

aspects of his nature are not necessary to the success of broadcasting, which concentrates on the average man's weariness after
a day's work as it does on the daydreams of women when husband and children have left them to do the housework alone. A
mixture of laughter, excitement, and sentimentality is indicated;
the audience must be receptive, as nearly passive as possible; as
a service to his clients, the broadcaster must paralyze the critical,
questioning faculties of the human mind. The commercial message will be delivered smoothly or peremptorily, it will appeal
to the customer's ambitions, offer him a way to success in life
and a solution to personal problems, or it will hammer hammer
hammer (in the triple rhythm of repeated assertions, with three
double-barreled adjectives) and the audience must never sense
the exaggeration, never ask for proof. This is "the engineering of
consent" carried to a high pitch, for it not only induces a mood
of friendliness, it blankets and suffocates all those faculties which
interfere with the creation of the empty mind.

Radio has a supreme advantage over the movies because its
fundamental rhythm is natural, it is based on the rising and the
setting of the sun, the division of time into days; and this is fortified by the common rhythm of the working day, the rhythm of
the recurrent days of rest. Five days a week we come home at
six-sixteen and are through dinner at seven-thirty and go to bed
at ten; into that routine the radio fits admirably. The rhythm of a
new picture every Thursday and Monday is artificial, and each
offering must be advertised as a powerful attraction because going to the movies is a break in routine for grownups, not a habit.
The movies, with nothing to sell but the entertainment they
offer, with no obligation to a commercial sponsor, might be freer
to induce the mood of contemplation or the mood of criticism
in the audience; they have not done so because they have chosen
to work for a minority audience, profiting by the habit of
movie-going before the years of maturity. Radio has a wider range
and a narrower objective. It must make more and more people
more and more suggestible. It does this not only by the quality

of its entertainment but by its mass. What one station cannot attract, another will; there is always something on the air; more abundant and more accessible than any other diversion known to man, its grand objective is to make man want diversion of no other kind or quality.

In *The Mature Mind*, Dr. Harry Overstreet has analyzed this aspect of broadcasting and noted that "from the advertiser's point of view" it is not good business to put on programs "that raise any basic issue about the economic structure within which advertising operates." This is true in practice, and it is not surprising; it points, however, to a remarkable psychological effect: the revolutionary new medium of communication is almost entirely in the service of the past. By a sort of internal pun, radio has succumbed to its first enemy: it has become static.

A review of the salient characteristics of broadcasting will demonstrate this. The repetitive beat is in itself an argument against change; it is an invitation to do the same thing at the same time, without end. The immortality of the daytime serial is only an extreme form of the permanence of radio types; the characters created by comedians are almost equally static—they may be old for the sake of a gag, but they do not age. Dramatic productions are drawn from the past or from the current movies glorifying the attitudes of the past, using characters which became stereotypes in the past. The resistance to change is reflected in the popularity of program types and of individuals: the ten highest-ranking programs of last year were the ten favorites of 1940, with only a slight shift in the order of popularity, and the programs were fundamentally unchanged in material and techniques. We are getting prewar entertainment in the postwar world.

Our present political temper is a reassertion of the American past against the Communist future; in this atmosphere radio does not need to be illiberal in order to slow down the tempo of change. It is enough to sentimentalize or glorify the past, and radio does this not only by using history and by reviving stock figures of the past, but, more subtly, by implying that the future will be based not so much on the present as on the past. "The same thing but more of it" is the essence of radio's promise. It requires no effort, the receptive listener at home need neither think nor act. He is being kept comfortable, he is being entertained, in an America gone static.

The fundamental American tradition is that we came away from the fixed world of Europe to create a dynamic country, with freedom to move, to change, to work; with opportunity to learn; with a chance to rise in the world; with a duty to keep the free spirit of the country free. Even the concentration of power in relatively few hands and the full development of vast industrial operations has not entirely checked the flow of Americans from job to job, from place to place, from the south to the north, from farms to cities to suburbs, from everywhere to California; and this persistence of change reflects the one emotion all Americans hold in common, that the future is theirs to create. It is a confession that the present is not perfect and an assertion that nothing in the present can prevent us from changing for the better.

### OTHER PEOPLE, OTHER SYSTEMS

The creation of a social apparatus for controlling the effects of our mass media will have to come from ourselves, but we can learn something from observing the machinery used elsewhere. In the Soviet Union the popular arts are in the service of the state and are recognized as creative forces; they condition people to be good by the Soviet standard of goodness. We maintain that this results in slavery, which is approximately what they think of our system. The grain of truth we can get from the Soviet critics is important: they see that our mass media do have a creative effect on our lives. That they do not like the effect is of small consequence.

In the British system of broadcasting, which came into being long before the Labour government, a corporation created by the state is allowed to function independently, subject to criticism and review. The listener contributes to the cost of broadcasting through an annual tax on receivers, and this probably tends to limit the distribution of radio sets; compared to one set for every two inhabitants in the United States, Britain has one for hardly every family. The listener has a choice of stations, and in addition to the erudite Third Program, popular and highbrow entertainments are balanced on the regular schedules. Although the BBC is licensed by the state, it has not been seriously accused of following a party line under the present government or its Conservative predecessor. It has been notably successful in dramatic experiments and, like our radio, has created popular personalities in the field of comedy. One of its signal achievements was the magnificent pioneer work done in television; by 1939 British TV programs were as far advanced as ours were ten years later.

The purpose of the BBC is to give the listener a great deal of what he wants and to give him a chance to want other things as well. The British fall below our standards of showmanship, especially in serious programs; on the other hand, the prestige of such programs is high, they are offered at hours of peak listening, not apologetically. Like the controlled radio of the Soviet Union, the responsible radio of Britain is engaged in the business of making good citizens; unlike the Soviet radio, the BBC holds with us that the citizen is all the better for exercising the right to choose what he shall hear; and, unlike ourselves, the British offer not only different programs, but programs of different kinds, reflecting many levels of experience, and offers them with equal enthusiasm. The "mixed economy" of British radio has not been entirely satisfactory to all the listeners, some of whom express admiration for the livelier air of America and tune in to the Continental stations, which carry commercials and are more competitive. The British system has been held up as a model to Americans, but no one has persuaded the American people that they can entrust any part of their entertainment to a government corporation which might become partisan or highbrow and take from us the double challenge of freedom to offer and freedom to choose.

Both the Soviet and the British systems confront us with the same problem: can we afford a completely free market in entertainment, particularly in those entertainments which are also means of communication?

The alternative to the free market is some sort of official control. Although the freedom of the market is only relative and real power tends to become concentrated in fewer hands, we are not yet in the hands of monopoly, and the regulation of the big entertainment business may still be possible without calling in Big Government. The number of broadcasting stations (AM, FM, and TV) has risen to over three thousand, and while few of the influential ones are really independent, the opportunity for individual action remains; the hold of the big studios on the big theaters has been relaxed. We are actually in a swing of the pendulum away from bureaucratic control, and only monumental follies committed by the exploiters of our mass media will persuade the average man, or the average congressman, that the movies should operate under federal license or television be policed for good taste by the FCC.

## THE "BOOK" BUSINESS

In one associated field the folly has been monumental enough, and although the action taken has been on a limited and local scale, the failure of law that is not backed by public opinion is clear. That is in the case of the comic books. In several respects these books resemble the other media I have discussed; they are pervasive, with some seven hundred million of them printed each year; they are readily accessible; they exist at a single intellectual level; and their mass coupled with the velocity of their circulation makes it difficult for printed material at other levels to overtake them. At post exchanges during the war they sold ten times as many copies as *Life*, *The Reader's Digest*, and *The Saturday*

*Evening Post* combined. Unlike the other mass media, comic books have almost no aesthetic interest.

They provide, on the other hand, the best example of the paralysis of public power, and it is primarily in that respect that I am considering them here. The reader knows that the comic books are a lineal descendant of the newspaper comic strip, which has itself undergone many changes in recent years. The self-contained strip of a generation ago, with a joke of sorts in the final picture, has been almost entirely displaced by continued stories, many of them of domestic life, and the Chicago school of comic artists responsible for this realism is also responsible for the most conspicuous use of the comic strip for fairly open political propaganda; on the other hand, the spirit of true fantasy which vanished when George Herrimann, the creator of Krazy Kat, died, has reappeared to a degree in the work of the gifted Al Capp. Like the comic books, strips are popular among adults.

After a number of strips had been collected and printed in book form, the potential popularity of the new form was shown when one book was offered as a premium by a radio advertiser; but the true comic book, a work created expressly for monthly publication, did not impress the public until "Superman" appeared in the June 1938 issue of *Action Comics*. When it became clear that the success of *Action Comics* was largely due to the "Superman" section, the hero achieved a remarkable eminence; he appeared in a quarterly, all by himself (he was also in a newspaper strip, on the air, and for a brief time in the movies—the wild laughter of the movie audiences may have frightened the producers). Dozens of imitators appeared, and some established themselves. Eventually a practical psychologist, deciding that America was becoming a matriarchy, created a superwoman. The preoccupation with crime foreshadowed by an earlier book, *Detective Comics*, did not diminish, and these books are, in fact, the ones that have brought down the fury of parents, police powers, and psychiatrists. As the business grew, other types appeared: the comic book has its economic background in the pulp-magazine business, and romantic stories, true confessions, and the other staples of the pulps have been adapted to the new medium.

Several of the publishing houses have provided themselves with distinguished advisory boards, including psychiatrists who defend the comic books on the ground that they stir the imagination of children, present life in the only terms the child can understand, and give the young a sense of security. Neither they nor their opponents can isolate the effect of the comic books from the effect of the movies and radio, from the headlines and the pictures in tabloids, from conversations in the street and the particular tensions which a child absorbs from his surroundings. The defenders concede the occasional appearance of a sadistic panel, but they assert that the bulk of the comic books is essentially serviceable to society. In the few instances where crime has been traced to the reading of this literature, the defenders say that the connection is loose, that a predisposition to delinquency must have existed, and that normal children must not be denied their rights because of the slight danger that a few may be badly affected.

The attack takes several forms. Attempts have been made to compete in the market, notably by Parent-Teacher groups who have encouraged the publication of historical or scientific books similar in appearance to the horrors; [1] small boycotts have been threatened; bills forbidding the sale of comic books to children under a specific age have been introduced in state legislatures; and in extreme cases summary action has been taken. In Los Angeles County, in 1948, an ordinance was passed to prevent the sale of any publications depicting "the commission or attempted

[1] Commercial houses have also experimented. In a comic-book version of *Macbeth*, the witches and murders and battles are faithfully exploited; the poetry is adapted to the style of the drawings. Thoughtful readers, however, will note that Shakespeare is corrected, his speech and his grammar being considered improper for the young. "Lay on, MacDuff" is acceptable; the rest of the exhortation has been changed to read: "and cursed be him who first cries 'Hold, enough.' "

commission of the crimes of arson, assault with caustic chemicals, assault with a deadly weapon, burglary, kidnaping, mayhem, murder, rape, robbery, theft, or voluntary manslaughter." Before the law had gone into effect, the sheriff of the County learned from a fourteen-year-old boy that a recipe for poison in a comic book had given him the idea of poisoning an old woman, and a hanging and a burglary were also traced to the inspiration of comic books. In half a dozen other communities, within the space of a few months, similar cases were reported. Agitation flared up, the Association of Comics Magazine Publishers, representing only a limited number of important houses in the field, announced a code of minimum editorial standards which emphasized indecency as much as violence; the bathing suit was accepted as the norm for nudity, and "sexy, wanton comics" were banned. The presentation of crime was accepted, but a warning was issued against throwing sympathy against law and justice, and comics were urged not to show details and methods of crime (when committed by young people); sadistic torture was not to be shown, and "divorce should not be treated humorously"—a hint that the Production Code of the movies had been remembered. Two years later juvenile crimes were still being traced to comic books, laws were still being proposed, and parents were raging helplessly. If violence had diminished in the comic books, it still had a long way to go. An early tabulation based on a hundred comic books to which had been added a thousand comic strips, gave the following figures: major crimes depicted, 218; minor crimes, 313; physical assaults, 531; sadistic acts, 87; physical monstrosities, 165.

One comic book of 1948 examined by Albert Deutsch "demonstrates to the child reader how to gouge eyes with the thumb, choke off the windpipe, kick an opponent in the stomach . . . flatten his arch with the heel, bite his ears, kick him in the liver area, punch him in the spine . . . all this under the protective title 'self-defense' with the explanation that this is the way T-men render their enemies *hors de combat*." The late George Orwell, who had a fine eye for popular iconography, connected American comics with the dollar shortage. "Are we actually using dollars to pay for this pernicious rubbish?" he inquired, and proceeded to describe: ". . . a beautiful creature called The Hangman, who has a green face, and, like so many characters in American strips, can fly. . . . A picture of . . . an ape-like lunatic, or an actual ape dressed up as a man, strangling a woman so realistically that her tongue is sticking four inches out of her mouth. . . . A python looping itself around a man's neck and then hanging him by suspending itself over a balustrade; . . . a man jumping out of a skyscraper window and hitting the pavement with a splash. There is much else of the same kind." The testimony continues: Sterling North noted "women strapped while sleeping, women thrown to their deaths from skyscraper windows, men shot in the back . . . children being tortured, specifically named poison being slipped into drinks. . . ." G. Legman, analyzing the comics in *Neurotica*, says, "With rare exceptions every child in America who was six years old in 1938 has by now [1948] absorbed an absolute minimum of eighteen thousand pictorial beatings, shootings, stranglings, blood-puddles, and torturings-to-death from comic (ha-ha) books. . . ." The Queensboro Federation of Mothers Clubs finds "manifestations of brutality, cruelty, and violence, . . . sexy portrayals and abominable English. . . ."

I have quoted the testimony of others because my own list is limited and because most of these outcries represent the attitude of parents searching for a way to cope with a powerful business enterprise which they consider positively evil. Even if they are exaggerating, even if the effect of the comic books on their children is not corrupting, the basic situation is still that parents have not been able to impose their will upon the publishers. Not enough parents are concerned, and those who are have not yet found the way to make their pressure felt. In that respect they are an ominous example; for the urgent need of the moment is precisely to discover new modes of applying pressure, to persuade a sufficient number of people that their own immunity from any ill is only an illusion, to persuade them to observe the facts and to act. The occasional flurry of good resolutions that follows even partial action against the comic books is a good sign; but, like the code of the broadcasters, the lofty promises of the publishers flourish on violations. Year after year Dr. Fredric Wertham brings forth panels showing new ugliness and sadistic atrocities; year after year his testimony is brushed aside as extravagant and out-of-date. The paralysis of the parent is almost complete.

The economic situation is a simple one. The newsstand receipts for comic books totals seventy-two million dollars a year; the wholesale distributors of these books count on them for a third of their total magazine sale; the spending money of the young runs to seventy million a week, and this vast sum (about three billion dollars a year) must be absorbed; the drug and candy and stationery stores that handle comic books profit by additional sales (of sodas, fountain pens, mouth organs, and ukuleles), and the books must be carried to attract the trade. The field is dominated by a half-dozen houses each of which publishes a wide range of books: Western, romance, "scientific," murder, and so on. Like the movies, they have developed a system of block-booking which prevents the retailer from exercising any discretion: if he wants the best-seller, he must take the others as well; he cannot eliminate those which bring disrepute.

The comic book is often compared to the dime novel of fifty years ago, chiefly by friends of the publishers and by independent admirers of gore for the little ones; it is not altogether a safe comparison for them to make. The dime novel was a printed text, sparsely illustrated, if at all, and therefore had to be read; the number of different ones available to the average child was small compared to a selection of dozens of comic books at every stand, out of a total of over two hundred and fifty published each month; and the dime novel was severely criticized precisely because it was different in tone from everything else the child could enjoy; there were neither serial movies nor murder-and-suspense programs on the radio to reinforce the lessons in violence. Present-day sentimentality over the Nick Carter stories is, finally, a throwback to youth; and the comic book, as we know, does not give up its hold as youth passes. It appears to be the most satisfactory kind of reading matter when one cannot go to the movies or listen to the radio.

We have here perhaps the real reason for the paralysis of the parents. In a Midwest city nearly two-thirds of the comic-book readers are adults; in the low-income group, nearly one-third of all adults are readers. It is possible that some of these enthusiasts will keep their favorite reading from their children, but not probable. The parents who wish to keep the comic books from their children are non-readers; they may outnumber the fans in a specific community, but they cannot take effective action unless they bring to their side the childless who dislike the comic books and the parents whose children have grown up—they have to convince that part of the general public which has no immediate personal interest in the matter, the same public that must learn the truth about all the popular arts: you cannot, by avoiding them, escape their effects. But the citizen who thinks himself untouched because he excludes any influence of the mass media from his life is harder to reach, unless, perhaps, his protected child is attacked by a gang of boys who have not been protected. He believes that some things are bad for people, but he thinks of "people" as "other people." There are, to be sure, private vices which by common consent are tolerated—such as gluttony. There are offenses against custom which are punished privately, as divorcées are ostracized at Court; an extensive local option is invoked to protect a township or a county where the variety of opinion in an entire state prevents a general law; and by a wise tradition federal laws are limited to such actions as no smaller body can cope with. Of all crimes against the person, only kidnaping is punishable under a federal statute; murder and reckless driving are local affairs. But recognizable danger eventually brings the appropriate defense into play; no appeal to State Rights will stop the government from acting against a plague, and the citizen seeing contagion spread across his boundary line will demand action at the highest level, by-passing local authority, if panic sets in.

Crime is the spectacular feature of the comic books, and since I am interested in public reaction, I have used it to illustrate a point. But it would not be entirely honorable if I did not note that after some ten years of unavailing public protest the emphasis has shifted; in the first half of 1950 dozens of crime, Western, and other comic books became "love books," comparable in material to the confession and romance pulp-magazines. I cannot say with certainty that this change was caused by objections to the horror magazines, of which an ample number remain in the field; I do know that parents have begun to object as seriously to the tone of these books as they did to the others. Those I have seen appear to range from the innocuous to the vulgar, but I am not yet familiar enough with them to say whether they will do anything more than repeat the conventional love patterns of the other mass media.

## CORDON SANITAIRE

The good and the evil of the communications arts have often been assessed; their special quality, which on the bad side can be called contagion, is not fully understood. If we become suddenly aware of it, if demagogues exaggerate the evil for their own purpose, we can get an hysterical cry for the government to step in. We can avoid the disaster if we know precisely how great the danger is and find the means to contain it, moving deliberately to isolate the danger spots; we can do it only if we know there is no immunity for ourselves, there is no place to hide.

Although the comic book in itself is not as spectacular as other media, it is an excellent proving ground for all the forms of pressure and control. The dispute between psychiatrists and the conflicting testimony of other authorities can be resolved, and the serious charge that psychiatrists are paid to defend the comic books can be impartially examined. A body of fact is ascertainable, the potential evil can be estimated. If the facts warrant, action can be taken step by step, without permanent damage to any civilian right, because any law that limits the circulation of comic books can eventually be brought to the Supreme Court. Local ordinances are naturally directed against the seller. As many states have a law against the publication and/or sale of indecent and lewd books, the courts can be called on to determine whether the ordinances are legal. Some of the fifty communities which have taken this first step have tried to ban comic books entirely or to forbid their sale to children under eighteen. In California and in New York attempts have been made to pass a state law against the sale, not the publication, of offensive literature. One law, vetoed by Governor Dewey, required a seal of approval from a state agency, which would have meant, in effect, that the state was exercising a censorship in advance of publication. Local boards, operating as various state boards of censorship do for the movies, have been set up to sift the acceptable comic books from the objectionable, giving the seller immunity from prosecution if he handles only those that are approved. In all cases of action based on local or state law, two possibilities arise: the law invoked locally may head off any appeal to higher authority or—the reverse—the acceptance of a local law may be only the entering wedge for state or eventually federal action.

The slightest appeal to law brings up thorny questions, the first of which is whether any community can forbid the sale of any printed matter *to minors alone* without violating the First Amendment; the appeal to law also reflects the feeling that no other power can be completely effective. In Hammond, Indiana, the newsdealers eliminated thirty-eight books against which religious and civic leaders had protested—a threat of total boycott went with the protest. It was pointed out that children could still get what they wanted by taking a five-minute bicycle ride to adjoining Calumet City. It was also pointed out, in connection with using the code as a form of protection, that only thirty per cent of the industry subscribed to it; the publishers of some of the best and of all of the worst are not members of the Association.

The sudden spurt of anger, the quick decision to do something, accomplish limited objectives. They prove that public opinion can be massed and that pressure can be effective at isolated points. The opponents of legal action invoke the principle of clear and present danger; when an ordinance is passed or other summary action is taken after an overt act, the danger is presumed to exist, but the spasmodic action is usually temporary and local, and we have something like the Eighteenth Amendment on a small scale with bootlegging not far behind. The publishers are untouched because fundamentally the public is untouched; the problem of eliminating a social danger without destroying the right to publish has not been met because the danger is still considered a private one.

## THE LAW OF THE LAWLESS

I have omitted adjacent but vitally significant problems of the comic book because I wanted to concentrate on the one aspect that can lead to intelligent action, the connection with crime. I have not even assumed that the connection is proved; a spokesman for part of the industry has entered a blanket denial. I assume only that proof or disproof can be found, and if the connection is established attention will be focused on the inadequacy of our present social apparatus to deal with it.

To that weakness the other aspects of the comic book contribute, by creating an atmosphere favorable to their prosperity. It is an atmosphere of violence, of contempt for the processes of law; not only is the criminal central to action, but the hero is himself lawless; he beats up villains, he kills enemies, without benefit of trial by jury. He parlays hero-worship into Führer-worship, and in this he is enormously aided by the figures who defy the laws of gravitation and smash the lightning with their fists, destroying malefactors and monsters, annihilating, on their way, "the armies of unalterable law." Children have always doted on the impossible, but at the same time they erect a logic of their own by which to judge what they hear. They accept the conditional mode of the old fairy tale where everything is given to the hero provided he does not forget to touch a certain flower or to say a specific word; they accept penalties and forfeits, which reflect something perilous in the adventures of life. The comic-book "heros" are outside all conditions. "At the rate I'm going," says Superman, speeding to prevent a bomb explosion on a train, "we're sure to be on the scene of the disaster *wherever it happens*." This is more than omnipresence: it is a super-Einsteinian binding of time and space. This world of supernatural power in which beings constantly fight, but never work or think, is contrasted with the world of men, and the men come off badly; Superman has a human alter ego, Clark Kent; Kent is not very interesting.

In this world of scientific marvels, the scientist is either "mad" or works for the general good, and obviously in a world where science is in itself sane enough, but has been put to the uses of mass destruction, the comic book version is reassuring. Science is reduced to the fabrication of gadgets which reverse the laws of science—in this the sane and the mad do not differ—and on the side of society or against it, science is used to do what human law, and civilization based on law, cannot do. It is a complete surrender to the philosophy of power. That is the sum of the comic-book report on society; about the individual it tells us that the criminal is a monster, which justifies any atrocity practiced upon him.

As Mr. Legman has pointed out, in his "Psychopathology of the Comics," the punishment that followed the escapades of the Katzenjammer Kids is no longer required; their butt was a human being, Der Captain, and justice was done at the end of each series; when a monstrous menace was substituted for a human being, no punishment, but rather reward or honor, follows the most violent brutality. I should note that Mr. Legman believes that the aggression enjoyed vicariously by children is actually hostility against their fathers. In "The Three Little Pigs" (comic-

strip version) "the wolf is papa, tricked out in animal false-face
so he can be righteously beaten to death"; and on the basis of
this analysis he raises an interesting question: "The admission . . .
that children *need* these aggressive outlets in fantasy against their
parents, teachers, policemen, and total social environment is an
admission that this social environment does not have a place for
the child. The necessity for the same escape by adults then means
that the social environment has no place in it for adults. For
whom has the social environment a place?" It is a serious question,
and it suggests another: is the comic book less an outlet for aggression than an instigation? In a society that respects neither
the laws of nature nor of nature's God, that transfers all dignity
and power to anti-Man whom it calls Superman, and that is built
on the certainty that all encounters must be hostile and end in
violence, we are confirmed in our fears and encouraged only to
seek power from the unnatural, which is called the supernatural.

In that world who can care what happens to children? Who
can care what will happen to the world the children will inhabit?

There are, no doubt, dozens of steps parents can take to
counteract the influence of the comic books, and the fact that
appeal to law is futile makes personal action all the more imperative. I have overemphasized the weakness of social action deliberately, using the comic books as the best illustration of a
dilemma that occurs in the other popular arts as well: the liberal-
minded citizen dislikes coercive action, tries to escape from corruption privately, and discovers that he cannot escape if his
neighbors, his community, are infected. The same problem has
become acute in relation to the hours spent watching television
by high-school students—about as many as they spend in school,
it appears. When the facts became known, Jack Gould, radio
critic of the *New York Times*, said that the broadcasters cannot
escape their responsibility; while John Crosby, of the *Herald
Tribune*, offered what he called "an old-fashioned" opinion that
"the parents have no one but themselves to blame." There is, at
present, no satisfactory social apparatus for compelling the net-

works to bring more useful programs to the children, and no one dreams of asking them to stay off the air at stated hours.[1] On the other hand, parents who limit the TV hours of their children will see those children grow up into a world of the half-educated, possibly into a world managed by the half-educated, if millions of other parents do not do the same. In self-defense, parents may move to areas of bad reception, but that is a Maginot Line, dangerous because they will think themselves secure and will not work out the necessary controls. The other danger was marked when the chairman of the FCC, Wayne Coy, warned telecasters to keep their programs clean of scatalogical jokes under threats of public protest and ultimately federal interference.

There is a sad footnote to this story of the comic books. "I remember," writes John Houseman, "the time when Disney and his less successful imitators concerned themselves with the frolicsome habits of bees, birds, and the minor furry animals. Joie-de-vivre was the keynote. Sex and parenthood played an important and constructive role, illustrated by such cheerful fertility symbols as storks, Easter eggs, bunnies, et cetera. Now all this is changed. The fantasies which our children greet with howls of joy run red with horrible savagery. Today the animated cartoon has become a bloody battlefield through which savage and remorseless creatures, with single-track minds, pursue one another, then rend, gouge, twist, tear, and mutilate each other with sadistic ferocity." This indictment is too harsh; the shorter Disneys often preserve the tenderness of his early work, even if the surface is violent; but the induction of fear or horror has become a deliberate purpose of his major pieces. As the imaginative powers have dwindled, excitement has been pumped up; too often, when he is not exciting, Disney falls into a depressing area of sentimentality. What was once a unique bedazzlement of the

[1] Mr. Gould's stinging rebuke to a network for permitting a horror drama to appear in the midst of several programs for children was promptly effective. The offense was rank, the criticism exceptionally harsh and direct. Mr. Gould deserves the gratitude not only of parents, but of the entire community, for the demonstration he has given of the power of protest.

senses has become routine and stale. The shorts, even *The Three
Little Pigs* and greater masterpieces like *The Band Concert*, did
not pay well, distribution of shorts being controlled by major
studios interested primarily in their features; Disney elaborated
his techniques, built a huge studio, and drew in the kind of investment that finances the major companies. He was compelled to
go into quantity production, into making long features; he also
found himself involved in a strike he could not understand
("Why, they all call me 'Walt,'" he said, honestly bewildered),
and the sweetness and the lightness went out of his work. The
conviction was gone too; he made pictures with human beings, he
did nothing after the war that reflected the brilliant techniques
of his military work. In 1950 he released a picture he was destined to make, *Cinderella*, which was an affirmation of an old
faith but without the miracle the old faith had worked. How
much Disney was affected by the change in children's tastes and
how much they were affected by the comic books are matters of
surmise. We only know that the one powerful countervailing
force to the ugliness and the brutality of the comic book has
retained a superficial prettiness without growing in range of
imagination and warmth of heart.

# A MODEST PROPOSAL

At the beginning of 1950 Dr. Arthur H. Compton, who had been associated with the first of our atomic-bomb projects, declared that the decision to make the hydrogen bomb should be left in the hands of the American people. It is, perhaps, the most complicated question of our time; it requires not only vast information and steady judgment, but a keenly developed moral sense as well. If the decision is made without consulting the people, we take a step toward the authoritarian state, losing our rights and our responsibility. If the decision is brought to us, have we the qualities of mind and character to understand the problem and to find a good answer? Considering our absorption in mass media, can the problem be fully exposed without the use of radio, the movies, television, and comic books? Are these media capable of conveying the problem intelligently to us, and are we capable of receiving it from them?

Or have our mass media prepared us to acquiesce, without question, in any decision made?

The news analysts have spoken about the cold war and the consequences of a real war between the Communists and the democratic nations; some of them have been eloquent and statesmanlike, some have played politics with the lives of the next generation at stake. There have been special programs giving the background of precisely such a problem as the hydrogen bomb presents. The movies snapped at the atom bomb as a good subject; two studios approached it, one surrendered to the other, and a totally negligible picture resulted. Since then the movies

287

have used a ravaged continent as the background for romance
and have not even been able to make a moderately popular picture about the five-year struggle of ideas that we call the cold
war, their best efforts being concentrated on spy stories. The
great audience, the people of the United States, has been worked
into a mood of indifference. The mass media have not created the
atmosphere in which grave decisions can be made.

The grave decision in the case of the hydrogen bomb was not
left to the public; so far as I know, only one reference to Dr.
Compton's proposal was made on the air, by a non-political commentator on a local station. After the President's announcement
was made and received in the usual unresponsive way, the obligation of the broadcasters became more pressing than ever to make
the public aware of the decisions which must follow, a series of
critical moments leading to peace or to annihilation. There was
only a little evidence that either radio or any other of the mass
media was aware of this duty. It was considered better to leave
the public undisturbed. Nothing in law or custom or the atmosphere of postwar life in America compels the mass media to act
otherwise. The single ill-defined phrase about operating in the
public interest is the only limitation on the broadcasters; a few
local boards of censorship hold a threat over the movies; the
police power has occasionally been invoked to check the sale of
comic books, and now and then a law governing their sale to
minors has been proposed. Everything else is left to public pressure, which means, in practice, to public indifference. *Ad hoc*
groups have publicized their hostility to individual films, and
newspapers have at times whipped up (and greatly exaggerated)
protests against individual performers, as the Hearst press did
when Paul Draper appeared on a television program after he
had been accused, also by the Hearst press, of Communist lean-
ings. But constant observation of entertainment with unremitting
criticism is seldom practiced and, except in the case of movies
listed by Catholics, is usually ineffective. The work of the National Board of Review in singling out good pictures and the

work of the American Civil Liberties Union in noting limitations on free expression seldom reach the public; smaller local groups sometimes have influence, in minor matters, on radio stations and movie exhibitors, but it is diffused, sporadic, and tainted with uplift. This taint may be synthetic; the interested parties like nothing better than the impression that only Hokinson women concern themselves with the social effects of movies and radio and comic books; other kinds of criticism are dismissed as highbrow or Communist; the final argument, against which there has never been a satisfactory rebuttal, is the statistical proof that the great majority either like, or are indifferent to, the entertainment called into question. *So long as mass media are considered as private entertainments,* with negligible effects on those who enjoy them, and with none whatever on those who pass them by, this situation will continue; its evils will, moreover, be aggravated, because the mass media will consistently try to increase the numbers of their patrons and at the same time will steadily undermine the capacity to question, to criticize, and to protest.

So far as they do this, our mass media are lowering the political vitality of the nation, and they are doing it at a time when the same media are being used to fortify the citizens of the non-democratic countries. Our system is based not merely on freedom to choose, but on freedom to act; it cannot survive if we choose paralysis instead of action. If the Communist system is founded on the duty to obey, the use of mass media in the Soviet Union is a masterpiece of adapting the means to the end; if the media are correctly used they will assist in turning out the ideal Soviet citizen precisely because, according to our lights, he is prevented from knowing anything the state does not want him to know and from enjoying anything that does not make him a more contented slave of the state. By their own standards, the rulers of Soviet Russia have a perfected instrument in radio or the movies or the printed page. Our standards forbid the state to use these media as instruments; but if they are used to destroy the state, what will happen to them? And to us?

We have preferred a less-than-perfect system in politics and economics, in education and in the care of the sick, in our mass media and in our war machine, because we believe that the blueprinted perfected system does not allow the individual to develop freely, and this free development is the ultimate objective of our society, not the abstract idea of freedom in itself. From the day the Constitution was adopted we have used the method of checks and balances to prevent any free activity from running wild; we knew then that disorder and anarchy are enemies of freedom. Whenever individuals have been unwilling to check themselves, the state has checked them, and always to the same end, that no one should with impunity stunt the growth of anyone else. What is our plain duty if we discover that a small group of men is stunting the growth of the entire nation?

Americans believe that a democratic-capitalist nation can survive the attack of any state not founded on freedom of the individual because capitalism is the most effective way of producing wealth, and democracy is the most effective way of letting human beings develop all their latent powers. Whenever the two conflict, the system of things gives way to the system of people; that is the principle, and although it has had its setbacks it still governs our society except in wartime. In the Communist states we are now facing a society which is eager enough to use our methods of production, but which is bent on creating a new man, differing in vital respects from the democratic man, in order to establish the perfect state of the future. During the next generation this new man is our enemy in the field of ideas; he is psychologically conditioned to be different. It is the moment when the essential features of the democratic man must be sharply defined, when no action that blurs the outline can be permitted. Against the Communist state we have so far set up the strength of our productive system; against the Communist man we have done little to strengthen the democratic man; yet he is the foundation of our state; it is the man that creates the system of production; democracy created capitalism, not vice versa. Our first and last line of defense is the independent, searching, questioning, intelligent individual, supplied with the machinery he produces.

I am proposing a revaluation of the popular arts in terms of physics rather than aesthetics, in terms of social effect rather than private pleasure. The ethical principles we apply to radio and the movies were developed in the days of the theater and the newspaper, our standards of decency for Hollywood are those of the 1890's, when Edison was working on one-minute films for penny peepshows; the ethics of fair play in broadcasting were known, if not always respected, when the first editor opened his pages to letters from indignant subscribers. We have not had time to create new standards; the sudden spurt of anger that demands censorship is the hammer and the fight for absolute freedom of expression is the anvil on which a new morality is being forged. It is a slow process because we are constantly looking backward, to abstract principles of the past, and so cannot look steadily at the present fact.

The fact in broadcasting, for instance, is that what enters the microphone with the speed of sound travels to the ends of the earth at the speed of light, so that a hundred million people may hear it simultaneously and may never hear anything to challenge what they have heard. The fact in the movies is that the film can be endlessly duplicated and can produce emotional disturbances in widely separated crowds of people who have no chance to balance any other influence against it. The availability of these forms and of the comic books, the amount of time that can be spent on them, the negligible demand they make on the purse and the mind, are new phenomena in the world; their capacity to effect the lives of people who never see or hear them is the result we get when we multiply all these new factors. A new social force has been created by high-speed printing presses and by the power-driven projector and by the electronic system, which may master all the other mechanics of the entertainment industry.

The number of people who accept these entertainments, where they are at the time, how much they absorb, what power they have to resist, how much time is left for the cultivation of other interests, are the vital questions. I have recorded what is known, but it is not enough; we need to know more. The movies were both attacked and defended for a generation before the actual age levels of the movie audience were known; the size of the radio audience relative to its total potential audience has been known, as a matter of statistics, but has not been related to any study of the effects of radio, and virtually no researches into the non-listening population have been made. What we call our "social attitude" toward the popular arts is the expression of our moral sense, and it has been based largely on prejudice—morality stemming from aesthetics as often as from religion. The people who came closest to the problem were, I regret to say, the censorious, the pressure groups who were defending their special interests; they, at least, did understand that you cannot have entertainment without having influence, they saw the movies bringing into play a new force that might diminish the influence of the school and the church. They were dangerously wrongheaded in the methods they chose, and they imposed standards on all our popular arts which stunted their growth. The enemies of divorce compelled the movies to undermine the institution of marriage, the educators allowed broadcasting to belittle the intelligence of man. But if they were wrong and weak, at least they were aware of the power of the new media, while the defenders put forth the remarkable paradox that these media were essential to the lives of the people but had no effects. The moralistic censors hated the pleasure given, the enthusiasts for pleasure were unaware of the moral problems.

We now see that judgment on the place of the popular arts in our lives cannot be left to the moral philosopher and to the aesthete, even if they should ever agree; a third judge must sit on the bench: the statesman. We move beyond the aesthetic question of the quality of a movie and beyond the moral question of whether the movies are good for people; we have to inquire what kind of citizens, what kind of society, all the popular arts tend to create. And whether, in the present state of the world, we can afford to give virtually absolute freedom to virtually irresponsible individuals, letting them create, by their whim, the temper of the citizen's mind, his outlook upon life, the moral and intellectual climate in which he lives. This aesthete-moralist-statesman does not exist, and even if he did I would hesitate to place authority in his hands or in the hands of Congress or the commissions and bureaus appointed by Congress. The delicate balance among the three qualities must come from a great number of people who are aware of the nature of the problem and who can persuade an even greater number to right action. Perhaps the first thing to understand is that the arts for which they want to find a proper place, through democratic processes, are themselves making it harder, with each day, for the democratic process to function. For if the mathematics of democracy can be reduced to "one man, one vote," the moral assumption is still that no man will be excluded from knowing the facts and no one will be prevented from using his intelligence.

By "the present state of the world" I mean the tension between two systems of social and economic life which have not yet decided whether they can or cannot live together. I make no assumptions concerning the cold war and its possible conversion into actual war, and in a sense it does not matter whether the cold war itself is a phony war, artificially induced by either side or both. We need certain qualities of intelligence, of steady nerves; we need the habit of trying to see things as they are, and the second habit of penetrating to underlying truth; or, if we cannot do that, we need the attitude of mind that respects those who can. We need these things, which are among the criteria of maturity, to survive the cold war, to prevent a real war, to be victorious if war comes, to make peace thereafter. We may win a war without these things, but only by sacrificing the freedom for which we will be fighting. I do not know what maturity can mean under any form of society not founded on the principle of individual freedom, but I suspect that the citizens of Communist countries are being conditioned to be useful to their governors and I feel that it is up to us to let our citizens develop so that they can be useful to themselves and to their fellow men. When freedom destroys freedom, we shall be fulfilling the Marxian prophecy that our own inner contradictions will bring us down. We must move to prevent it.

Everything I have written here of the power of the communications arts compels me to a hard conclusion: there are a hundred preliminary steps to be taken, but the decisive move must be to use the mass media as counterforces—against themselves. It is not a romantic dream of seizing the enemies' guns and turning them; it is actually dictated by the logic of the situation, for the rationalized use of mass media can create a powerful democracy; the wild dream is to work from the outside, leaving the strongest weapons unused.

It is not necessary for radio or the movies to undermine themselves; it is necessary for them to change, and for the managers to be brought under pressure to change in the right direction. The three principal media are today on shaky financial foundations, and the fourth, the comic book, has always been exceptionally vulnerable. The moment for action is propitious.

It must begin with those people who have not yet succumbed to mass pressures, and they must begin with a simple act of awareness: that the entertainment arts have a public as well as a private character, that pleasures taken individually have profound social effects. Nothing effective can be done so long as the old concept of a purely personal relationship between the citizen and his diversions remains unchallenged. The justification for public pressure is public danger.

This pressure can begin with the older forms of communication and propaganda: in the schools, which have denounced the mass media more often than they have studied them; in the pulpit, which has been lofty in tone but unfriendly; in those newspapers which do not appeal exclusively to the audience of mass media; and, with most effect, in the large-circulation magazines which are the rivals of the mass media and have accomplished the spectacular feat of attracting and holding large sections of the mass audience while doing what the mass media conspicuously fail to do—they give their readers a real variety of choice, presenting to them subjects of significance as well as amusing trifles, simplifying without debasing, appealing to many different levels of human interest.

The popular magazine is in itself a demonstration that a genuine intellectual curiosity exists even among the moderately educated, that the appetites are not completely dulled. It is a demonstration also of the way to use the techniques of popularization to attract attention. It does not matter if nine-tenths of all the readers merely glance at an essay on medieval philosophy in *Life* or a diagrammatic study of the incidence of taxes in *Look;* ten-tenths have been exposed to these presumably remote and forbidding subjects, which have been presented not pompously or apologetically, as a documentary is presented by radio or the movies, but with a combination of authority and showmanship that is impressive; and one-tenth of the total of their readers is a much larger number than any equally sound presentation has ever attracted in the past. At a moment when every report indicates that television stands a good chance of destroying the habit of reading altogether, the intelligent popular magazine may be the last fortress of those who believe that we cannot survive unless we preserve our capacity to think. We are being suffocated with sameness and should be grateful for every indication that the wants of the average man are not entirely satisfied by those exploiters who think of him as part of a mass.

The reduction of man to mass is not an irreversible process. Some twenty years ago a sort of mass rebellion took place in the United States, a rebellion against the chief architect of robotry. For a generation Henry Ford had imposed his indifference to superficial charm on the buyers of his cars; he was in a strong position because he sacrificed everything to economy—and he was defeated. The American people were no longer amused to hear they could have any color so long as it was black; in the years of prosperity, competition had come up and had exploited purely aesthetic qualities in their cars; the appetite for brightness had not been destroyed, and the Model T vanished. This could not have happened if rival manufacturers had failed to use the methods of large-scale production, or if they had used them as Ford did to impose a single level of taste upon the public; actually they did precisely what I now am convinced must be done in the mass media: they adapted the methods, the system of quantity production, to a wide variety of interests. It was a victory for the independent man achieved through the simple economic pressure of buying what he liked. The kind of reconversion this victory forced on Henry Ford is not impossible elsewhere.

The movies are making the great discovery now; because they turned out their Model-T pictures, the audience drifted away, until there came into existence an audience ten times as great as the remnant in the movie houses, ready for many kinds of entertainment the movies did not supply. It may take broadcasting longer to learn the lesson, but the present instability of the business, with radio frightened and television still unsteady on its legs, can be used to advantage. The first symptoms of panic in radio were not reassuring, they were all within the concept of the single mass audience; for this audience its favorites must be bought, and when a network lost a popular program, the first move was to replace it with another program as like it as possible; old standards were lowered, and the economies imposed by the costs of television were most keenly felt in those departments of broadcasting that reached out to the unmassed audience. The first moves in television were in the same mode: use whatever is certain to be popular, do not try to gather in a non-radio audience. We have to face this natural reaction. There are prophets who say we have already passed the golden era of television, that everything first-rate will go down within a year or two and we will have nothing but the crudest forms of entertainment, while radio, they believe, will make ever more degrading compromises to hold on to its remnant. Against this despair I have noted the relative success of TV programs that are true to the characteristics of the medium, the arrival of reasonable human beings and of plays based on character, the failure, already marked, of some of the efforts to reduce television to illustrations of bad radio programs. About radio itself I am not too sanguine, but it is possible that broadcasters will be forced to search out their missing audiences by being imaginative and that programs for such audiences will not be as costly as those they are now putting on. Poverty may compel radio to overhaul its methods, to use new techniques, to let us hear a new voice on the air.

In these circumstances I think it is premature to be defeatist. If radio goes down, as it may for purely technical reasons, the opportunities for television and the movies will be all the greater and the lesson of radio's disaster will be learned: that no great entertainment industry can live on a mass audience alone. It will be reinforced if, at the same time, the existence of the great audience is made manifest in sustained, sympathetic, and critical contact with all the mass media.

From working in nearly all of the media myself, I have learned how sensitive they are, how responsive to influence, and also how hardened they can become. I am a believer in organized pressure, although I have little experience in its management. I am convinced that nothing else can be effective in dealing with such highly organized, entrenched, and well-defended enterprises as these media are. There are elements in each of them that see the possibility of more favorable public relations and some degree of profit to be gained by a change of direction; these mavericks have seldom received enough support from the intelligent public because, it seems to me, the intelligent public has never recognized its own interest. And the independent minds among the managers have long recognized the danger of bureaucratic control; the fight of the NAB against the Federal Communications Commission whenever the faintest suggestion of program control has been made, the first powerful reaction of a conservative like Louis B. Mayer against pressure from the Rankin Committee, indicate a general apprehension that freedom may be jeopardized by abuse. I do not think that the threat of government interference or control should be lightly made by those who want the mass media to become better servants of the public; not to destroy any democratic institution, but to reinvigorate the whole democratic system, is the objective. It needs to be accomplished before the fanatics of freedom or the fanatics of bureaucracy go too far. A sufficient but not clearly defined apparatus of control already exists; it needs a new kind of public support. But threats of bureaucracy are not evidences of support; they abandon the fight and turn everything over to invisible powers. Even without this last-ditch argument, pressure groups attempting to make our mass media democratize themselves will be ridiculed as reformers if they aren't denounced as Reds. They will have to take the risk.

At stake is simply the future of this country as a creative democratic society. If a nation cannot survive half slave and half free, a democracy cannot endure if the forces making for free minds are apathetic and the forces of invincible ignorance are aggressive and brilliantly managed and irresponsible. If it is already inconvenient to attack them, it will be dangerous in five years, and it will be impossible in ten. They multiply, and their critics have been sterile too long. If the breakdown of the independent spirit of the individual citizen is to be averted, it must be done promptly.

The phrase about "bread and circuses" is familiar, but its full meaning cannot be understood outside the context. Juvenal had witnessed the degradation of a great race; he knew that the mind of the citizen was being distracted, that a crafty manipulation was going on, and his savage indignation turned against the managers of public opinion who were stunting the growth of the individual. But there is pity as well as contempt in his voice when he speaks of the mean life to which the Romans had been reduced: "That sovereign people which once bestowed military command, counselships, legions, and all else, now bridles its desires and limits its anxious longing to two things only—bread and the games of the circus." He composed in these words an epitaph. For us it is still only a threat. *Absit omen.*

The unspoken fundamental promise of American life is that the opportunity to grow to maturity, to become responsible men and women, will not be denied to anyone. It is an extremely personal and urgent matter that this promise should not be broken, and we cannot be indifferent if it happens to others and not to ourselves, because in our complex and highly integrated society there is no immunity. Our strength cannot survive the weakness of others. We have lived through too much to be frightened, and we hope for too much to let ourselves be defeated.

"Master, we have not come through centuries, caste, heroisms, fables, to halt in this land today."